Inside
FILM MUSIC

COMPOSERS SPEAK

Inside

FILM MUSIC

COMPOSERS SPEAK

CHRISTIAN DESJARDINS

SILMAN-JAMES PRESS | LOS ANGELES

First Edition
10 9 8 7 6 5 4 3 2 1

Library of Congress Cataloging-in-Publication Data

DesJardins, Christian, 1977-
   Inside film music: composers speak / by Christian DesJardins—1st ed.
       p. cm.
   Includes index.
   ISBN 1-879505-88-6 (alk. paper)
   1. Motion picture music—History and criticism. 2. Film composers—Interviews. 3. Motion picture producers and directors—Interviews. I. Title.

ML2075.D48 2006
781.5'42—dc22

2005035932

Cover design by Melanie DesJardins

Printed and bound in the USA.

Silman-James Press
3624 Shannon Road
Los Angeles, CA 90027

To Chris Young for his enthusiasm and love for film music and life. He is my inspiration. Without his insight, guidance, talent, and passion, my journey with this book would not have been.

I also want to dedicate this journey to my cousin Canaan. He is a warrior in heart and soul, fighting with the United States Special Forces with pride and glory. From the time we grew up together through today, he shows me the way. As my best friend and mentor, this one is for you.

In memory of Elmer Bernstein, Jerry Goldsmith, Michael Kamen, Basil Poledouris, and David Raksin

Contents

Contents

Foreword
by Christopher Young

Film music is an amazing thing. We are told that it was born out of necessity more than a hundred years ago to cover the racket of exposed projectors. And then, almost by accident, it was discovered that having music accompanying moving pictures made the audiences connect emotionally to the images in ways they never had before. That's when all the magic began. I do believe there is nothing more rewarding for a film composer than watching someone cry to a scene that's scored by his/her own music. Or laugh harder, or scream louder . . .

A film composer is no different from any other artist. In the final analysis, we all do it for love. We present our music to millions of viewers/listeners hoping desperately for a positive response. Unfortunately, all composers have to face the age-old dilemma of film music: At best, it plays third fiddle in the audio-visual experience. The picture comes first, the dialogue is second, and the perpetual battle between music and sound effects sits in the third position. But no one really listens, do they? Isn't the best score one that goes by unrecognized? God forbid, no!

I think you will find Christian's book is both as informative and, more importantly, as passionate as we film composers are ourselves about what we do. What makes this book unique is that it is written by someone who truly is madly in love with everything that pertains to music written for movies. This book is a testament of that affection, and its primary goal is to educate those who previously had no idea of what really goes on behind the scenes. He once told me that he lost his naïveté about film music while researching this book. I know now that he's taken the journey, and he can never go back.

So, beware! You will never think of film music the same way again.

Your Friend,
Christopher Young

Preface

For as long as I can remember, music has been an integral part of my life. My enthusiasm for film music, however, did not begin until I encountered the film *The Prince of Tides*, with its score by James Newton Howard. Prior to this movie, I recall hearing John Williams' music to *Indiana Jones* and *Star Wars* and humming his themes from them, as I did with Beethoven's Fifth Symphony. But it took the strongly emotional score to *The Prince of Tides* to bring me to a true understanding of the marriage of music and film. This was a turning point in my musical life, and the music of James Newton Howard and Thomas Newman soon consumed my CD shelves, which Wagner and Berlioz had dominated before.

My passion for larger-than-life, richly emotional film music, which has grown to be a major part of my life, drove me to develop this book with the hope that, through it, I might kindle a similar passion for this music in others. I hope that through my writing, readers will discover a greater appreciation for film music when viewing movies or simply listening to the scores by themselves.

Too many filmgoers overlook the talent and craft involved in writing music for film. Too often, we fail to think about the emotions we experience when watching a movie—laughter, tears, and so on. Would our experience of films be the same without music? What role does music play in the highly collaborative filmmaking process?

Answers to these questions can be found in this book's interviews, in which each interviewee shares stories about their techniques and experiences and the crucial role music plays in a finished film. Through these stories, I hope that readers find the personalities behind the names we see credited on the screen and develop an understanding of these composers as important artists working within the excitingly collaborative medium of film.

With *Inside Film Music*, I also hope to build a stronger awareness in film-music fans of what actually goes on when a film is scored. Not too long ago, I visited websites and conversed with film-music fans around the world about aspects of film music that I knew very little about. But I soon realized that to evaluate a film score properly, one must try to learn all one can about the whole collaborative process from which it grew.

I am—and will always remain—a film-music enthusiast and a loyal listener to the many composers who inspire me, but I don't hear their music quite the same as I did before I undertook the writing of this book. And I hope that, after reading it, you will hear film music in a new way too.

I hope that this book also fills a need for those musicians who dream of making film music a career. Although the feature-film scoring environment is an extremely competitive and grueling one, as you will hear from the many professionals who discuss it in this book, I believe that if you have the desire and the willingness to pursue your dream (and a bit of talent certainly doesn't hurt), you can do it. Learn what these masters of their art have done and follow in their footsteps.

Acknowledgments

My warmest thanks to Jeff Atmajian, Samantha Barker, Marilee Bradford, Cat Celebreeze, Holly Church, Ray Costa, Mychael Danna, Brad Dechter, Robert Elhai, Robert Folk, Alan Frey, Neil Kohan, Richard Kraft, Robin Phillips, Jeff Rona, Jeff Sanderson, Dawna Shinkle, Ryan Shore, Brian Tyler, Monique Ward, and Christopher Young, all of whom went well beyond the call of duty to help me. I'm deeply indebted to everyone interviewed in this book for freely giving me their time and insights. I also extend my thanks to the many wonderful composers whose schedules did not allow them to contribute to this book, which I might not be writing were it not for the inspiration of their scores. Thanks to Jim Fox and Gwen Feldman for helping my dream become a reality, and to Michael Schelle, whose book, *The Score*, truly inspired me.

I thank my dear friend Tom Kiefner, who has been my strength. I owe so much to him for always listening, sharing music, and—most of all—being a true friend. And I thank everyone in my family: They stood by me, offering their own great excitement, through the completion of this project. I can't thank them enough. Most of all, I thank my father, who is an artist, and who taught me to appreciate the finer aspects of life; to live with my heart and soul; and notice of the often-unnoticed inner beauty of life and music. I love you all for showing me the way. Last, but certainly not least, I thank my loving wife, who has in all ways contributed selflessly to the dream that this book has been for me.

Film composer Ryan Shore discusses the basic terms and techniques of film music

Why is there a need for film music?

The magic of why music works so well with visuals to affect human emotion is probably as mysterious as any aspect of human nature. However, it certainly works quite effectively and has done so for thousands of years. Prior to accompanying film, music accompanied other forms of dramatic visuals, from opera to plays to musicals, and even earlier forms of live dramatic performance, including dance.

When filmmaking was in its so-called "silent era," films were never actually silent. Although the technology to synchronize music and sound to film wasn't available in the beginning, early films were usually accompanied by music played live to picture by a theater house organist. These organists often had large books of thematic pieces of music that were organized by situation—love, chase, celebration, sadness, etcetera. The organist would watch the film along with the movie patrons and perform a live score created from pieces found in such a book or perform other pieces from memory, which, in many cases, might include a popular song of the day. In this way, if you went to see a movie more than once, you might get different scores each night, and you most certainly would if you saw it in different theaters. The purpose of this early film music was twofold. It not only provided a musical accompaniment to and comment on the actions in film, but it also helped mask the noise of the projector, which was not able to be effectively isolated from the audience in the early days of cinema.

Generally speaking, the role of music in a film is to support or extend the emotions within the film. At its most basic, it is there to make you feel. However, music has the ability to not only support or extend scenes, but also to provide additional information via such techniques as foreshadowing and the red herring, to name but a couple. At its best, it can help to bring a film together as one piece, helping to shape its dramatic arc and increase its overall effectiveness.

Describe the basic process of writing a film score?

The process begins when the composer meets with the other filmmakers to discuss the film. In this early stage, discussions usually include such topics as the overall intended effectiveness of the film, the kind of music that should be in the film, the role that music should play, and the places where the music should be heard. In today's film marketplace, this list of topics may also include the film's intended audience.

The meeting at which the filmmakers watch the film and discuss the specific placement of music in it is called the "spotting session."

Once the filmmakers are in agreement about what roles the music should play and where it should occur, the composer begins by translating what has been discussed into actual music. Often-times, a composer will begin by writing the main themes and choosing instrumentation, i.e., the instruments that will be used in the score. Then he/she will begin scoring the music to the scenes, tailoring the music to specific timings for actions and emotions. Early in the process and continuing throughout it, the composer usually meets with the filmmakers to preview themes and portions of the music. This is often done by creating score mockups—performing portions of the in-progress score on synthesized instruments played back synchronized to picture—or, at times, with a live performance by a small group of instruments.

It goes without saying, though, that discussion can be an important and effective way to make sure that filmmakers are on the same page. Often, a healthy dialogue can be even more effective than the best "mockup."

During the Golden Age of Hollywood, it was not uncommon for a composer to preview for the filmmakers only the main themes on a piano and possibly a few key scenes to picture, and that would be it. The filmmakers would then hear the complete orchestrated score for the first time as it was being recorded by the full orchestra in the studio. This process was easier to facilitate at that time because the movie studios had their own orchestras, which were available to record any music that was ready for recording, be it for the film on hand or another film that had its cues ready to be recorded. It wasn't uncommon for the same orchestra to be recording one film's score in the morning and another film's score in the afternoon.

Returning to the present, once all the music has been composed, it is prepared for the recording sessions. This includes completing the orchestrations and creating all of the printed scores and parts for the musicians and the conductor. (Sometimes, music preparation can also involve taking electronic music files—MIDI files—from synthesizers and transcribing them so they can be converted into printed music.) For a full orchestral score of substantial duration, this job can often result in the creation of thousands of pages of printed scores and parts. Then the score is recorded and mixed and delivered to the final film mix, where it is mixed into the movie with the dialogue and sound effects.

What is a "temp track"?

A temp track, or "temp score", is a temporary score for a film. It's usually created by piecing together recordings of other existing pieces of music.

Temp tracks are often used by film editors to help guide the pacing of a scene or to add the emotional carriage that it will have later on when it is actually scored. They are often used to help the filmmakers decide on the musical direction for the score because they are a quick way to try out different kinds of music with the scenes before composing and recording an original score. They can be an effective way to "discuss" music in film, particularly for those filmmakers who may might find it simpler to refer to an effective piece of music without having to explain its function in musical terms.

Temp tracks are usually used in test screenings to help audiences feel the intended effectiveness of a movie before its editing is locked and the original score is composed.

Before the advent of all of the current computer technology, which greatly helps in creating very refined, seamlessly tailored temp scores, temp music was commonly only used in a few scenes of the test-screened film, for example, in a main-titles sequence, a montage that might be completely silent without music, and/or the film's climax. Now that computer technology and digital audio editing tools are relatively inexpensive and readily available, a temp score is commonly created for all scenes in which an original score is to be composed.

Who chooses the composer?

The decision is most often made by the director. However, in some cases the decision is also aided or made completely by producers or studio executives, depending on the arrangement they have with the director.

Why is a particular composer chosen?

Usually, these choices are made based on previous working relationships or on a previous score that a composer has written that may be similar in approach to that of the desired score for the film at hand. The director (and/or producers and executives, as noted above) also often meets with prospective composers to find their best match musically and/or personally.

How does a composer know in which scenes, and where in those scenes, to put music?

These decisions are made through discussions between the composer and the director and/or other filmmakers. (See note about "spotting session" above.) The decisions may have been influenced by the effectiveness or ineffectiveness in an existing temp score. Sometimes when a composer begins writing the score, after scenes and timings have been discussed and agreed upon, he or she may feel things differently and suggest other options to the director.

When does instrumentation enter the picture?

This is a creative decision that is usually made very early on in the process. However, as with any creative process, changes to instrumentation are sometimes made throughout before arriving at a final result. Instruments are colors, and are chosen based on the emotions or feelings that they can convey.

What is the process of finding the right instruments? Do guidelines exist within each genre?

This is probably the hardest question because it truly cuts to the very core of creativity. Many genres have become associated with specific instrumentation and compositional styles: romance with strings, action with percussion and pounding brass, comedy with a "bouncing" orchestra, period films with period instruments, Westerns with sweeping, expansive orchestral themes or simple guitar and harmonica, films set in exotic lands with ethnic instruments, horror films with wild and dissonant splashes of orchestra, religious films with choir, science-fiction films with synthesizers, and the list goes on and on. There is no limit to the human imagination, and there will continuously be new ways to score and orchestrate music in order to tell the story of the human condition.

Many credited positions appear in the notes to today's film-score CDs. Why are more names credited on today's recordings versus earlier recordings?

These days it is not uncommon to credit everyone—all orchestrators, editors, engineers, copyists, coordinators, etcetera—who work on any aspect of bringing the score to fruition. The same number of people may have been involved in the process years ago, but it used to be the fashion in film to only give screen (and recording) credit to a very select few.

Many films from the thirties, forties, and fifties gave all screen credits up front on very few cards, and the end of the film was nothing more than a "The End" card. Those credits did not necessarily reflect how many people actually worked on the film, including the music. As a matter of fact, during the Golden Age of Hollywood, it was not uncommon for numerous composers to work on the same film. One composer might write all the main themes and begin scoring the film, but then the head of music for the studio would assign him to another film, so a second composer might finish the score. However, even though this took place, it was usually decided that only the main composer would receive the credit. This was all during a time when composers were not as high-profile as many composers are today, when some film composers are nearly household names. The changing status of film composers is also reflected in composers' fees. Many years ago, composers on films made significantly more modest fees compared to composing fees during the last twenty-five years.

What does the orchestrator do?

The composer creates the notes, melodies, counterparts, harmony, accompaniments, and so on, which can be played on any instrument or instruments from solo piano to full orchestra. The orchestrator's role is to translate what the composer has written to the chosen instrumentation. This job requires a complete knowledge of all of the instruments: their ranges and special timbre and dynamic characteristics, the styles that are idiomatic for them to play, how they interact and blend when combined with other instruments, and so on.

[See also "Orchestrators and other members of the film-music team" on page 297.]

What does the music editor do?

The music editor wears many different hats throughout the scoring process. In the most general summary, the music editor is the composer's right-hand person and the liaison between the music and the film.

At a production's early stages, the music editor can create a temp score.

During the film's spotting session, the music editor will take notes about all that is discussed. He or she then compiles those discussion notes into a set of coherent notes that often are referenced to a detailed set of timings from the picture. These are called "spotting notes," which the composer can refer to while writing the score. The music editor also will keep up with any picture editorial changes that may occur while a composer is writing the score and let the composer know what has changed in the film and how the score's timings may be affected.

During the recording session, the music editor often is responsible for the "clicks" and the onscreen cueing known as "punches and streamers," by which the composer or conductor and musicians synchronize the music to picture. The music editor may also help take notes on the individual takes that are recorded of each cue, so that the best performances may be quickly selected and edited together later. Often, a music editor will make those edits of the best takes so that the composite best performances can be mixed. The music editor may also edit into the film any pre-existing songs that will be used.

After the music is mixed, the music editor will attend the film mix and represent the score, being on hand to answer any questions the film mixer may have about the music and to help make sure that the music is applied to the film in the way that the composer intended. After the film's mix, the music editor will prepare "cue sheets," which list in detail all the pieces of music and film-score cues used in the film along with their corresponding composer, publisher, use type, and timings. These cue sheets are submitted to performance rights organizations, such as ASCAP or BMI, which in turn pay royalties to the writers and publishers when the film is played on television and in foreign markets.

What does the music engineer do?

The engineer records and mixes all the music that the composer has written. After preparing for the sessions by making sure the studio has all the necessary gear required for recording and mixing the score, the engineer will choose the most appropriate microphones, decide microphone placement and isolation of instruments in the studio in order to achieve the best possible recording, and so on. A film music engineer's skill also includes the ability to mix music not only in stereo but also in the surround-sound formats.

What is a "mix"?

A mix combines all recorded audio elements in a desired balance with one another. These elements may include recordings of musical instruments and other sound sources made at different times during the scoring and recording process, including many "overdubbed" sounds—sounds added to an existing recording (e.g., perhaps the sound of a triangle is added to an already-recorded orchestral chord that needs more "sparkle").

Mixing involves balancing the levels of recorded instruments and applying to them such sound processing as reverb, equalization, compression, and so on, in order to achieve the best possible representation of the music for various types of venues—movie theaters, television, even airplanes—and such different delivery mediums as 35mm film and DVD.

Why do composers in the States sometimes travel to foreign countries to record orchestral music?

This is done for a variety of practical, creative, and financial reasons. A practical reason may be that it is more convenient to record the music in the same city or country in which the film is being produced or where the composer lives and works. A creative reason could be the desire to record at a specific hall or studio for acoustical purposes. Another creative reason could be to record specific specialized foreign instrumentalists or unique artists. Economic reasons may include recording in a country where the musicians work for lower rates than they do in the States and/or are not tied to such union obligations as reuse fees, which may be incurred when creating a CD soundtrack, or additional payments that are due when a film generates revenues from additional markets or video sales.

Who pays the musicians' salaries and how are these salaries determined?

The salaries are paid for by the producers or studio. Salary rates are most often standardized by the music unions.

What is the average time frame for a film-scoring project, from beginning to end?

It can vary greatly. On average, it's between four and eight weeks from the spotting session to the delivery of mixed music. In some cases, such as a television movie or a replacement score, this time may be much shorter. If, however, there is time in the production schedule to allow for it or if there is a need for a very large amount of score, more time may be allotted.

Why is the composer often brought in so late in the filming process?

The score is most often the last substantially new creative effort to be added to a film. It is composed after the film has already been written, cast, shot, and edited. Therefore, the composer is often hired very late in the filmmaking process, which is when the his or her services are needed. Most are chosen during the time when the film is being edited.

In some cases, a composer may be hired early on when he or she has an existing relationship with the other filmmakers or when there is a need for original music elements to be addressed before a film is shot, as is the case with a musical or when an actor needs to perform music onscreen.

Composers have publicists and agents. What are their roles?

An agent helps a composer be in touch with the industry. Agents keep composers aware of what films are in production and who may be in need of a composer. They also negotiate the terms and conditions for the composer's work—fee, music budget, credit, ownership rights, and so on.

The publicist's role usually begins once a score is completed. His or her job is to raise awareness of a specific composer or score. This may include developing a strategy for raising a composer's profile or campaigning for awards. At times, publicists are hired on a per-project basis, whereas an agent has a full-time commitment to a composer.

What ownership rights does a composer have after his or her music has been used in a film?

A musical composition's ownership is divided into two parts: writer and publisher. Except in rare cases, the composer owns the composition itself, which is referred to as the "writer's share." The "publisher's share" is often owned by the entity who commissioned and paid for the score, which is usually the film studio. In some cases, the composer will retain the publisher's share to make up for accepting an unusually low composing fee on an independent film.

In addition to the ownership of the writer's share and publisher's share, there is the ownership of the "master," which is the actual recording itself. This is usually owned by the entity who commissioned and paid for the score, but, at times, its ownership can be retained by the composer to make up for a low composing fee.

In general, the standard arrangement is that once music is written for a film, its rights are permanently connected with that production and not available to be used in other productions.

How is it that a composer can be removed from a project? What legal agreements protect the composer whose score is rejected?

The decision to fire a composer is usually made by the director or the producers. The only legal agreement that the composer has is his or her composer's agreement. In most cases, if a composer is let go, they are paid for their work in part or in full, depending on how much of the score has been completed. A composer may agree to not take the full composing fee, in the best interest of retaining a relationship with the filmmakers or studio.

If a composer is hired because his or her style is deemed to fit a picture and/or because of previous working relationships that have been successful, why is it an all-too-common decision to fire that composer just days or weeks later?

Good question. You are correct, a composer is usually hired for his or her style, sound, and scoring sensibility. However, filmmakers may go into the filmmaking process thinking that they want a specific composer's sound or approach for their film and then change their minds for a variety of reasons that range from creative to commercial.

When the direction of music in a film changes, the composer is sometimes asked to adapt to the new direction or is let go from the film. Sometimes, filmmakers feel that it may be easier to begin from scratch with another composer, rather than re-conceive a score with the same composer. This situation is unfortunate because most composers, unless they are not enjoying the film or the collaboration, would probably rather start from the beginning themselves and compose in a new direction rather than be let go.

Often, movie soundtracks that do not include the score are released. Who decides on this? What is the reason for not releasing a score on CD?

By and large, song-based soundtracks sell far more CDs than score-only soundtracks. If the studio feels there will be a significant interest in a soundtrack, the decision of what to put on it is usually made for economic reasons.

They may compare, for example, how much it will cost to pay for the songs to be on the soundtrack with how much it will cost to put the instrumental score on the soundtrack. If a score is recorded in the United States on a union contract, when it is released as a CD, a reuse fee must be paid to the performing musicians for using that recording. If there are a large number of musicians on it—perhaps a large orchestra—the reuse payments can potentially add up to a prohibitive amount, thus making a score soundtrack uneconomical if the studio doesn't anticipate selling enough copies of the CD to pay back the reuse fees.

Reuse fees are determined by the number of minutes of music that appear on the soundtrack CD, which is why a score soundtrack is sometimes less than thirty or forty-five minutes long, even though there may be more score than that in the film.

PART I

Composers

Klaus Badelt

Klaus Badelt grew up in Germany, but in the late 1990s, his film-music talents brought him to Hollywood, where he quickly became one of the most sought-after young composers in the industry, first working under the wing of Hans Zimmer at Media Ventures. He collaborated with Zimmer on several films, including *The Pledge* (2001) and the dark, introspective film *Invincible* (2001). Badelt has since moved on to such solo projects as the sci-fi epic *The Time Machine* (2002) and the intense *K-19: The Widowmaker* (2002). In 2003, he wrote a bold, rollicking score for movie producer Jerry Bruckheimer's powerhouse adventure film *Pirates of the Caribbean*, and since then, Badelt's list of big-film credits, including *Catwoman* (2004) and *Constantine* (2005), which was a collaboration with composer Brian Tyler, has grown steadily.

Tell me a bit about Media Ventures, and how you became involved.

The main idea was to have a creative community made up of composers and people in affiliated fields, such as music editors, production designers, visual-effects designers, casting agents, and so on. This creative vibe is super-appealing to anybody who is interested in filmmaking. For the filmmaker, it is just incredible to have a place like this. I always see myself as more of a filmmaker than a composer; I just happen to express myself in music. After all, I'm doing one part of the movie.

How I got involved? I just showed up one day while I was on vacation from Germany. I simply asked if Hans [Zimmer] had a second. I saw on his website that his way of working was very similar to mine in terms of synthesizers and high-tech production. Anyway, I showed up and for some reason they let me in. I got to meet him and we kind of hit it off. I remember sitting on his couch, listening to what he does when he's writing. He would turn around and ask me a few questions about different approaches. I remember asking myself, "Why is he asking me?"

From then on, I started hanging around and being useful. I was very willing to come here and start over again—so I did the whole story of cleaning the kitchen and hanging around as an intern just to see how the big guys were doing it. Then I started working with Hans. I also was working with Harry Gregson-Williams at the time. Things developed, and at some point I started doing my own films.

Were you always interested in film music?

I didn't begin with music actually. When I was twelve, I saved enough money and bought my first film camera and started shooting short feature films. I was always interested in film. And I did music since I was very little, so I would combine them. The educational system in Europe, especially in Germany, didn't really support this art form at the time, though, so I started studying composition and recording engineering, and I discovered that this was actually what I wanted to do. It was horrible, though, because they wanted to make me a concert piano player. I was way too lazy and I didn't really want to do it. So I started working with film composer and music producer Ralf Zang, basically starting the same way as I did here in L.A. I showed up and said, "I am interested in music. I never did this, what do you think?" We talked a lot. And, at some point, I started writing for him. It was a great collaboration. I did that for a few years until the first vacation I ever took, which catches up the whole story to now.

What have been your strong musical influences?

Many different ones, but mainly the masters in the classical world, the romantic works of Wagner and Mahler. But then, I like lots of rock music and pop music, too. There's this new guy called Jack Johnson, whom I really adore.

When you watched films when you were young, were you conscious of the score?

I have to say I always listened with two brains, so, yes, I was. At the same time, I liked to get immersed into the film, which I still do. Then, when I watch it a second time, if I really liked it, I listen to the music. There are only a few films where I consciously listened to the music while it was playing from the beginning.

Do you have any examples?

I remember very early on I saw *Once Upon a Time in the West* [score by Ennio Morricone]. It was like a music-video clip to me sometimes. I was totally fascinated by that. I remember that as one of the first times I listened to the music and became aware of it in film.

Producer Jerry Bruckheimer seems to have a certain sound that he expects. Can you tell me what goes on behind the scenes when you're working on his projects, as opposed to other projects?

Good question. Jerry does expect a certain style. He has certain tunes in mind, even though he is really not a musician. If you would ask him, I'm sure he would tell you he has no clue about music, but he does have a very good feel for it and for what he wants. The music in his films has a certain style, and you can recognize them by that. If you write a score for him, you expect to deliver that. Yet, you know, there are still opportunities to put your own personality in there.

For film music in general, you can't have an ego because it's the film that's first, not you. The trick is not to lose your personality either. That thin line is quite tricky.

With *Pirates of the Caribbean*, the overall sound is very Jerry, and I'm proud that I can actually deliver that. At the same time, there are a few things in there that are not Jerry. The ethereal, abstract tension themes for the curse, for example—it's almost not music there. When we proposed that, we thought for sure it wasn't going to go by him, but he was even more excited. In the end, he is always full of surprises. He even pushed me to do different things sometimes. In another episode in the film, we used the tuba and the piccolo together, which is something I've never heard in a Jerry Bruckheimer film, and we thought, "We cannot do that." We actually hid it from him until the very end, so there was almost no time to change it if he disapproved. By accident, we played the wrong mix for him, and it was in there, and we looked at each other while it was playing, really scared. He looked around and said, "This is brilliant." He really loved it. So never believe what you hear about people.

Moving ahead a little bit, there's a director, Werner Herzog, who I'd heard was supposedly a slave-driver who made people suffer. I was told, "This man is mad. He's going to drive you crazy." I ultimately got to work with him, which was quite an honor, and I haven't had a more rewarding experience with a director ever. He knows exactly what he wants. He doesn't have to prove himself. He just lets you create, and is very cautious about making suggestions. He didn't really spot the film with me or ask me what to do. So, my experience was quite the opposite of what many people told me about him.

The Pledge is an edgy and unique score that leaves the listener almost unsettled. What brought you to use the desolate solo female voice?

I watched it without music and was immediately inspired. What came to my mind was a Scandinavian hymn I once heard. It has this pureness and this innocence in it. I wrote a very simple tune, basically like a Scandinavian hymn of the eighteenth century. Of course, it has nothing to do with the film. I just saw Jack Nicholson's character ice-fishing in the beginning and I thought, "Wow, this could be very interesting." The director [Sean Penn] was immediately hooked on it, too. He felt this gave his film another dimension.

In general, voices seem to be the most intense instruments. I found the solo voice through our violin player, who came to me and said, "I know what you're looking for. I heard my wife singing in the shower, and she is great but she never did anything professionally."

We had her come in, and she was so untrained, so innocent, and yet so fascinating. She was amazing. She was very talented. She was absolutely perfect for it.

This was a project where I had ten days to write the whole score, record it, produce it, and mix it. So I took one day to write the themes they needed. Then we got a handful of players in the recording room in this chaotic hustle. Sean Penn would come at night from San Francisco, where he was still cutting and in post-production. He would come from there almost every night, bringing a few bottles of wine. He'd listen to the cues, make some notes and opinions, and then he would go back to San Francisco in the morning. We didn't really sleep much, but it worked well.

If you had had more time, would you have taken a different approach?

That's always a question, isn't it? While I was doing it, I thought, "This isn't a good way of making a film, because what I would have liked to do was be able to make mistakes and try something knowing that I had time to actually go back or try a different approach." Now, looking back, I think, "Wow, I can't believe we achieved this in such a short time." Should we have done it differently? Maybe not. Regardless of time, it was the right thing to do. It kept the composing minimal, which I think it was appropriate for the film.

Invincible **is an operatic-style score with strings blended with a powerful, dark choir. How did this style fit the concept of the film, and was this your first intention?**

It is a saga of a national hero. It's like a story you want to tell for generations. Producer Gary Bart was related to the great- great grandson of the hero in the film. He just wanted this film to be done about this man and his family. So I wanted something that musically lifted this story up to become something like a bedtime story you tell your children of your mother or something that happened to your parents or to your grandparents. So my approach was to lift this character up to this larger-than-life hero, even though the movie is very intimate and very close. It's not thousands of shots on the battlefield, it's just this one guy who, by accident, turns into this hero.

The music is such complex music because I thought of it as tunes that wrap around the action like a cancer. It's suffocating. It almost has an uneasy feel to it. You cannot use this music in any other movie really. You cannot temp any movie with this kind of music because it's almost too important, which I usually don't do. But I just felt it was right to give this guy, who is very simple, yet very straightforward and very honest, the complexity and the depth that he actually has and the story has.

Hans Zimmer was involved in both *The Pledge* and *Invincible*. How much of a role did he play in these scores, and what was the reason for the collaboration?

First of all, it was the beginning of my career. *The Pledge* came to me through Hans. Sean asked Hans for help, and Hans said, "Look, I can't really do much on this. But here, I know this guy, why don't you try him?" So that's how I met Sean. Hans got a little bit involved here or there, but he just didn't have the time to really do it.

Invincible was the same thing: Hans introduced me to Werner [Herzog]. On *The Pledge* more than *Invincible*, Hans would come in and write a little or share with me the way he looks at film, which is very interesting. I basically had to do them myself. It was very scary. I thought I wasn't ready for this kind of music and this kind of director for *Invincible*.

The first music of yours that captivated me was your score to *The Time Machine*. From the themes to the orchestrations, it feels as though you sunk your teeth into this one wholeheartedly.

It was fantastic. It was enormous. The opportunity was great because it was a film happening in the future—but in a very primitive future. We're not in Africa or in South America; it's a primitive New York of the future. So what do you do? I thought we needed music with familiar elements, but with something new. So that's what I did.

For the main theme I recorded an orchestra and a real opera choir. At the same time, I had one woman vocalist sing all the voices of what the choir would sing, just herself 150 times. I built a choir from this one voice and combined those two to create this unique sound of two different worlds, at the same time creating one new song—not a duality, but one.

It's a dream to do an adventure like that. There was a love story in there, so I could write a love theme. It was so emotionally driven in a way. Whenever a film has such emotional reasoning for the characters, it's wonderful to work on it.

Your scores are often thematic. Where do you find your inspiration? Do you often write from your own emotions instead of directly from what is on-screen?

I always do. I never actually write the themes *to* the picture. My way of writing is like this: I get involved early on in the film, sometimes even before the script or when the script is being written. I read it or watch the film maybe once or twice. I don't look at it for a while and just try to have it sink in, and write the themes or maybe a few pieces. If I have the time, I'll take ten days or three weeks maybe, to write these themes, maybe longer if I have the time, because it's defining the vocabulary. Then, after I do all of this without the picture, I put the picture back up and see if it sticks somehow—if I wrote for the right film or not. This way, for me, I don't get stuck in details. I don't try to do the twists and turns of the film yet. So I have time to create emotionally valid material. Then I can adjust it.

K-19 is a score that is inwardly emotional and dramatic with regard to the characters. How much research did you do for the characters?

A lot, actually. I had this wonderful director, Kathryn Bigelow, who also did a lot of research. She developed this film for seven years. And I just tried to catch up with her and did the same research.

The Russians of the time had a very different way of thinking, a different way of looking at honor and the military and happiness. She went to Russia to find only a few survivors, and went to the original *K-19*, which, by the time the movie came out, was destroyed for obvious reasons. She insisted that scenes had to be shot in Moscow. Like, for example, the cemetery scene, which you could shoot on the Fox lot, of course. But, no, she insisted on going to Moscow. It was really cold there, really freezing. And it really has this character that you cannot find somewhere else.

Another thing that helped a lot was that we had access to the Kirov Orchestra under the conductor Valery Gergiev, who is quite a unique and strong voice in the classical world. We had the chance of going to St. Petersburg to record the score at the Mariinsky Theater, where Tchaikovsky's *1812 Overture* had its premiere. That was quite exciting.

The Kirov Orchestra had never recorded a film score or even knew how to record to picture. But I didn't want to put them in a situation that they were not familiar with, so I handed the score to the conductor and said, "Here, just do it." He would look at the scene, have the score in his hand, turn around, and from there the picture was turned off, and he would just conduct the piece like it was Tchaikovsky. In many ways, this is very different from how we would have done it with a studio orchestra. So I had to get used to it, and I loved it. Then, of course, we had a major job making the music work again to the picture, because the timings were all different. The cue that was supposed to be three minutes was now six, because they just played it slower, the way they normally would play it. Gergiev gave the signature of Russian musicianship history to it. You cannot tell anybody what to do there, so you have to just be happy that you're so lucky to be able to have access to that. It was quite an amazing experience.

John Barry

The name John Barry speaks for itself. His film-music career spans more than four decades, during which time he has composed some of the most amazing and well-known film scores in cinema history, including his immensely popular music that defined the character of the celluloid James Bond.

Barry's keen insight into the emotional heart of film stories has made his music—which skillfully runs the gamut from jazzy to deeply dramatic—a major influence on many film composers and makes him practically a household name to the filmgoing public.

I am ever grateful for the time that he shared with me, allowing me a glimpse into his unique musical world.

When did you actually know you were to become a composer?

I think when I was about nine. I took piano lessons at school with this large lady who used to smoke all the time. She had this huge blonde hair but the actual front of her hair was kind of brown. If you played the wrong note, she'd hit your knuckles with a ruler. I always thought that this was a strange behavior for a piano teacher, but that was her style. Nevertheless, it was about that time that music became a strong interest to me.

When you first look at a project, what is your approach to scoring that picture?

I always look at it as if I'm a member of the audience. I never look at it from a professional point of view. I act as though I am sitting myself down and I've paid my bucks, so entertain me. I find that very useful. If I get engrossed with its story, its performances, or whatever, and then it holds me, I want to do it.

How did you usually communicate with a director prior to the days of temp scores?

The big thing I used to do upon meeting a director was surreptitiously find out how much he actually knew about music. What is his musical knowledge? And then I'd adjust myself according to my assessment of that. I didn't do it in an arrogant, brash way, but in a helpful way. I found that worked. So you either listen to the guy or take the reigns. Richard Lester, for instance, knew a lot about music. The Bond directors, none of them knew much about music at all. I didn't mind that.

Did you just basically come to the table with your ideas and play demos?

After a very short time in the business, I thought that the more the director knows about what the music is, the better it is going to be for everyone. So I used to ask for a pre-recording budget so I could go in and record maybe three or four things, not the whole score, because I base most of my scores on themes, and some of them are very broad, wide-open kinds of thing.

There are a million ways to arrive at a point of view, and I always try to get a point of view. If I didn't get it, I felt there was something missing for me.

You've worked with so many filmmakers through the years. Has the younger generation posed any conflicts or challenges to your scoring process?

I found the directors of the past that I've had the pleasure of work-ing with had more knowledge of music. They couldn't detail music in musical terms, but they had very exacting ways of explaining what needed to be done with a theme.

I much prefer if a director can give me some strong indications as to what he wants the audience to react to in a scene. There are things in certain scenes where the dialogue is saying something that we know is a devious behavior. They're going to be betrayed later on in the movie. Those kinds of things are wonderful for the composer to have and to play with.

I had the good fortune to have been born into a movie environ-ment, so a lot of these things came automatically to me. But I've found that a lot of people who decide when they're in their twenties that they want to be filmmakers lack a lot of warmth. A lot of pas-sion about movies isn't there. To a lot of the people, but not every-one, it's just a job.

What composers have contributed to your rich sound?

I'm a huge fan of Russian composers. And, strangely enough, many of the successful ones, like Prokofiev and Shostakovich, did Russian movie scores—and wonderful scores, too. Those are the people I really loved and worshipped one way or the other, and not only what they wrote for film, but also all their symphonies.

How much of your own experiences inspire your themes, and how much is taken strictly from the content of the film?

We don't necessarily have the exact situation, obviously, that's going on on the screen, but we've had similar experiences. When I see a movie for the first time, sometimes I call on my own experiences, which are not exactly the same, but similar in many ways, and I very much draw on that well of emotions.

The Bond films have a unique voice. How did your Bond sound come to be?

You must know that I'm a very big jazz fan. And I had an older brother, Patrick, who was a really big jazz fan. I've loved contemporary jazz, and that played a major role in those movies.

GoldenEye was composed by Eric Serra. Why did you not continue with the Bond films?

I think I had done enough. One thing was great about it, and one thing wasn't so great about it: After virtually scoring the same movie ten times, which was basically what it was—always the hero, the woman, the villain—I just felt exhausted, like I had run the course. So I backed out.

Your shoes are nearly impossible to fit into. Did David Arnold ever seek your input for his first James Bond score, _The World is Not Enough_, for a smooth transition?

Yes. David was very sweet, and he called me. I said, "Look, if you want to meet with me, I'll tell you as much as I can. I can't tell you note for note, but I can tell you what my attitude was." We spent some time together, and I explained how I went about it. I think he was very grateful. I'm not a teacher. I can't go into the details. I just told him what to look for—what I always looked for—and gave him whatever advice I could that I thought would be useful.

I was intrigued by _Jagged Edge_'s early synthesizer sounds. At the time I saw it, I only knew the orchestral John Barry, so I'm curious: How challenging was this project?

I wanted to use the synthesizer. Everyone was starting to use it. It had a certain flexibility where you could just put things a little off, and that made it kind of interesting. You could bend chords, you could do weird stuff with them. And it seemed appropriate in that movie.

Everybody uses synths now. They don't use them in a very imaginative way. It's like a wall of sounds and everything blends. The thing about an orchestra is that you have this wonderful separation of the orchestra fabric: You can choose to do the themes on the strings, on the woodwinds, the solo trumpet, or whatever. But you don't have that wonderful orchestra fabric with the synthesizer—it all blends into one movie sound. I'm not crazy about it as a primary instrument.

You seem to have a great fluency with jazz music, as found in your scores for *Hammett* and *Body Heat* and *The Cotton Club*. Do you enjoy writing in a jazz style?

Oh absolutely. I hate the jazz thing when it's inappropriate, but when it's appropriate, it's a wonderful thing.

I don't think I write in a jazzy way. My approach is more orchestral, so it comes down to a matter of the musicians you get—whether it's an alto sax player who I know is going to be great, or a trumpet player like Chris Botti. *Body Heat* was all built around the alto sax, and it had a lovely, personalized quality throughout, which I liked very much. I remember alto sax player Ronnie Lang would play these great solos that were fascinating.

Do you find your musical inspiration in a film's characters or its settings?

It's very much the characters. It's their reactions and their behavior to the situations that I go with. And that's very much an emotional thing—love, hate, and so on. It's the ambiguity of human behavior that you go with. That's what makes things so personal. Even though *I'm* writing this thing, I'm writing the *reactions of the characters* to the situations they're in.

In *Dances with Wolves*, your music is picturesque, but it also incorporates the character's reaction to his surroundings.

Right. It was very much about how Kevin Costner's character observed things. He wanted to see the West before it was gone. I was struck by a line in the script about how he was going to see something that was passing from the sights of the Earth—it was never going to be the same again. I virtually based the whole score on that. It was the key to the whole score.

***The Deep* has a unique musical flavor. It has an unusual flute sound set amid intimate orchestral themes. Why did you choose that sound, and does the use of the flute have any particular significance?**

Well, it was just that thing about being underwater. I've dived; I live in Oyster Bay right on the water here. Floating around is almost like flying, but you're in water. It's the freest way we're able to move, unless you want to jump out of a plane without a parachute. When you dive underwater, the world becomes the mumbles, and it shuts out light and movement. I just tried to capture that kind of thing with a lot of reverberation.

Two of your scores—*My Life* and *Chaplin*—fill me with warmth and tragedy in the same breath. Would you talk about your music for *My Life*, and what fed your heartbreaking themes for it?

I'm always attracted to that sense of sadness. It's just something that's always been there. It's just a natural thing. I don't force it. Michael Keaton was wonderful in that movie and the music was about the oncoming sense of loss—that you're not going to be there anymore. You really can't talk for hours about it. It's a very felt thing.

I think the composer must have the ability to see a character and really get him, really understand and comprehend what it is that he must be going through. That's why I love music. I don't sit down and write a thesis on what's going on in this guy's mind. I sit down and write music, and it's far clearer for me to do that. I am moved by it, and that's what I work with.

Your *Chaplin* score opens with a sorrowful theme that sums up Charlie Chaplin's life. The music tells the real story. How much research went into finding the right music for this film?

I had seen all of the Chaplin films—from *The Gold Rush* onwards—in my dad's theater. I just loved them and grew up with an appreciation of Chaplin right from the beginning. So, there wasn't research, but rather, I had an awareness from the start.

Chaplin had this wonderful directness and wonderful simplicity in the way he acted and in the way he directed. He never did anything that was complicated when you analyze it. I think the sadness of Chaplin was when he found his voice. I think he was wonderful when he was totally silent and just dealt with the visuals.

Chaplin and W.C. Fields took the art of comedy to new heights. They are my comedic gods. Of course, Fields was very different. He was very verbal and very interesting. I don't know whether you know this, but women don't like W.C. Fields. He said things like, "Women are like elephants: I like to look at them, but I don't want to own one." I remember when he was in The Plaza and *The New York Times* interviewed him as he sat in the bay window there drinking his champagne. The interviewer asked him, "You have all this success now and all these movies. I wonder, do you ever think back about those times and the people you worked with in those movies?" He replied, "You know, I do. I think, "Fuck 'em." It was so W.C. Fields, so in character.

What do you look for when you choose a project to work on?

I read about some artist, I can't remember who it was, who years ago talked about having a nervous reaction towards a visual phenomena. I thought, "Oh my God, that's exactly what I feel when I see a movie!" It's something that makes me nervous, which is not necessarily a bad thing. It's something that pricks you, makes you sit up. If I get worried or disturbed or moved or happy or whatever by what's going on, then I know that I've got something to write about. But if I sit down with a movie for twenty minutes and nothing is happening, and I get a distinct feeling that it's going to go on like this, I say, "Excuse me, gentlemen, I don't think I am the right composer for your movie." Sitting through something that you know isn't good is the worst thing.

There are two CDs of your music from outside of the film world that I find unbelievably captivating—*The Beyondness of Things* and *Eternal Echoes*. Both have that sentimental sound and lush orchestration that is uniquely yours. What inspired these works?

I just love the title *The Beyondness of Things*. I don't know whether I read it somewhere or whether I came up with it. But I love that and *Eternal Echoes*. Father John O'Donohue, an Irish priest whom I know rather well, wrote this wonderful book called *Eternal Echoes*. I phoned him to see if he would mind me using the title.

In a strange way, if I don't have a film, I make up my own scenes, as it were, to whatever I'm going to write. I take the words that I like for the songs and what is "the script" behind those words—the meaning and emotion behind those words. I can't just sit down and write music. I've tried, but I just find it very difficult. I want to write *about* something.

What does it mean to you to have impacted so many lives with film music that is adored around the world?

I'm very flattered. It's kind of a silent confirmation, if you'd like, that you've reached an audience with what you've felt and your assessment of what the story was about—that you put your finger on the nerve sensor. That's the way I communicate. I just don't write a lovely melody or something like that. There's a lot of storytelling behind each melody. I can see somebody walking down the street, a character for instance, and I look and find there's a lot there in that person. It's in the way they walk and the way they smile—something springs out of that. My music has everything to do with people. I don't write for castles, I write for *people* in castles. Why are they there and what are they doing?

Marco Beltrami

Beltrami is a master of "dark" music who he has lent his unique voice to many thrillers and horror movies. His scores seamlessly weave together traditional orchestral and experimental electronic textures. One must listen to Beltrami's scores for _The Minus Man_ (1999) and _I Am Dina_ (2000) to fully appreciate the talent and originality of this young composer. These are scores that break with film-music tradition. In _I Am Dina_, which could be considered an effective avant-garde chamber work, a coldly emotional solo cello and a female voice breathe a soul into the story. In _The Minus Man_, the composer uses a glass harmonica and strings to provide a desolate emotional quality. The ambience and the surreal nature of this music will give you chills. Marco continued on this same path with his score for _The Crow: Salvation_ (2000). Beltrami's score to _Terminator 3: Rise of the Machines_ (2003) is a pure adrenaline rush. But in the midst of the battle between humans and robots, he weaves a poignant sense of life and human emotion.

Film is the perfect vehicle for Beltrami's music. He has the ability to translate the pulse of a film into the deepest, darkest of human emotions.

Let's talk about your interest in music and how it led you to scoring films.

I never intended to score films when I started out. I got a master's from the Yale School of Music and was mainly interested in doing concert music. I knew very little about film music, but my teacher at the time encouraged me to pursue it because he said that a lot of the stuff I did had a cinematic flare to it.

With lack of anything else to do, I came out to California in 1993 to do the USC program that Jerry Goldsmith guided. It was good. I learned about technical stuff and a little bit about the business. The people who came in to talk to the class, like Chris Young and Bruce Broughton, I found to be very inspiring, and the more I learned about film music, the more I liked it. I started hearing some film-music things that I thought were great musical achievements, regardless of the field they were in. I thought it could be something worthwhile pursuing.

After the USC program, I did an internship with Chris Young, getting him coffee or something and xeroxing his scores. Then I did proofing stuff for Pete Anthony. Then, it came time to put together my own music and get things together. I did a short movie called *The Bicyclist*, which was funded by Sony. It was a good little movie, and Sony provided the orchestra. It turned out to be a great little demo. After that, I did some TV stuff: a series called *Land's End* and some *Red Shoe Diaries* and some TV movies-of-the-week. Then, in 1996, I landed *Scream*.

How much of an influence has past film music, such as that written by Bernard Herrmann or Christopher Young, had on your style?

I'm a huge fan of Bernard Herrmann. His stuff is so visceral, and it even works without the film. He had a very big impact on me. Chris Young had a big impact on me, too. There were scores he was working on at the time I interned with him, such as *Dream Lover*, and things that he was doing with the orchestra that used it in a non-orchestral sense or, rather, in a nontraditional sense, which I found to be really interesting. I was definitely influenced by that.

But I was influenced as much or more by concert-music stuff. I was really unfamiliar with the whole film medium. In fact, I never really saw movies as a kid. I certainly never saw a horror movie. I didn't like the thought of going to a movie and getting scared. I remember seeing part of one when I was little and walking out because I couldn't take it. But it turns out that twentieth-century musical styles easily lend themselves to horror movies, and you can afford to be a little bit over the top and take liberties and just have a lot of fun with horror movies.

Nino Rota was a huge influence on me. His was music that didn't take itself too seriously. He obviously had fun writing a lot of the stuff. It was innovative. It used different ideas. It took from the past. It took from things that were happening currently. He used everything available, and that's what really appealed to me. That's what I view as film music. I just sort of grasp everything that's available and sort of steal ideas when I can from anywhere I can find them.

Your experiences and influences are orchestra-related, yet your music often seems to have a metallic or synthetic texture to it.

It's funny, because when I went to get the job for *Scream*—which was not a huge-budget movie at the time (in fact, it was a low-budget movie)—I didn't have any orchestral music on my reel. So, after I asked a few questions about the movie, I put together this demo that had absolutely nothing orchestral or even remotely orchestral-sounding on it. I used the palette of sounds I had: Instead of having violins and woodwinds and stuff, I had non-orchestral sounds, which I put together and gave to them. They liked it. That's what they responded to. So they called me in on a Friday and asked me to score the opening Drew Barrymore scene, which is a thirteen-minute cue, and bring it to them on Monday. So when I finally got hired, I had to continue the score in that same vein, which was basically an orchestral and electronic mix. It was the nature of the job and what they were looking for.

I didn't have a studio when I came out here. I had to borrow other people's studios. Even on *Scream* I didn't have a studio. As I started working on it, I bought some equipment. Now, one of the things I enjoy a lot is creating sounds. We spend a lot of time working on them: For *Terminator 3*, we spent about three weeks just taking acoustical sounds and manipulating them and working with them and coming up with a palette of non-orchestral sounds that would work organically with the orchestral stuff.

How comfortable are you coming to the table with your own thoughts now, versus when you first started doing film scores?

A lot more comfortable. I think that as much as this process is about writing music, it's also about social skills and figuring out what it is that somebody is looking for. It's such an abstract business that you have to be able to read into what a director says to you and figure out what the director means, which is a skill that I was not terribly adept at when I started. But the more you do it, the more you figure it out. Even when a director says that this is exactly what we want, and they play you a temp score, you know that that's not really what they want, it just happens to work with the picture in some way. So you have to be sort of a detective, finding what the clues are and what really is *needed*. That's something I feel I have really grown at. Now, when I see a picture, I have my own ideas about it, and I can then talk to them and find out specific things they want. And when I come to the table now, I can present my ideas and defend them, which I may have had trouble doing in the past.

Brad Fidel wrote great scores for the first two *Terminator* films. I'm curious why they changed composers.

The first two scores, which were synth scores, worked. I also think Brad wrote a very strong theme for it. On this movie, what they were trying to do was different. Jonathan [Mostow, the director] was not trying to redo *T2*. He was trying to do something new. In its scope, this movie was little bit bigger than other two movies. It really needed an orchestral score, and perhaps not a copy of the first two scores.

I did do an arrangement of Brad Fidel's *T2* theme for orchestra, though. It's at the end of the movie. So there is an homage paid to Brad's score, but the feeling was that if we just did an update of the music from *T2*, it would bring the viewers back to *T2*-land, and that's not what this movie was about.

Jonathan had heard my music because the editor had temped a lot of it in from other scores that I had done. In fact, it was about seventy percent temped with my music. So Jonathan asked, "What is this stuff?" And the editor said, "It's this guy Beltrami." So I met with

Jonathan, and he said, "I just wanted you to know that I liked your music a lot, but, being politically honest, you're probably not going to get the job because it's a big movie, and that's the way it goes. But I just wanted to let you know we are temping with your music." But, over the next month or so, he was able to sell the producers and everybody on the idea that I would be the guy to do this. That's how that worked out.

Would you like to move your music away from its predominantly dark character?

Yeah, my music definitely has a dark character to it. I don't know that I am really interested in doing romantic comedies. Being like a wallpaper thing is not interesting to me. I've always said that I like to have fun with what I do, even though it may be dark.

Not everything I do necessarily has to be dark. I still want to explore a lot of things. My interests are varied. I have sketches for things. I have sketches for non-film projects. In the next year or two, I will be working on some non-film projects as well. I certainly don't want to just be typecast. Nobody does.

Which scores of yours are you most fond of?

One of my favorites is *Mimic*. Even though it's a dark sci-fi/horror movie, I think the score was able to reach a very human element. I think *T3* is a really good score. I think *The Minus Man* was kind of cool. I did it all with prepared piano, viola, and percussion. It's a fun score.

I like them all for different reasons. There are different things I did in different scores that I like. I like *The Crow* for certain reasons. *Dracula 2000* has this Middle-Eastern part that I really like.

I think your music in *Joy Ride* works so well for the movie.

With the score before that, *The Watcher*, I really started to experiment with creating sounds that were integral to the movie. I spent a tremendous amount of time creating a palette of sounds that would define the score. That's something I continued in *Joy Ride*.

The Watcher **seems to mark the point at which your music evolved in a more experimental way.**

That's one of the most intense scores I've done, but I had to search a little for my inspiration there. It seems to work really well for temps.

Bruce Broughton

Bruce Broughton has been composing for TV and films for more than four decades, and he also created the first symphonic score for a computer game, *Heart of Darkness*.

He wrote for such noted television series as *Hawaii Five-O* and *Quincy* for many years before he gained wide audience recognition with his exciting first major-motion-picture score, *Silverado* (1985). He has followed this with many Americana-flavored scores, including *O Pioneers!* (1992), *True Women* (1997), and *Roughing It* (2002).

Broughton's signature style is predominantly lighthearted, beautifully orchestrated music. During his long, varied career, he has worked in almost every conceivable film genre, and his impressive oeuvre includes wonderful music for the mystery movie *Young Sherlock Holmes* (1985), the suspense-laden *Narrow Margin* (1990), and the emotionally charged, delightful *Miracle on 34th Street* (1994).

What was your exposure to music when growing up, and did you ever see yourself becoming a film composer?

I came from a musical family. A grandfather was a composer of band music, a grandmother was a trained singer; all of my grandparents and both of my parents could read music, sing at sight, and play two or three instruments. An uncle was a songwriter; his sister was a pianist. My brother is a professional trombonist/composer. I started playing the piano and the trumpet when I was six or seven, and I started composing when I was twelve. But I never considered composing for films or anything else until my last year of college.

Your career started in television. How did this come about?

I got a job out of college as an assistant music supervisor for CBS Television in Hollywood. My job was to track and supervise music for series that CBS produced. At that time, I worked on shows like *Gunsmoke*, *Hawaii Five-O*, *The Wild Wild West*, and many other shows you've probably never heard of. I began composing for TV while I was at CBS and eventually became Assistant Director of Music for the network. I left when the job became too immersed in the business end of music. When I left CBS, I knew TV, so that's what I went into. I started working immediately on *Quincy* and then *How the West Was Won*.

Your first major film score was for *Silverado*. Was the transition from television to motion pictures difficult?

It was not a difficult transition, because, by that time, I had done many, many Western-style and Americana shows: *Gunsmoke*, *How the West Was Won*, and *The Blue and the Gray*. I knew the musical style well. But, because it was my first major feature, it was somewhat daunting. I didn't want to screw it up.

What are the major differences between TV scoring and film scoring, and which do you prefer?

It's mostly a matter of size. Movies are scaled toward large images, whereas television is generally more intimate. Movies are meant to be seen in theaters, where the image is huge and the drama is shared with other people. There are generally not many distractions when watching a movie. With television, it's much the opposite. The images are smaller and the programs suffer the distractions of not only people walking in and out of the viewing area, but of commercial breaks, poor transmission, and rigid time constraints. In the case of television series, there are also rigid story formats with well-developed characters and relationships.

For a composer, one of the main differences between the two media is that there is generally a little more time on a feature film to think things over before committing to a direction, though not always. Television is practically always done on the fly. There also tends to be much more attention paid to detail on a movie than on a television show. When recording a movie score with an orchestra, hours can be spent agonizing over one musical gesture. There's rarely anything like that in television.

I like working in both television and movies, assuming the stories are interesting. Television often has more variety in stories than movies. But for capturing an audience and having the maximum effect of your music felt, there's nothing like the movies to do that.

Although you have proven yourself to be a most versatile composer, you often seem to score films that require an Americana sound. Is this a purposely chosen direction or do you find yourself pigeonholed a bit because of your early scores in this style?

I just happened to have done a lot of Americana-themed projects early on in my movie career, and a couple of these, most notably *Silverado* and *Tombstone*, got the most notice. Because of this, I think I may have been sometimes pigeonholed as a certain kind of composer. However, I have a versatile technique and can write many other sorts of scores.

What are your musical influences? Do you ever turn to the old film-music masters, such as Steiner and Korngold, for inspiration?

In general, though I think they were good composers, I don't go to film scorers like Steiner's or Korngold's or anyone else's for inspiration or for stylistic influences. Most film composers borrow a lot from concert composers, because the concert composers have the opportunity and time to be more musically original than film composers. Both Steiner and Korngold, for example, were admirers of Wagner's music and borrowed a lot from that composer, as well as from other composers' styles.

My musical influences are pretty eclectic and span a lot of different composers, techniques, and time periods. These influences get funneled and sifted through me, eventually becoming part of my style; but the process really isn't all that different from what any other composer does, no matter what medium he or she is writing in. I usually know where I picked up a specific technique or whether it was something that originated with me. Sometimes the sources are pretty weird. Having said that, I occasionally hear an interesting film score by someone who takes an approach I would never think of, and that sort of influence is often inspiring aesthetically. You can always learn something from someone else, even if it's what not to do.

What is your film-scoring process, and is it the same for all areas of your writing, from TV to films to concert music?

My composing process, in whichever medium, is usually the same in one respect: I start at the beginning and work my way to the end. I essentially through-compose. Some composers start on the big cues; some of them start on the hard cues. I just start. I will work out my main theme first and then see what comes up later. If I have spent enough time with the story, there's a part of me that knows when to do what, and I find there's no use in trying to figure everything out before I start writing. As the story develops in the film, so does my understanding of it, and so does my music. It's an interesting process.

In concert music, I work a lot slower. I will go back over a piece and add or subtract measures or phrases for better timing. I'll rewrite sections. It's usually not necessary or practical to do that with a film.

In television, I just sit down and write. The eraser is the busiest part of my pencil.

You have also composed the music for a game. What was this like?

This was a lot of fun for a couple of reasons. First of all, the game was good, the story worked well, and it was very well-executed. Secondly, the production team was French, which meant that I made many trips to Paris. I developed some really great relationships with some very creative and interesting people, whom I have continued to see ever since. We all stay in touch.

It seems that composing for film has changed quite a bit in the past couple of decades, with more reliance on synths, more hands involved, and a shortening of the composing time. Does this affect your more traditional style of scoring?

Synths are just musical instruments, so that's not a big deal, once you figure out how you can use them.

There have always been many hands involved, though not as much micromanaging as there is now. I think the anxiety is very, very great now for directors, who do not work as often as composers and are in charge of spending a lot of money that belongs to other people. The anxiety is also great for the studio executives, who are relying upon the director to come up with something that will sustain their careers for a little while longer. Every aspect of a movie gets minutely examined and re-examined, and it very quickly comes down to someone peering into the composing process. If you've ever worked in television, you're used to a shortage of time, though sometimes it gets ridiculously short in movies through a lack of foresight or understanding of the composing process.

Most of the above issues have always been around. What is different now is that, due to digital technology, much is possible for filmmakers that was never possible before: Temp-tracks are easier to do. Making picture edits up until the last minute, even during the recording of the score, is easier to do. Making changes in the soundtrack is easier, as is changing one's mind at the last minute. All of the above can make scoring a lot more time-intensive.

What are your feelings to using a synthesizer versus a full orchestra? Is it often an attempt to lower the costs of recording, or is it merely a tool, an instrument in itself?

The synth, as I said, is basically just another musical instrument, and a really useful one at that. However, to some people, it is thought of as a way of getting cheap and quick scores. To some composers, it is a way of not having to learn how to deal with an orchestra or acoustical music. The synth gets in my way from time to time because I can't always demonstrate what the orchestra is really going to sound like from a synth mockup. I'm a good orchestrator and a more-than-adequate synth player. I can make an orchestra sound very, very specific, but I can't do that with synths. So, when I do a "synth score," I often feel limited by fewer aural opportunities. I know some synth-oriented composers feel the opposite. Doing a decent synth-based score is expensive, even if a composer does it himself in his own studio. It's very time-consuming. But he or she doesn't have to pay a great mass of musicians in order to get the fat sound that his or her index finger can get by pressing the right key that connects to that specific fat sound on a keyboard. This is essentially what's considered as money-saving.

The best synth scores are those that are either integrated into the overall orchestral fabric to produce unique and special sounds or effects, or are produced by people who live, work, and think more comfortably in that specifically creative environment.

In your score for the 1994 remake of *Miracle on 34th Street*, you created a warm mood that makes me want to snuggle under the blankets with a cup of hot chocolate. How did you create this emotional mood?

The first thing you have to do is to buy into the story. The second thing you have to do is to find the notes that express the way you feel while helping to tell the story. Then you have to find the right instruments and timbres that will carry the emotion to the audience in the most convincing way. Holidays are associated with a certain sound, like Westerns are associated with guitars and harmonicas and horrors with screeching violins and so on.

You also wrote some of this film's cues in the voices of Vivaldi and Handel.

Christmas music is partly associated with music of the Baroque. Think of Handel's *Messiah*, for example; it's played more at Christmas than it is at Easter. In any case, I chose to write ersatz Baroque for all of the Christmas source music. Besides, I really like to work in other composers' styles when I can. I learn a lot by doing that. I think my faux Handel and faux Vivaldi work pretty well musically. For the TV movie *Eloise at Christmastime*, I chose to write much of the music in Tchaikovsky's style, and incorporated bits of his *Nutcracker Suite*, another great Christmas piece, as accompaniment to the Eloise theme.

In *Homeward Bound*, you gave an Americana-style voice to the main characters.

There was a definite country flavor in the score, given the outdoor surroundings. The cat had a theme that was, to me, the musical equivalent of a cat coming up and rubbing against your leg. The theme for Chance, the young dog, was giddy, bouncy, and country-like. The overall *Homeward Bound* theme, however, was big, outdoors, and inspirational. It is, after all, subtitled *The Incredible Journey*.

I find it unfortunate that the moviegoers are not exposed to your work in blockbusters. Are you where you want to be in your career, or do you feel underappreciated in the industry and want to be attached to larger projects?

Though I don't feel left out in the industry, I'd certainly like the opportunity to work on a blockbuster movie. I have no control, however, nor does anyone else, over what the next mega-hit will be. I try to work on things I enjoy with people I like and respect and whom I enjoy working with. I like working on all sorts of pictures: serious drama, action, comedies, animation, period stories, whatever. But I particularly like working with people who are passionate about what they're doing, and in this respect I've been very fortunate. There's still a lot to come.

It's taken me many years to realize one essential reality: It's not only about the music. Whatever success as a film composer means, it's not just about whether someone writes well or not. Just as the three rules of real estate have much to do with location, the three rules of success in the movie business have much to do with relationships. Having said that, the choice of whether or not to take "the big picture" isn't one that any of us gets to make. No one knows which one is going to be "the one," but we're always hopeful.

Which musical projects or areas do you most enjoy being involved with?

I like writing music. Period. All sorts. I like composing for the movies; it's interesting, challenging, and exciting. I also like composing concert music. It brings me into direct contact with my audience.

What one word would best describe you as a composer?

Versatile.

Teddy Castellucci

There is much to be said for the talented Teddy Castellucci, who is perhaps best known for his work on comedies starring Adam Sandler, a teaming of star and composer that started with *The Wedding Singer* (1998) and continues to this day. Castellucci, however, is not just a "funny music" guy. His score for the Sandler vehicle *Mr. Deeds* (2002), for example, is made up of epic adventure motifs and heartfelt love themes. And his score for *Little Nicky* (2000) has a slight horror-genre edge to it. It is a lighthearted orchestral score with a clever "tongue in cheek" thriller/horror tone, and his blend of these elements works perfectly. His score for Sandler's *50 First Dates* (2004), with its Hawaiian-flavored music, shows us yet a slightly different side of Teddy Castellucci.

You were a professional performer, a session player for movie scores, at an early age, which eventually led you to becoming a musical director for network television. How did all of this fall into place for you?

I grew up in New York, on Long Island. I've been playing since I was nine years old. I started off as a drummer, then switched to guitar a couple months later. I played guitar and drums through all my

formative years, studying and working on both instruments. I started
playing sessions in New York when I was fourteen or fifteen. That
was my passion and my love growing up. I never wanted to be a rock
star, never cared about any of that kind of stuff. Now, I'm thirty-nine
years old, and when I was younger, there were a lot of variety shows
on television, like *This Is Tom Jones* and *Donnie & Marie*. I thought
the coolest thing were the musicians who were playing behind all
these acts. My desire was always to be a studio musician. That happened for me in New York at an early age.

When I moved out to Los Angeles, I was fortunate because my
career took off very quickly. I became musical director for the show
Into the Night. I was told that I was the youngest musical director in
television history. I don't know if that's true, but that's what ABC told
me. Then this other career pops up. I think it's very important in the
music business in general to be adaptable and open to things that
might come your way.

As a session player for movie scores, what did you do?

Generally, I would play guitar just on the sessions, and later on I
started arranging and doing orchestrating for some composers.
That's really how you start to learn the business. If you're fortunate
enough that your time comes to get in as a composer, you've already
seen the process from the inside. Especially if you're arranging and
orchestrating, you're a little bit more aware of the internal process.
If you're fortunate or unfortunate enough, it depends, to be part of
meetings with producers and directors and things like that, you can
really start to see how the mechanism of film works, which is different from some of the other recording mediums. It's very different
from records. It's very different from television. It's an entity unto
itself. So I was very fortunate to kind of see some of the things from
the inside, so when the opportunity came for me to have a shot at
scoring a film, I kind of knew somewhat what to expect. And that
was invaluable.

How did you land your first scoring assignment?

I got hired to do all the pre-records on the movie *The Wedding
Singer*, which is essentially a musical. It's wall-to-wall music. It's an

eighties' period piece. I got hired to do the arrangements and kind of oversee all the pre-record sessions before shooting started, and they went really well.

I was introduced to Adam Sandler and we got along famously. He's an East Coast guy, like me. We're of similar age and we just hit it off. At the end of the sessions, he said, "We had a problem with my last movie, and we ended up throwing out most of the score. Would you be interested in doing this score, because I really like working with you?" I said, "Absolutely!"

So that was my first film. I know people reading this are going to hate hearing this, because I was fortunate enough to hop right into things. I didn't do student films. I didn't do B-movies.

How that fell in your lap is amazing.

It is. And that's what I mean when I say, "You just never know." If you're in the fray of things, working with people who are part of the creative process, you just never know what kind of opportunity is going to come your way. So you should prepare as best you possibly can because, as we all know, getting an opportunity like that is very difficult. When it comes, if you're prepared, that's your shot.

Prior to *The Wedding Singer*, what was your knowledge or awareness of music in films?

It was pretty high because I had played on films for six or seven years. So I'd gotten to see a bunch of different situations, and talked to the other studio players, like Tommy Tedesco, who I was honored enough to know a little bit before he passed away. There is no more legendary a person than Tommy. Later on, I got to know Chuck DeMonico, who passed away a couple of years ago. These are giant people in their fields, and I was fortunate enough to be in the position where I was around these kinds of people all the time. I found that if I kept my mouth shut and my ears open, I leaned a whole lot. These were also super-nice human beings who were open to questions, which is the only way you find out about things.

I had no contact with composers, except for working for them as a player. But I obviously had a ton of contacts, because of the musicians I'd see all the time.

One of the most rewarding things about being a composer now is that I get to be part of the process that gives employment to tons of people whom I spent a lot of the years on the other side of the glass with. So my sessions always have a great feeling of camaraderie. I always want my dates to feel real relaxed and have a great vibe. But there's always underlying and not-so-underlying pressures: the time pressure, the creative pressure, all of that stuff that has to happen because film deadlines keep getting pushed up farther and farther until you're really at the eleventh hour. This is becoming more of the norm than the exception these days.

Those pressures are a shame because they don't allow the creative process to really flow.

Right. Film composers really can't afford to have days when stuff doesn't come to them. Missing days is not an option in this profession. It's not like concert works or things of that nature. It's a create-on-demand profession that requires making changes at the sessions themselves. Being a session player is such amazing training for being a film composer because the jobs have such huge parallels to each other: It's create it now, on the spot. You have to have the ability to do that or you won't survive in the business. That's just the hard, cold reality of it.

Have you ever run into writer's block or challenges that put you in a panic state?

Oh sure, absolutely. But generally, I'm pretty lucky. I try to work through that as best I can, and it really doesn't happen that I hit a wall and nothing comes. Sometimes, I might have to spin my wheels for an hour or two, but then the floodgates usually open and stuff starts to pour out, thank God. Not having that happen is really not an option. It's just not.

Another thing, besides deadlines, is the rejected score, which not only tightens the schedule further for the next composer but also has to be discouraging. I know you haven't had this happen yet, but what are your thoughts about having a score rejected?

I've been fortunate again. I've just had great relationships with some of the people I've worked with. Sure, sometimes you'll have something that you think works perfectly, but a director or someone else in the process will go, "Naw, why don't we try something different?" As a composer, you can be passionate about what you do and try to take a stand, but at the end of the day . . . I would imagine it's different for John Williams or Jerry [Goldsmith], rest his soul, than it is for some of the guys.

In general, a composer is a facilitator of someone else's vision. If that person allows you to bring your creativity to the party, that's a win-win all the way around. But if you get into a stalemate, the director wins or else he will replace your score. That happens so much nowadays. A lot of that, I'm sure, is not a reflection on the composer; it's just a difference of opinion. At the end of the day, you have to please the person who has the final say. No matter how good you think a piece of music is, how great you think it works for a particular scene, or how well it serves the movie, if the filmmaker does not agree with you, that piece of music will never wind up in that film. That is what is so different about film composition as opposed to other kinds of composition. It's a whole different headspace to be in.

In general, this confounds me. It seems to me that when a composer is selected, it should be for a reason, correct?

There are so many political minefields one must cross as a film composer. Sometimes, if something gets torpedoed, you might not ever know where it came from or why. That's a hard reality to live with. I haven't had any of my stuff get replaced yet, but I'm still early in my career. I would make a bet with you that, unfortunately, sooner or later, it's going to happen to me, because it happens to virtually everybody.

Often not the fault of the composer and their abilities . . .

Right. Generally, I don't think it's a reflection on the composer. Sometimes, it's not even a reflection on the director. Some people have the luxury and the option of changing their minds, which could happen after you've spent a whole lot of time and effort giving them what you think they want. But if they decide it's not what they want, they want something different, they can ask you to do something different or they can just say that they want to try it with somebody else. That is their prerogative.

I'd like to talk about temp scores. Here's a hypothetical temp-score situation: Say a filmmaker temps a movie with some of Thomas Newman's music but hires Chris Young or James Newton Howard to score it. Young and Howard quite clearly have their own voices, which are different from Newman's. Why wouldn't a filmmaker always hire the composer whose music was used as temp? I know they often don't.

That particular situation would have me scratching my head, too. But they might have tried and maybe Thomas wasn't available or he said no or something like that. That' s a very interesting example, because when you talk about a composer like Tom, his music has a very specific kind of sound to it. It's very unique, very specific unto him. So when a film is temped with his music, but they don't hire him, yet they want that style, it's going to sound like a rip-off, and it's going to sound generic. What he does, he does so brilliantly that if you get anybody else to do it, it's just going to be a secondhand version of him.

People have to realize, too, that composers are sometimes asked to rip themselves off. I've had that happen. A film is temped with my music, and then, after I write the score for it, the filmmaker might say, "Yeah, that's okay, but I really like your other thing." So you wind up ripping yourself off. You try not to, of course. Composers don't want to rip themselves off or do the same thing over and over again, or worse, have to emulate somebody else. But there are instances, certainly, when a filmmaker wants a certain style. If the filmmaker is set on that, you have a choice: You can give them that style and try to infuse it with as much originality or creativity as you can, so it's not generic, or you can say, "No, I'm not going to do that," in which case they will replace you. You always have that choice to make. And that's not an easy choice.

Have you ever been distracted going from a temp score to your own music?

I'm sure if you ask many different composers this question, you're going to get many different answers.

For me, it's not really a problem. Here's how I try to deal with temp music: If a director says to me, "I like the temp score in this spot," I'll generally try to listen to it one time and say, "Okay." I'll listen stylistically because most filmmakers can't talk, nor should they be expected to talk, to you in musical terms. It's generally hard for directors to explain to you what they're looking for, especially if they've been watching a film in the editing room with the same temp music every day for months. When you come along with a fresh perspective, which obviously is a good thing, and write something that could be 180 degrees different from the temp music, it is sometimes very hard for them to wrap their mind around. It's not what they're used to hearing.

Temping is just part of the film process nowadays. Films have to be temped because the filmmakers do recruited audience screenings, which have value to the studio for marketing and all kinds of other things. But what happens, of course, is that the temp music, regardless of what it is, starts to get engrained into everybody who is involved with the film.

I know that the temp score is valuable tool, but I think that filmmakers ought to refrain from temping with other film scores and use just source music.

That would certainly be better. But, source music will never sound like good film music. And because test screenings have an enormous impact on the whole process of making a film, filmmakers certainly want the best test-screening results that they can get. If you're testing a thriller and you're using thriller music from several films that have been successful in the last five years, that music could have a subliminal effect on audience members, who might subliminally think, "Oh, this is familiar to me, so it is good." I'm sure that a lot more people have put a lot more thought into the psychology of this than I have, but that's how it strikes me.

I can get around that if everything on a certain project aligns so that I can write early in the game. I've done it both ways: I've come in way late in the game after all the audience previews are done and written a whole score in three weeks or whatever. And I've been on a film very early on. Both ways have advantages and disadvantages.

The advantage of being on a film very early is that your demos go into the temp screenings, and if you're fortunate, the screenings go well and the film seems to be working and everybody is happy. In that case, there is no actual temp music. About half of *Mr. Deeds* had no temp music. The audience screenings were done with demos of my score. If the filmmakers use your demos for the main thematic elements of the film and the main sound of the movie, be that very orchestral with electronic elements or whatever the particular sound of that movie is, they will get used to hearing your music when they see the scene. That's certainly the upside of it.

The downside of coming onto the project very early is that there's a very good chance most of the stuff you write will have no bearing on what the final movie is. You'll write music for scenes that will not be in the film and scenes that will be unbelievably truncated from the original version of what you wrote. So you could spend a lot of time doing things that, depending on the project, could be for nothing.

If you come on too early in the process, the filmmakers probably haven't thought a ton about music yet. When you start showing your music, it could be like, "No, that's not what I want." Or it can go the other way. Obviously each director and each situation is unique. Even on productions with the same people, the dynamic of each movie is always a little bit different.

A great relationship with a filmmaker seems to be very productive, because it allows the composer to free up the "what ifs." You already have a sense of what that person wants. The strongest scores often seem to be those written for directors and producers with whom the composer has had an ongoing relationship.

Making movies, in my view, is such a team sport. It is so between a director and a producer—if the producer has a strong opinion about things—and the studio. In the best-case scenarios, people will lead you to a place where you wouldn't have gone by yourself. They might make a comment and you might go, "Oh, I didn't see it that way at all, but I get what you mean. Let me try that." It could turn out to be great. I always like getting another person's opinion because one word or one phrase could spark an idea in my head and

I go, "Oh, you know what, I would have never thought of that! That's a cool idea, so let me run with it." Boy, you never know where a good idea is going to come from. If you're not open to that, you're just closing down some of your options.

Which composers inspired you as you developed your style?

The people whose music I most relate to, whose music—pretty much everything they do—just resonates with me immediately. Three people come to mind: James Newton Howard, Alan Silvestri, and the king, John Williams.

I don't mean to suggest that you take from James Newton Howard, but in your more lighthearted scores, I can hear a certain tone or style that might be somewhat similar to his.

That's actually a nice compliment because that's the level I aspire to. Everything I've heard him do is on such a high level. His career is, again, what I would aspire to.

I have been very fortunate. I've had a lot of success in comedy. This is still early in my career, but if you listen to some of my scores, hopefully you'll hear my skill levels in other genres, even though the music comes from comedy films.

I have noticed a lot of styles in your music that would be great in other genres.

I certainly hear that in James [Newton Howard]. My god, *The Devil's Advocate* sounds nothing like *Dave*. It sounds nothing like *Snow Falling on Cedars*. And all of that sounds nothing like *Major League* if you go back to his early career.

He comes from a record background, too. So maybe that's also why I relate to his music—because of its production values and its interesting use of color, not just acoustic color, but soundscape and textural kinds of things. I just very much relate to virtually all the music that I've heard him do.

What is your writing process?

It differs on each project, and it really differs depending on what the schedule is. If you come in late in the game, you have to start writing some projects immediately. I work well that way. I work well under pressure. That's one kind of creative head to be in. You can be in another kind of creative head if you have the luxury of maybe a week or so to watch the film a couple times. Then you can really think about it and try to get your head around it before you start writing and developing thematic ideas and just what you think is sonically going to serve the film the best. I can work either way. But, generally, the first time I watch a film, and sometimes when I read a script, I'll start to get a sense in my head of what I think the score should sound like. Very often I'll get thematic ideas right off the bat, and a lot of those wind up being in the final version of the movie.

Do you sit down at the piano with a pencil and paper?

I start with pencil and paper first. I find that the music comes out the best that way.

Do you think that happens often anymore?

I think that varies greatly from composer to composer. I do pretty much ninety-nine percent of a cue with pencil and paper before anything goes to synth. I just find that that works best for me.

Some people might never even pick up a pencil. Film composition is such an individual thing. I'm always curious about how other people's processes work. With what you're doing I'm sure it's amazing to hear all the different answers to this question from all the different composers. I can't wait to read your book because I don't know a lot of other composers. Again, I come from being a musician on the other side of the glass. So I know the all people whom I would play for or whatever, but that's a different kind of relationship.

Yes, it is exciting and intriguing, really. There is so much creativity going on that is often taken for granted. Some may wonder why I interviewed all these composers who, like you said, have their own stories and processes and so on. I hope these interviews will ignite some reader's unknown passion.

That's great, man. I am excited to hear these stories.

The film industry often seems to pigeonhole composers by genre. Since you've scored so many comedies, have you been frustratingly pigeonholed or are comedies your favorite work?

I'm not here by choice; it's just kind of what happened. It's frustrating in some respects, and in other respects, I kiss the ground every day for what's happened to me. I had a really successful career as a player. Then I started to arrange records and had success that way. Then the film-scoring thing happened and my first film was a hit movie, and I've been lucky enough to have a lot of hits and a lot of success in this genre. To bitch about it is ridiculous.

Having said that, I would love to do other genres. I think that will happen, but I also understand the business enough to know that people hire you to do what you've already been proven successful doing. It's very hard to get them to take chances. If they hire people with proven track records in the same genre of film that they're making, that takes their stress level down a couple notches.

I was offered something that was totally different from anything I've ever done before, but I don't want to be too specific about it because I wound up not taking the film for several reasons. It would have been amazing to do. There was almost two hours of score in the film. There were no songs. It was not a comedy at all.

That was the first offer I've gotten that was 180 degrees away from what I've proved doing. I've got my fingers crossed that there will be others. It's way early into my career though. I mean, my first film came out only six years ago. I've scored thirteen films at this point.

This is where temp music can actually help you. A composer often gets hired if a film is temped with his music and the music seems to be working well and all of the parties involved think that the style fits the movie. I've certainly benefited from that, because my music is starting to be used as temp in a lot of films. I get calls from music editor friends and different people all the time, telling me that so-and-so temped half their movie with this score or that score of mine. I've gotten hired because of that.

The only problem with that is if they are using your music, it is probably being temped to another comedy, right?

Well, yes, this is probably true, unless somebody takes some of my non-comedic music from a comedy and temps it in a different genre.

Another way you can break out from a pigeonholed role is if a director or producer or somebody whom you've worked with and formed a very strong bond with works in a different genre from one you've worked with them before. You know, for me, I'm dying to do an adventure movie, like an *Indiana Jones*, that kind of stuff. Hopefully, one of the directors whom I have a good relationship with from doing comedies will think of me when he does an adventure movie and give me a shot at it.

I can hear your dramatic abilities, and I hope a director will read this and ask for a demo from you/your agent. A prime example of your dramatic music is in *Little Nicky*. You spread your wings from comedic work into a dramatic, somewhat epic work that is bold and almost "superhero-ish."

Thank you very much. That was a fun movie for me to score because it was a very broad canvas to paint on. That's a score that has a ton of combinations of traditional orchestral music with a ton of electronic stuff.

Hopefully those opportunities will come. I feel good about them, and there is definitely progress being made that way. But, generally, people think of me for what people already know me for—comedies. When I talk about James Newton Howard and Alan Silvestri, those two guys in particular, that's such a thing to shoot for in my view because I think their music is always on a high level. And look at their careers—they do all kinds of varied films. They have very strong bonds with several directors, and those directors use them no matter what genre film they're making. That's a wonderful thing. If I could pattern my career—in terms of the kinds of films I'm offered— after anybody, it would certainly be those two gentlemen.

What do you find most rewarding in your career?

That's a good one, and in some ways a very tough question to answer. I try never to take for granted the fact that I'm lucky enough to be working on things that go out to the world and hopefully give people enjoyment. And sometimes give them enjoyment when they're not in the best situations or have had a crappy day or any of that kind of stuff. Maybe I help in my little tiny contribution to brighten a person's day a little bit. That's a wonderful thing. That can have far-reaching effects. You're not curing cancer with this stuff, but at the same time, if you can make people laugh or cry or touch them in any way with your little contribution to the filmmaking process, that's pretty damn cool.

Another upside of this work is that you get to work on the highest level, with the people who are on the highest level in all of their particular fields. That's an honor and a privilege. I get to have my music played and recorded by the best people in the world all the time. I never take that for granted. This career and this field allow you to provide a nice life for your family. It's a wonderful thing if that happens while doing something you love. That's win-win.

I feel like I know you well from your music, because I figured you would answer my questions the way you have. You are a composer who brings this quiet passion to life. Also, it's exciting and fresh to hear you being so humble about your accomplishments. You are right: Your music affects many, consciously or subconsciously.

This is wonderful to hear, thank you. You know, sometimes it's really easy to lose sight of that fact when you've been up for two days and you're battling a deadline and the picture keeps changing and all you want to do is throw all the shit against the wall.

Another good thing about this profession is that you can have time off. You can have a couple months at a time off to be with your family and to take a step back and look at your work.

I'm so fortunate. There's not a day that goes by that I can't flip around the channels, with all the cable channels and stuff, and see something that I was lucky enough to work on. Sometimes on cable there are three or four movies that I've worked on playing at one time. Then you get your BMI or your ASCAP statement and you see that your music is being played literally all over the world in the theaters and on television. If you can step back from it a little bit, you can go, "My God, how cool is this?!" It's a cool thing. But don't get me wrong, it's also a tough business. Being a film composer is not for the faint of heart. I'm sure I'm not the first person to say that to you. It's a hard, demanding, pressure-cooker job.

Pointing out the job's negative aspects is easy. I think too many do get caught up in that and forget what they have accomplished. You're doing something you're passionate about and, at the same time, able to provide for your family and have fun doing it.

God bless you. How many people in the world are in that position? Not many. If you're one of them, you kiss the ground and say "Thank you," even on days when you're not so psyched about it. Everybody has those days, and if they say that they don't, they're lying. It's just life.

Jeff Danna

Jeff is the younger brother of film composer Mychael Danna. Amazingly, they work in the same field without any signs of sibling rivalry, and sometimes even collaborate on projects. As a team of two, they scored the film *Green Dragon* (2002), beautifully blending together their distinct musical styles. They have also collaborated on two non-film-related CDs released on the Hearts of Space label, *A Celtic Tale* (1996) and *A Celtic Romance* (1998).

Jeff Danna's great musical strengths are his abilities to sculpt striking melodies and construct vibrant, colorful orchestrations. For *Uncorked* (1998), Jeff wrote a lovely stream of melodies that flow from the harp, strings, guitar, flutes, and hurdy-gurdy in such a way that they beautifully heighten the film's emotional character. His praiseworthy score for *The Gospel of John* (2003) uses the same approach to express the intimate side of a much more epic story. For this movie, Jeff chose not to write an epic score a la Miklós Rózsa. Instead, he took us on an introspective journey into the events found in *The Gospel of John*.

In 2004, turning 180 degrees from his biblical style, Jeff composed a dark, textural score for *Resident Evil: Apocalypse*. This is a synth-heavy score with orchestral cues that are far from angelic (or melodic), but like all of Jeff Danna's work, it is very well done.

You started your musical career as a performer. What type of music did you play?

I was into the songwriting, the pop music world. I started out as a guitar player, and my interest first lay in band arrangements, and then in songwriting. That was where music started for me really.

You worked with your brother Mychael on two non-score projects titled *A Celtic Tale* and *A Celtic Romance*. How did these ideas blossom?

I had recently moved to L.A. and was working on other projects when Mychael and I discovered that we had the same time off that summer. We had done some movies together back when we both were starting out in Toronto. As we talked about those experiences and how much fun they were, I mentioned that, since we had some time, we should do something else together again.

At the time, I was working on a project that used a lot of Chinese instruments, while he was doing a project that used Indian instruments, so we talked about mixing Western music with these other cultures and combining orchestras with native instruments and voices. We both loved this style of music, but we hadn't really heard it done the way we thought it could be done, with that kind of orchestral element added to it.

For the first one, we said, "Let's just do whatever it is that we do with the Celtic music and see how that turns out." When that first album did as well as it did, we were then asked to do another, and we agreed. We changed it up a little bit by adding Gregorian chants and early music elements as the story called for them.

Where did the words come from?

The words come from some fragments from eighth- and ninth-century poems we found. We had our lyricist, John Stuart Dick, clean up the translations for us. We wanted something that was historically accurate.

Collaborating seems like it would be terribly difficult. How did you blend your work?

Usually one guy starts a tune. He'll start the seed of the idea and he'll bring it in some kind of form to the table, and then we'll both start hacking away at it.

You undoubtedly have different approaches to music, different sounds, so how did you combine your efforts to create a united finished product?

Well, there is commonality. You might be able to listen to both Celtic albums and tell who had the bigger role in certain pieces, but I am not sure. You are right in that we do have our own sounds, but there is a foundation of common interest that seems to connect our music.

Your music is heavily acoustic. Talk about your relationship with the orchestra versus the synthesizer.

I tend not to like synthesizers that often. But I have worked on projects where I needed a cutting-edge sort of electronic sound that could not be done acoustically. If I can achieve this sound with an unusual acoustic instrument, I would rather do it that way. I feel it ages better, among other things.

How did your film-music career begin?

I was a guitar player, but I hurt both my hands with a couple different injuries, and it was starting to look like I wasn't going to be able to be a player for a living. I was told that I would never play music again. At that point, I started to wonder what I was going to do, outside of jumping off a building, which definitely was something I was considering. Eventually, I just fell into films. As a player, I had played on some soundtracks and saw how it worked. So I thought I would give it a shot myself.

How were you injured?

I basically got serious carpal tunnel syndrome and tendonitis in both my arms. Those injuries can get to the point where you can't really do anything. I had taken piano lessons while I was young. Then I discovered the guitar and put the piano aside for a little while and taught myself to play guitar incorrectly, apparently. I could play fine, but I was doing things that were not good for my hands, and after about twelve years that caught up with me.

Does this affect you now?

When scoring a film, you're not required to play guitar eight hours a day, seven days a week. When I first started scoring and I was doing TV series, I didn't really play guitar at all for years. And that really let everything settle down and heal. Those injuries took a long time to heal, so I was away from guitar for quite a while as I started my film career. It is better enough now that, in fact, I'm playing today, all day, on this sci-fi film that has some very industrial Nine Inch Nails sort of things going on, lots of guitar. There are still aches and pains, but it's not like it was. I'm just careful with it and I can get through it fine.

Your instrumentation makes your music uniquely yours. It has a bit of raw sound and abstract ideas that blend in such beautiful creative work. What is your fascination with sound and where does this come from?

Well, I guess I always like something a little left of center, even in orchestral music. In straight-up orchestral music I try to find a way to come at the orchestra a little differently. One way is to inject the orchestra with different kinds of instruments that aren't usually found in orchestral settings. That creates a tension that I find lends itself to interesting sounds and interesting music. But I try above and beyond anything else to write good melodies and themes—to have solid melodic content. I think that you can get quite unusual and abstract sonically if you have a good melodic base to hold it together.

Uncorked **is a score with an Irish flavor. But it doesn't sound like a traditional folk score. You added a mysterious presence with the hurdy-gurdy and other instruments. When you write a score like this, what do you set out to accomplish?**

Remember, when we're film composers, a lot of factors play into the music. The director of that film came to me because he had heard one of the Celtic works. So that was one of the things he immediately started talking about.

In that film, Nigel Hawthorn played a character who was rather eccentric and made references to St. Augustine and some other ancient presences and such. So it was a good excuse for me to drag out the hurdy-gurdy. But, again, a lot of it just goes back to me trying to find something unusual or some slightly different way to come at things if that's possible.

All of your music has flowing themes and melodies. This aspect of music seems to come so naturally to you. Is this true?

I would say that it comes easier to me than other aspects of composition. And, like I said earlier, it's also something that I think is very important. It's something I hold in high regard. I spend a long time—days sometimes—tweaking melodies, trying to make them as flowing and effective as possible.

Which composers have inspired you most?

I tend to think more in terms of films when we're talking about film composition. But, of any one composer, Bernard Herrmann stands out for me. I really love his sound. He's not necessarily the most melodic composer in terms of your standard straight-up melody, but he does a very interesting thing, and I love it. And then I think of individual film scores that I love, such as Elmer Bernstein's *To Kill a Mockingbird*, which has a lovely melody, and Alfred Newman's *The Razor's Edge*, Rózsa's *Double Indemnity* . . . I could go on and on.

Were you aware of film music as you were growing up?

Yeah, because music was such a big part of my family and my upbringing. I was always aware of music in any context, because I grew up in a house with so much music in it. I remember going when I was very young to see Gilbert and Sullivan musicals that my parents were singing in. I remember going to movies and noticing music. It never occurred to me for a long time that film music might be how I could make a contribution, but certainly it was something that I always took note of.

Let's talk about *Green Dragon*. How did you and Mychael come to collaborate on this film score?

It just sort of happened. I don't remember exactly what he said, but I was available and he was available and we said, "Yeah, we'll give it a shot."

This score strove for an authentic Vietnamese sound. How much research went into the sounds and instrumentation?

It's probably the most research I'd ever done for anything up until *The Gospel of John*. We spent a good month driving back and forth from L.A. to Orange County, where there's a large Vietnamese music community. We had a translator who was a Vietnamese musician, and he filled us in on a lot of things. It's a fascinating culture. I don't think we quite got as much of the musical culture into that score as we might have, given the beauty of that sound.

***The Kid Stays in the Picture* utilizes a complex group of sounds. By the time I got through the middle of the CD, I was so impressed by the many levels to which you took this music. Tell me what I'm hearing and how difficult was it to combine all these flavors for one story?**

The challenge in it was also the thing that was really fun about it— spanning about five decades musically. It is something you would never do in a conventional film score. You would rarely write tarantellas, waltzes, gangster music, and carnival music in one score. I was really attracted to the film because there was room for all those different sounds to sit next to each other amongst the source music—Cat Stevens, Steely Dan, and the other things that the filmmakers were using to tell the tale of Evan's life. I really enjoyed that project. There was some sweating, as it had a very short turnaround, but it was really a rewarding film to be part of.

***The Gospel of John*—I believe that you were meant for this movie right from the beginning. Your emotional and heartfelt music seems truly inspired. What was this project like for you?**

That's an interesting take on it. I think you're probably right. I remember that one of the producers had heard my score to *O* and had liked it. And that was the beginning of our conversation.

They liked the fact that I had done some things with Renaissance instruments and the orchestra. Their concept for *Gospel of John* was that it would have the ancient music of the biblical era and the geography of the place mixed with large-scale modern-orchestra sound. Then, when I saw the film and saw how they were handling the subject, I thought that the score shouldn't really be *Ben Hur* or something like that. It should have some of the scope of the vintage bible flicks, but it should also have the real period instruments injected into it. A music supervisor who had already done research on this project for a year tracked down a lot of the players. Then it was just a matter of my absorbing the book of information that he gave me and going to London to meet with the players and talk about their instruments and their craft. I came back to Los Angeles to write it.

Will you continue to write for films or do you have aspirations in other areas?

I like film. I have been asked to do a couple of concert things, but film is a really good place for me to work right now, and I am comfortable doing it. I still have other things I do on the side: I still play a little guitar on sessions and that kind of thing. I do some album work. But I think that film music is in some ways the classical music of this generation. I'm happy to be here, making whatever contribution I can.

Mychael Danna

Aside from his younger brother, Jeff, Mychael Danna has had another very significant collaborator—filmmaker Atom Egoyan. From 1987 through 2005, Egoyan-Danna collaborations have included the films *Family Viewing*, *Speaking Parts*, *Montréal vu par . . .* , *The Adjuster*, *Gross Misconduct*, *Exotica*, *Felicia's Journey*, *The Line*, *Ararat*, and *Where the Truth Lies*. From among this list of great films, *Ararat* (2002), about the Armenian Genocide of 1915, stands out as an unparalleled work of art. Danna's heartbreaking score for this unsettling film was recorded in Armenia by Armenian musicians performing on indigenous instruments, lending the score a unique depth of feeling and an authentic sense of geographic color.

Mychael Danna's compositional voice stands apart from the traditional Hollywood sound. Far away from Los Angeles's chaos, Mychael lives amid a serene Canadian landscape of water and trees, where his music thrives on his fresh, creative energy and unique sensibility.

Why film music as a career?

It was kind of an accidental thing. When I was growing up, a film composer wasn't really a career path in the sense that now it is kind of a viable option. In fact, even the university where I studied music now is offering film-music courses, which are becoming more and more popular on university calendars today. When I went to school for composition at the University of Toronto, that wasn't really an option, and certainly the local film industry at that time was pretty small and Los Angeles was a long way away. It wasn't something that people really thought about. While I was at school, I wrote music for all kinds of different things and places—from advertisements and industrials to theater. That's where I met Atom Egoyan and then did my first score for a small National Film Board of Canada film that he was doing called *Family Viewing*.

How do you approach a project?

The most important thing is to take a lot of time to think and talk to the director before you write a single note. It's really important to come up with a concept—to really let things kind of form together, especially in the subconscious, which I feel is a major part of the creative process.

Watch the film, talk to the director, and try to understand the underlying themes, or what is required by the film, and also what the director is trying to say so that you can help through music. I generally start by trying to figure out what instruments to use, where the music is placed, and how hot and how cold it is. But sometimes I get ideas that just jump into my head right from the beginning.

Of course, there's this whole new and destructive element of the temp score. It kind of screws up the whole composing process because a lot of your choices seem to be made before you even come on to the film, and half of your work as a film-score composer is getting people to stop listening to the temp score.

Quite often filmmakers feel it's a compliment to temp with your own stuff, but I find that's even more disturbing and confusing. It actually doesn't tell me anything. I turned down a film last week because the director was very attached to the temp score, which I felt was a wrong fit, but they had already made their decision: It's what they wanted. That was unfortunate because, if they had brought the film to me without the temp score, I probably would have done it. It was a well-made film and I liked the story.

Temping is one of the two very disturbing current film trends that work against film music. The other, while we're on the subject of bad things happening in film right now, is the incessant editing and changes that go on way past the date when they should stop. That has really made it difficult to make a good score.

What sort of storyline or genre suits you or your style best?

That's a good question. For every composer, there is an ideal sort of setting that inspires him. Not everybody is lucky enough to be able to find or be able to work in that setting because people are cautious, and once you've done one, say, a romantic comedy, you'll be doing them for the rest of your life—whether you want to or not. But, for me, the films that I really get excited about, inspired by, and are reflected by my best scores are the films that have layers of meaning, that have subtext. These are complicated films in the sense that they may have paradoxes and contrasts in what is on the surface and what is going on underneath. Those are the films that I find most fun to score and, I think, I'm best at.

You've collaborated with Atom Egoyan on several projects. What is your relationship with him like, in comparison to other people with whom you've worked?

Well, I've had long relationship with Atom. We started out together. I learned about film scoring with him, and he learned about film-making with me. It's a very special, treasured relationship, one where I'm trusted, and that means I get the most excited. Atom trusts me more than anyone. He gets excited when I get an idea and encourages me to follow it. It's very inspiring. So I've done some of my most interesting things for him.

The other long-term relationships I've had are with Mira Nair and Ang Lee. With Mira, I did *Kama Sutra* and *Monsoon Wedding*, and I'm now starting her new film. I think I've been able to do some nice stuff with her as well. Ang Lee and I have worked on three, and perhaps I'll call *Hulk* a half. I think when somebody comes back to work with you again, it's a sign of trust and a sign that they enjoy your work. That's inspiring. You want to try and preserve that.

Tell me about working with Denzel Washington on *Antwone Fisher.*

I expected a first-time-director experience, and it quickly became apparent that that was not what it was going to be. The man has spent his whole life in the filmmaking process—on the front line, as an actor dealing with directors, and obviously he is one of the greatest actors alive. And all he did was take his extraordinary skill and sensitivity toward acting and apply it to music, and he became a fantastic director of music. It was really a fun experience.

He would say things like, "I don't know anything about the music end of things," and a few weeks later, he'd be saying, "You know, I think that in take three the oboe was more in tune in bar eight." He really bowled me over with how quickly he picked up the technical side of the music process. His whole understanding of pacing and rhythm as it applies to acting was totally applicable to music. Sometimes he would show me something he wanted me to do by acting a scene in two different ways, a couple of times scaring the hell out of me, reliving a scene from *Training Day* in my little studio, as I cowered in the corner. He's a very smart, savvy filmmaker, and he just happened to be on the other side of the camera. You can tell by his performances that he puts a lot of thought into what he does and a lot of thought into what a good film is and how to make a good film. His directing is a natural extension of that, and I think it shows in the final product, a very beautifully crafted film.

What challenges does being in Canada present to you in terms of getting U.S. projects?

It's definitely a handicap in some ways. But, I think it's an advantage in some ways, too. It's an advantage to my work. I think I write better music because I live here. I've worked in Los Angeles, and I find that it's really impossible to live in that city and not be aware of what everyone else is doing and what everyone else is thinking. And, you know, it's only human to be affected by that. For the kind of work that I'm probably best suited for, it is best for me to live like I do in the middle of nowhere. I live in the woods on a lake, which kind of makes my whole worldview a little bit different. It just frees up my mind. It takes pressure off of me in a sense and probably makes my work a little more original, a little different. The disadvantages are obvious. Obviously, it's hard for me to take meetings immediately. For Denzel's film, I relocated to Los Angeles for six or eight weeks. I've done that several times. It's something that I adjust to when I need to. I worked on *Girl Interrupted* from here and hardly ever came down to work with James Mangold. I would send him MP3 cues that he would put up on his end, and we'd discuss them on the phone. It was very efficient. He'd press Play at his end, and I did the same. We'd watch it, and he'd give me his feedback. Then we'd both put down the phone and go back to work.

What has influenced the creation of your sound?

I grew up and started working and continue to work far from the center of American filmmaking. I think that's the biggest thing right there. I've discovered how to make film music without any help or instruction—without any influence, really. I didn't even watch films very much when I was growing up.

How about musical influence outside of films?

As you can tell from my body of work, ethnomusicology is a huge passion of mine. I love traveling and meeting and working with different musicians from different cultures and different places. It's a real excitement for me. It's something that I've tried to bring into my film music and make valid and reasonable and artistically intelligent as added colors and choices. That's one of the most exciting things for me.

Would you explain your use of ethnic sounds intertwined with a pulsating percussive synth sounds in *Exotica*? Why did you choose to give your music that Middle-Eastern edge?

The Club Exotica in the film is supposed to be kind of otherworldly. It's not supposed to be a typical bar in your town. There's supposed to be something very odd and a bit twisted about it, but also something enticing and very elegant and beautiful and sexy. I think the atmosphere of the film has a sort of tangible quality to it that is very important to the effectiveness of the film. And I think that my musical choices were really a big part of that.

Most of your projects are serious and intense, but *Bounce* is a different story. It seems like a natural transition, though. How was it breaking away from your more offbeat style of movies?

The interesting thing is that I found it a lot more difficult. I don't know if there's something perverse about me as a human being, but I found it really difficult to write lighter, more fun music. I don't even think I want to think about that too much. I found the experience really difficult and challenging. I'm glad you think it worked and was effortless, but—believe me—it wasn't.

What I liked most was the edge it had. It wasn't a typical love story or light drama with soft string melodies. You held to your sound and dared to take a different approach. I respect that.

Well, thank you. I think that a lot of American filmmaking is very afraid of that kind of color, that darker element. Studio executives criticize it. They don't think that it's an attractive emotional choice.

Bounce was a film where the director wanted to play up some of the darker elements of the story. And there is some very dark stuff in that film, but the studio typically will want to gloss over that kind of thing and make the music kind of happy and fun. That's a conflict that I deal with a lot.

I found it very interesting that on the *Bounce* CD cover, for instance, every single picture is of somebody smiling. That's no accident. And I find that really absurd, so I'm probably not very comfortable with those sorts of films.

Which one of your own works are you most proud of?

That's a tough question. It's like asking a mother to pick her favorite kid. I love *Monsoon Wedding*, and I think part of the reason that I love it is because of where it came in my life. It's a really brilliant film, and I think the music really works. Believe it or not, I wrote that score in only one week. Then I got on a plane and went to India for seven days to record all the instruments there. When I came back, I mixed for a week. So the whole score took three hellish weeks. At this same time, I was engaged to an Indian girl, so we went to India together. It was just like we were living the movie. For sentimental reasons, *Monsoon Wedding* is way up there. *Ice Storm* is way up there. *Exotica* is way up there. *Ararat* is way up there. Those are probably the ones. *Regeneration* is one of my favorite films that I've ever worked on, although no one's ever seen it.

What is the most rewarding aspect of your career?

The most rewarding moments I've had are when I do things that are really unusual and that nobody else would have thought of and they work and are good. Those are hard moments to come by, and they don't happen very often, but once in a while they do. When you mix together instruments that shouldn't really go together or never have been together before and it works and does something really profound in the film, that's a huge thrill. And just working with certain musicians can be a thrill. Going to Armenia, for instance, and recording an Armenian choir in a sixth-century church in the middle of nowhere [for *Ararat*] was a thrill. It was just unbelievably moving to be recording something by candlelight in the country where the song was written twelve hundred years ago.

Don Davis

Don Davis has earned his reputation for being both versatile and influential the hard way: Before composing his own feature-film scores, Davis accrued an impressive list of allied credits, which included the prolific scoring of television movies and series (*Hart to Hart*, *Star Trek: The Next Generation*, *Tiny Toon Adventures*, *Beauty and the Beast*, etcetera.) and orchestrating for Randy Newman, James Horner, Mark Snow, and others.

In his futuristic score to *The Matrix* (1999), the first installment of one of the most successful trilogies in film history, Davis molded an extremely eclectic, colorful soundworld that mixed pop music elements with both avant-garde and traditional orchestral and electronic elements. This pioneering score created a new musical landscape that perfectly paralleled the film's new cinematic landscape. Davis also created highly imaginative scores for this film's two sequels, *The Matrix Reloaded* (2003) and *The Matrix Revolutions* (2003).

In 2001, Davis was presented the daunting task of scoring *Jurassic Park III* (2001), following in the footsteps of one of the greatest film-music masters, John Williams. In this score, Davis craftily married his own voice to John Williams' themes, keeping the film's well-known musical fingerprint while making the music his own.

A composer with widespread musical interests, Davis has always kept a foot solidly anchored in the concert-music world, writing prolifically for noted chamber ensembles. Currently, he's writing an opera. We may not know what lies in this talented composer's future, but we can be sure it will be exciting and new.

You have had music in your blood from an early age. What were your influences while you were growing up?

I started out as a trumpet player, so my early influences were more jazz-oriented than anything else. I was attracted to popular and rock music as well. I had fairly limited exposure to classical music; it was really jazz that got me involved in writing instrumental music.

How did your jazz writing evolve into your writing for movies?

When I started writing jazz big-band charts back in junior high school, I began to develop a camaraderie with a number of other composers who were also writing in that medium. In the course of discussing music, our conversations would inevitably turn toward scoring for films, since that was the career arc for a number of film composers. At the same time, I was starting to wonder what sort of career could possibly evolve from writing for jazz ensembles. Although there was something of a big-band revival at the time, I was pretty sure that it wasn't going to continue long enough for me to make a career out of big-band arranging. This was one of the reasons that film music eventually seduced me.

Did you have any interest in films prior to your career?

Yes, film music had definitely made an impact on me, although it may have been primarily a subliminal one. When I was a child, I used to watch a lot of *Twilight Zone* reruns when I came home from school, such that I eventually was able to recall each episode by name, and I specifically remember the effect that the music had on me. Later on, when I started to study music seriously, I became aware of who Bernard Herrmann and Jerry Goldsmith were, and I noted that these giants of film music were the same composers I had heard on that show. That was when I started to become aware of the cross-pollination that was going on between television and feature-film music, and between jazz and dramatic music.

Did any film composers inspire you?

I think those two composers in particular, Jerry Goldsmith and Bernard Herrmann, are pretty hard to dismiss—they're absolutely seminal to the art of film-composing. John Williams has been a big influence on me, if for no other reason than the incredible integrity he puts in all of his work. More recently, James Horner has written some remarkable scores that have made an impression on me, as has James Newton Howard. I think Randy Newman has written some incredibly wonderful music. I think that he is the most naturally gifted melody writer who's writing at this time. I also think that he's really the true successor of Alfred Newman, much more so than David and Tom Newman, who I believe are actively trying to distance themselves from the influence of their father.

Many may not be aware of your collaborations as an orchestrator, particularly with Randy Newman.

I'm not really sure that you can accurately call those collaborations. Randy's sketches, like John Williams', are very complete and fully elaborated. In spite of that fact, he is always open to suggestions. I might have suggested a different layout that would have possibly been better for a certain situation once or twice, but I would be hard-pressed to call what we did together a collaboration. I was orchestrating his sketches and certainly not co-composing.

It is true that in my trajectory as a film composer I came up through the ranks as an orchestrator. My very first job, after I graduated from UCLA, was orchestrating for Joe Harnell on the television show *The Incredible Hulk*. After that, I worked for Mark Snow in the same capacity on the shows *Hart to Hart* and *Crazy Like a Fox*, and when he became unavailable, he was able to throw a few shows my way. So I started composing TV show scores under Mark, and that sort of experience eventually led to a lead-composer position on a

TV show called *Beauty and the Beast*, for which I scored forty-six episodes. After *Beauty and the Beast* ended, my then-agent Mike Gorfaine introduced me to Randy Newman when Randy was looking for an orchestrator. I also had been orchestrating for James Horner by that time.

How did these two gifted melodic writers—Newman and Horner—differ in terms of technique or approach?

James is amazingly resilient, and he has always had a very strong picture sense. I think he is quicker to draw on different stylistic approaches than many other composers might be. You could say that James is more open to a broad view of what the film composer can bring to a film.

Randy is very much the traditionalist, which is due mostly to the fact that he had a lot of exposure, both personally and professionally, to a number of old-school film composers, primarily Alfred Newman and Lionel Newman. There's a pureness to the way Randy approaches dramatic situations. And since he became famous as a songwriter before he started to score films, he has retained a stature by which he can demand a lot of respect, and get it—not just for himself personally, but for the music itself. There are very few people left who are dedicated to protecting our art, but Randy is one of them.

Is your approach to scoring influenced by those composers you worked with?

Absolutely. Every time I orchestrated for other composers, I took advantage of that unique opportunity to dissect their work, and as such I tried to absorb their points of view while all of the time trying to inform my own developing and, hopefully, unique point of view. I tried to see how I could adapt their particular insights to my own work. There are many times when I have been asked to do something melodic, and I would think about the way Randy might approach something, with that purity of musical sense that he has. Other times I might try to embrace the kind of versatility that James Horner has consistently shown in his work.

What confounds me is that the body of your orchestration experience has been with thematic and emotional music, yet you are the action/adventure man a lot of the time. How did you get labeled so quickly in this genre?

It's pretty simple—the projects that I became known for as a composer have been action/adventure films. A lot of composers get pretty upset about the typecasting that goes on in this business, but I generally feel pleased that, even though I'm being pigeonholed, I'm not being forgotten entirely.

Following in the footsteps of John Williams, *Jurassic Park III* must have been a little intimidating. Did you set up a lot of pressure or expectation for yourself?

It was difficult, and more than just a little bit intimidating, there's no question about it. I definitely wanted to elevate the music that I was writing to the level of integrity that John Williams puts in all of his music. Just making the attempt to incorporate the melodic, textural, and orchestral integrity that John Williams routinely puts into his work was really quite an intense challenge.

How did this project present itself to you?

Originally they wanted John Williams to score *Jurassic Park III*, but he wasn't available. Still, since this was a sequel to a franchise in which he had established the original musical voice, and since it involved some of the people who are central to his stature in Hollywood, he justifiably wanted to maintain a certain amount of control over what was really his domain. So John and Mike Gorfaine discussed who they thought would be the best custodian of that domain, and my background as an orchestrator, along with my credits as the composer of *The Matrix*, convinced them that I could do justice to the project.

What an honor that one of the greatest film composers put faith in you to carry forward the musical integrity that he brought to the franchise.

It was a very big honor, and one that I did not take lightly.

Let's talk about your Matrix trilogy scores that have set a new standard or perhaps a new tradition in terms of scoring action-film music.

I had a number of conversations with film editor Zach Staenberg before we spotted the film. We talked about how exactly the music should be approached, and often we would discuss the possibility of utilizing what some might call the postmodern style that is heard in the music of Philip Glass, John Adams, and Steve Reich, among a number of other composers. After these discussions, and especially after putting some of that music up against the film, I felt very strongly that this approach would work especially well in that particular film. Actually, I had become interested in exploring that kind of approach in film scores quite awhile before I had the opportunity to work on *The Matrix*, but that movie was the first film to come along in which I felt that the approach could work in an organic way, without imposing a non-germane style to the picture in an obtrusive way. So I worked on developing an approach that incorporated the soundworld of that style, but all the time still enabled the music to function dramatically. Also I felt that, in general, the music needed a bit of a hard-edged veneer to it, to keep it from veering too far into New Age territory.

I felt that it was absolutely necessary to keep a consistent approach going through each film in order to maintain the stylistic integrity of the trilogy as a whole. Although there aren't any themes, per se, aside from Neo and Trinity's love theme, there is definitely an abundance of thematic material and motifs from the first film that I was able to develop quite a bit in the second movie. *The Final Flight of the Osiris*, the Anime short film that precedes *Reloaded*, establishes some thematic material that will find its development in *Reloaded*, and *Reloaded* establishes some new material that is going to be exploited further in *The Matrix Revolutions* as well. I definitely tried to keep a consistency of style and attitude throughout the three films, not just for franchise identification, but because I feel that sort of musical development over the course of the trilogy lends the kind of richness and integrity to the overall process that is in keeping with what Larry and Andy Wachowski were establishing with the trilogy in the first place.

Was it difficult to avoid repetitiveness and maintain originality throughout the hours of music you created?

It certainly required some thought. There is no question about that. It was never acceptable for me to simply rewrite the preceding score. I think there may be a certain amount of repetition that is acceptable when developing a score with this kind of scope, but I don't think anyone can claim that the later scores are simply clones of the first one.

That makes sense. When John Williams, for example, continues the *Star Wars* series, he has his recurring themes that tie together the whole story alongside a great amount of new material to fit each specific film installment.

Certainly, and that, along with the *Indiana Jones* trilogy, is among the best examples of that kind of stylistic development. I think that it's important for sequels to keep that consistency going throughout every installment, for all of those reasons.

You are working on something quite exciting outside of the film realm.

I am actually working on an opera now, for which I have received a commission from the Los Angeles Master Chorale, which will present it in November of 2005. The Chorale, along with an orchestra and five operatic soloists, will be performing what is essentially a preview of an opera-in-progress. It's kind of an unusual situation because I'll be writing the excerpts before I actually write the opera, in order to meet the deadline for the concert, and then I'll be going back and filling in the rest of the opera between the excerpts. I've been thinking for quite a while about the dramatic point of view that a film composer can contribute to opera. I think it very possibly could be a welcome and refreshing point of view that may not be obvious to a composer who hasn't worked in the theater of the absurd that we call film music. It's really a massive challenge to tackle such an enormous undertaking, so that's definitely where I am going to be turning my attention to when I am not working on any film projects.

How does a concert piece differ from a film score in terms of writing for each medium?

Well, for me, the difference between writing film music and writing concert music is as different as night is to day. I really don't want to be in the situation where I am writing a piece for the concert stage that is essentially no different from something that I might write for a film. I think there's a lot more opportunity to really detail the music in a serious composition. The important thing to remember about film scores is that film music is not about music, it is all about film. The focus of a film composer's attention always needs to be on what will make the film better, and if a composer gets too wrapped up in the music itself, the film will be worse off for it.

When I'm composing music for the concert stage, I'm able to give my entire thought process to the integrity of the music itself, and therefore, I'm able to justify everything I do in strictly musical terms. My goal is to infuse the music with such detail that deleting a measure or two anywhere in the composition would create an irreparable fissure, whereas film music, almost by definition, must be absolutely resilient to that kind of circumstance. It has to be created with enough modularity such that two bars can be taken out and it will still make perfect sense musically, because the structure of film is constantly changing with the re-editing that is always being done.

Aside from these mechanical issues, I also approach the creative aspect of the two mediums differently, in a physical sense. When I'm scoring for film, I'm always writing at the piano and synthesizers, directly into the sequencing programs that I use to synchronize music to films. By contrast, when I'm composing concert music, I almost always write the music at a desk away from the piano, and I only use the piano to check the music after I've written it out.

The film industry continually evolves, and composers have to adapt to its changes. How do you view yourself in terms of this evolution?

I'm actually very happy in the situation that I find myself in. I don't have any specific techniques for dealing with change, except that I try to be constantly aware that this business changes very rapidly and we all have to be ready to change with it. I like to think that I'm resilient enough to accommodate the inevitable changes that will

certainly come my way in this business. I suppose the most important thing to remember is that, although change is a frightening
thing, it's only the fear of change that will paralyze us, and if we can
learn to embrace those changes as an exciting challenge, then the
task before us becomes a happy one. When I first started working as
an orchestrator and then as a film composer, things were so different that it could almost be mistaken for an entirely different business. We had no sequencers, no synthesizers, no computers, not
even video machines-everything was done with a pencil. It's almost
incomprehensible that we could work back then without the benefit
of seeing the film we were working on in a videocassette player. We
would go to a screening room and watch a screening of the film, and
then go home and work to the timing notes that the music editor
prepared from a Moviola. [The Moviola was the primary film-editing
machine used from the 1920s through the 1970s. It allowed editors
and other film personnel to scroll through a film while viewing it
through a lens.] Also, there were no mocked-up demos of cues back
then. The directors would hear the music when they got to the scoring stage and the orchestra played it. Many of the composers who got
used to working that way weren't able to acclimate themselves to the
environment that we now find ourselves in, in which each cue has to
be demoed for the director before the scoring session. It seems to
me, then, that the best way to achieve longevity in this business is
to be resilient enough to embrace whatever comes our way, because
the only thing we can be entirely certain of is that the future is going
to be very, very different.

John Debney

John Debney is one of the most diverse and productive composers in Hollywood, capable of successfully doing anything that he sets his mind to. One of Debney's great achievements is his score for the epic adventure _Cutthroat Island_ (1995). This exciting, thematic music was written in homage to Eric Wolfgang Korngold, who, if he were alive today, would probably congratulate Debney for executing his score with such intensity and grandeur. Cut from the same cloth as his score for _Cutthroat Island_, yet certainly more modern in its outer appearances, is Debney's intense music for _The Scorpion King_ (2002).

Debney's work is not all on a larger-than-life scale; his intimate and emotional music is exquisite. _Dragonfly_ (2002), a film that deals with the supernatural/spiritual connections between life and death, is a complex tale for which Debney wrote mysterious, richly emotional music that weaves itself into the story's physical and metaphysical worlds. Perhaps the most inspired and captivating work that John Debney has created to date is his score for Mel Gibson's _The Passion of the Christ_ (2004), a controversial film of great impact that is forcefully driven by Debney's epic, heartfelt, soulful score.

Describe a little of your music background and how it led to film music.

I started playing guitar at age six. My mom was a musician, so it was natural that I would pick up an instrument. I did the normal guitar-playing thing during my adolescence, then I started to play some piano just on my own and was in numerous rock-'n'-roll bands. In my teenage years, I was in a band that had a record deal, so I kind of went that route for a while. Then I went to college at Loyola University here in L.A., where my double major was drama and music. I did that for my first two years. In my junior year, I decided that, of the two crazy profession ideas, music was the less crazy because it was my passion. So I transferred over to CalArts in Valencia, where I got a degree in composition. I then worked at Walt Disney Studios' music library department for about three years, copying and pasting scores, being a runner, and doing other things like that. Slowly but surely during the years I was at Disney I started to get some orchestration work. I orchestrated a lot of the theme-park things they were doing at the time. I then got married, left Disney, and started to do some freelance work as an orchestrator. That's what I did in the early eighties until I, started to get a television episode or two, then a series. In the early nineties, after being a television guy for many years, I started to graduate into features, and I've had a slow, steady growth into feature work since then.

You have a diverse career that seems to have kept you from being pigeonholed in a particular genre, although you have done several comedic score. What genre most inspires your creativity?

I am sort of known as the big comedy guy, or at least one of them. The genre that most interests me right now is anything but comedy, anything with a more dramatic emotional side to it. That interests me greatly. I love doing big, epic, adventurous things. Some of my favorite composers are guys from the Golden Age who did the big swashbuckling movies and, of course, John Williams among the modern-day composers. So I'm sort of at both ends of the spectrum. The very small, dramatic, emotional film is very interesting to me, as is the big, overblown, fun *Cutthroat Island*-type thing.

Being one of the busiest composers in Hollywood, how do you balance your projects and do they ever overlap?

First of all, being the "busiest composer" for a couple of years was never planned. It just happened. They do overlap, or I should say, they did. This year, consciously, I've made an effort to do less, which I think is important right now. Doing two projects at once is doable but difficult. Unfortunately, there have been situations where I have had to do three at once. That's horrible! That's really undoable. Doing two at once is not the most fun thing in the world, but schedules change, more so now than ever. It's almost like you can say yes to a project in any given timeframe knowing that it's going to move. So it just happens.

I'm one of those composers who doesn't use a lot of help. I call in a friend to do a cue or two here or there, but I'm not into having a lot of people work on a score. So I'm sort of doing it all myself, and that can become tough.

Especially when it interferes with your family and everything?

Yeah, you want to have a life. It's difficult to do that. I'm better at it now than I was a few years ago.

Did you choose to take on so many projects to gain wide exposure for your work and help yourself move into the bigger films and be able to be a bit choosier of your projects?

Yeah, absolutely. There was a period three or four years ago when I basically just wanted to work. I just wanted to get out there and work a lot and work hard, which I did. I was very fortunate with opportunities and representation to help me do that. Again, now this year, I'm looking to just slow down and try to do different things and do them more selectively.

Given the fact that you produce so many scores in a year, how do you manage to keep a constantly original sound without duplicating pieces?

It's been easy for me because so many of the projects I do are so different. Perhaps if I were doing two romantic comedies at the same time, but that has never happened. It's usually a romantic comedy and some wacky comedy or maybe it's a drama or a thriller, which I've done less of. In other words, I haven't had the problem of having two similar kinds of movies happen at the same time. In that sense, it hasn't been much of a problem.

Do you find it tempting to go back on your own work once in a while?

Absolutely. You know, when I'm writing themes for a given movie, I'll write a bunch of themes, and one or two will end up of being the theme that the director likes. But I keep the other themes and, if possible, revisit them. If one of these themes works for another movie, that's great. But that doesn't happen a lot to me. There are plenty of stories of themes that never were accepted for a movie that the composer uses for the next project and it's a big hit.

Is diversity the key to longevity in a film-music career?

I think it is. I mean, my gosh, I've had years and years of writing television music and churning it out and honing my craft. It was a golden opportunity for me. When I got my chance to get up to the plate, I was ready. I was sort of in the minor leagues for years, to use a baseball metaphor. So I'm fortunate in that I've had a lot of training and a lot of experience with writing a lot of different kinds of music. If you don't have that behind you, sometimes that can be a problem.

I've always loved your mastery with the orchestra, and the score of yours that first captured my attention was *Cutthroat Island*. It's an incredible epic score for a film that seemed to fall through the cracks.

It did fall through the cracks. It was quite a disappointment for me because, had that movie done well, it could be a completely different landscape for me. That's not a complaint; that's an observation. Actually, that film had a stigma to it. It was such a huge disaster financially that my agent at the time felt that they couldn't really send out the score on CD with the movie's title on it. In other words, we would send out the CD, but it just said, "New Music."

I appreciate what you say about the score. I'm very proud of it. It's probably one of the two or three that I'm most proud of. I think fans have discovered it, and I know a lot of people temp with that music. That's gratifying, but certainly, as you can imagine, if it had been a big success, it would have certainly helped my career a lot at that moment.

With *Cutthroat Island*, I hear the impact of Korngold and Alfred Newman. What other composers have impacted your sound?

Very good question. There are a lot of subliminal things that we all do as human beings in that we're all influenced by others' work. If I were a painter, I'm sure I would unconsciously be influenced by a lot of other painters. Things sometimes unconsciously come out of me that I feel sound like someone else.

Other composers? From that Golden Age, as it were, certainly Korngold, Max Steiner, Alfred Newman. David Raksin, in terms of melody. *Laura* is still one of the most gorgeous themes I've ever heard. I think David Raksin is quite under-appreciated. He's right up there.

My list is voluminous. I'm all over the map. I just happened to see the old *Superman* series on TV. Who is the composer of the original *Superman*? What I'm trying to say is that there are a lot of obscure people.

I think more in terms of scores. Hugo Freidhofer's *Best Years of Our Lives*, to me, is one of the finest film scores ever written. I just get choked up every time I hear it. What he did with the music was just astounding. You know, Hugo was mainly known as a master orchestrator. But boy, the few scores he wrote were great! Now, moving ahead in time, my two absolute favorites would be the two biggies: John Williams and Jerry Goldsmith. I'm also terribly fond of James Newton Howard. I think James is pretty amazing in that he's so good. There's something about what he does with a film score. He just gets right to the heart of things.

I credit my passion for film music to James Newton Howard, whom I became familiar with first. He is one of the most prolific composers in the industry, and he has a true ability to capture a film's emotion.

Yes, and I think he's almost under-appreciated right now. I mean, he's in the top five composers, but probably people would argue that right now in town. I personally think that he can literally do anything.

I want to mention Alan Silvestri, too. I love Alan. He's another one who can do anything. I just love Alan's sense of melody. His harmonies are amazing. Sometimes I write things that come out sounding similar to Alan's, I think. It's certainly not intentional. But I think I know why it happens. Alan is a guitar player, like I am. I'm sure he writes on the keyboard now, as I do too, but guitar players learn harmony in a certain way or the way to change chords or the way to write a melody. I may be wrong, but my guess is that may have something to do with it.

John Barry. Who writes a better melody? Randy Newman, too. You know, I really could go on and on because my problem is that I'm just a big fan of everybody, but those are some of my favorites.

It's nice to hear a film composer speak of how he admires other film composers' music.

Oh yeah. I'm sure you get a lot of them living in an unreal world. There are some great artists out there and it's terrific that they get a chance to speak their voices, as it were.

You're one of them.

I don't know. I just do what I do and it's fun for me to grow. I think that the key for me is that I'm really aware. I don't want to stagnate ever. There's always something I can do better. There's always a genre or there's always a cue specifically that I think that I can do better. So it's a learning process for me, and it always has been.

The Scorpion King **is an eclectic mix of powerful orchestrations, with electric guitars and voices. You experiment with some cool sounds while creating a complex score that is an intoxicating listen. How did you prepare for this film and how challenging was this project for you?**

It was very challenging, and I think it was very successful. There's a lot of *The Scorpion King* that I'm extremely fond of and happy with because it was really fun for me to write it. It was a difficult one though, and it bears out what you're hearing.

There were a lot of people involved in that movie. It was a huge movie, and it's a franchise movie with Universal. Therefore, we had a tremendous number of, shall we say, cooks in the kitchen. There were many ideas floating around. At one point, there was a big group that thought the score should be, in the main, pretty contemporary and pretty rock-'n'-roll based. I didn't have a problem necessarily with that, but the director did. So you had a couple of schools of thought, and they were not always agreeing on the direction. So I felt I had to infuse a lot of elements into the score, and I think it came out okay. I wanted to infuse some rock-'n'-roll and some guitar-oriented things. I wanted to infuse world music. It's sort of an amalgam of a lot of things. I don't know if that's good or bad, but it certainly was kind of interesting to do. Ultimately, the score ended up seventy-five percent traditional, twenty-five percent nontraditional, meaning kind of more rock-'n'-roll-oriented. I didn't plan on the blend. That's just what happened. It was the result of people wanting different things. Sometimes, as composers, we are hired guns. At the end of the day we have to please the director and the studio, etcetera. So that score was a result of kind of trying to make everybody happy, which we have to do.

I have a funny story about that score, which has a lot of choir in it. When we were working on the choir, I got a book on how to teach yourself Sanskrit, so the lyrics or the syllables that a lot of the choir is singing are Sanskrit, and they are saying things. It's kind of silly. It's kind of gibberish, but that is Sanskrit in there, which a lot of people don't know.

Dragonfly is my favorite work of yours. It is beautifully written, with a lovely theme and a nice flow between dark sound and an angelic touch.

That score is so close to my heart, and I really appreciate you saying that. I probably put more of my heart and soul into that one than I've put into a lot of them, to be quite frank with you.

The subject matter was very close to me. I, however, had very little time to do that score—probably three weeks. I totally connected with the movie because I had lost my mom about a year and a half before that score was written. So had the director, Tom Shadyac, and the editor. We all had lost our moms within a two-year period. So you can imagine the emotional experience. I think there was just some door opened or some channel opened in my heart, and I just came up with these little motifs that became the main theme. Tom was very happy with it.

I wish the movie had done better. I think it's a much better movie than people give it credit. A harsh reality, unfortunately, in Hollywood is that you're kind of judged on the success of the movie a lot of times, and that's normal. I recently had a conversation with James Newton Howard about this subject. He said, "John, it's always one film away." I thought that was very interesting. Meaning, if all of a sudden that film succeeds, then you're that guy for a while. Had *Dragonfly* been, let's say, *The Sixth Sense* or *Unbreakable* or something like that, I would be that guy now. I'd love to be that guy for a while in the sense that I'd love to do more movies like that. Now we've got the score and it's wonderful to hand it out.

Liar Liar, which has a completely different sound, is yet another great work of yours. It seemed to have a huge impact on the blooming of your career.

Oh it did, no doubt. It was big, huge gift from James Newton Howard. James was going to do the movie. He had written a theme, but, all of a sudden, schedules changed, so he was going to have trouble doing *Liar Liar*. Through his incredible generosity, he brought me in. It's kind of a wild story. I remember that he spoke to the director and producer and said that this guy, John, is great, and they were amenable to meeting me. We had this incredible lunch, James and I and Tom Shadyac, and I think the editor was there and a couple producers. At the lunch, James kind of did his thing and convinced them. He said, "Look, this guy can finish the score for you and I'll be in the wings. I'll help John with whatever he needs." Basically, I wrote a couple of little themes to go along with James's great theme, and that literally opened the big door for me. That was a huge, big, beautiful Christmas present.

Your scores for a lot of movies are not fully represented on those movies' soundtrack CDs, which may have only a couple tracks of your music. This must be frustrating for you.

It is. With *Bruce Almighty*, somebody said to me, "I thought I was going to get all your music from the movie, but I got a bunch of songs." I replied, "At least you got *some* score on there." A lot of times I don't even get a track on there, and we fight for it. *Princess Diaries*, the score, would not have happened unless we complained for months to Disney and whined about it and begged. I'm serious. They're not wild about having the score come out because, quite frankly, it doesn't make them any money, and they don't want it to compete with the soundtrack. It's dollars and cents, and they don't want to compete against themselves. That I understand, but I also think people are a little smarter than that. If you clearly market the score and clearly market the other one, the soundtrack songs, I think people know the difference most of the time.

You've been involved with Varèse Sarabande recordings on some of the older releases, including one of my favorites, *Superman*. What is this experience like, working with other composers' music, and how did you get involved doing this?

Bob Townson invited me to a party a few years back. At this party, Bob asked me if I would be interested in coming over to Scotland to conduct some scores for Varese Sarabande. I said, "Why not?" I just thought it would be really fun. So we worked on it and I brought the family over to Scotland.

Prior to this, Joel McNeely had done a lot of those albums for Bob. They're very close, but Joel had been getting much busier with his feature career.

I'll never forget the very first day, when the first batch I conducted was *The Golden Boys of Sinbad*. The first piece was the main title, and when we rolled tape, Bob and I were floored. I was just like, Wow! There was just so much magic in the room. I'll tell you honestly, I think the Bernard Herrmann stuff turned out really well.

With *Superman*, I did not have enough time. I felt some of the tempos were not correct because the music is so demanding, as you know, that the orchestra physically got tired. The cues to *Superman* were recreated from sketches. The score has gone by the wayside, destroyed. Somebody, years ago, had them in a file, but they were thrown out. Luckily the sketches exist and we've orchestrated all that stuff. That was all great.

Back to the Future was a complete disaster in that, unbeknownst to me, when Alan did that score, there were so many picture changes that they made so many cuts in the score, physically, that sometimes the scores wouldn't match. So the trumpets would have twenty bars missing. It was a mess. It took us a couple of trips to even get what we got, and it was still a mess.

Every situation is different, and sometimes you're recreating from nothing basically.

What is the most satisfying part of being a film composer?

That's easy. It's getting to work with the orchestra—to be able to stand in front of these incredible musicians and conduct, which I call a birthing process. There's nothing more thrilling. Still, to this day, I love it! I love the people I work with. I love standing in front of the group, and I'm just astounded every time they start playing. That process of hearing the music, finally, after I've been spending months or weeks in my little room on my machines, is just a fantastic payoff.

Are you taking Pete Anthony on as your conductor more now?

I love Pete. He's fabulous. He's a great orchestrator. We have a great relationship. I take him on on a case-by-case basis. There are scores that I need to be in the booth for because I feel I need to really communicate with the director. On others, if I feel it's a pretty good situation, I can be out front.

Sometimes, like for *The Scorpion King* or some of these other ones, there are so many pre-records that it's better for me to be in the booth with my assistant, Michael, and the engineer and the director so I can hear the mix going down. I conducted *Princess Diaries* because it just is what it is. It's a nice orchestral score and not a lot to think about. You just do it, and then run back and talk to the director and go out and do it again.

• • • • •

*[I had the opportunity to speak again with John Debney at a later
date once his score to* The Passion of the Christ *was complete. It is
a monumental work, not only from the musical aspect, but the
project as a whole. I wanted to get John's insights and experiences
on this controversial Mel Gibson film.]*

How did you become involved with *The Passion of the Christ*?

It's a rather long story, but I'll tell it very quickly. Last October, I got
a phone call from an old friend of mine, a gentleman I had grown up
with who happens to work for Mel's company. I hadn't spoken to him
in a couple of years, but he called to pick my brain. He told me that
they were having some problems with the music for a film he was
working on. He didn't tell me what it was at that point, but he said
that the director of the movie was not sure what kind of music he
wanted in the movie. I asked, "What's the movie?" When he replied
that it was *The Passion of the Christ*, I fell off my chair. I said, "Gee,
I read all the articles about this film. It's been talked about for almost
a year. Can I see the film?" He said sure. They sent the film over. I
viewed it. I was completely emotionally touched be it. I offered to
write some music for free, just on spec, because of my interest in the
film. I thought it would be an honor to write music for something like
that. It would be a dream, really. So I spent the weekend after I
viewed the film writing some music. The very first thing I wrote was
what became the trailer music with the female voice and so on. After
that, they liked what they heard, and it became my sort of the back-
door way into the project.

**When you first tackled this project, what was your approach or
inspiration?**

I got a lot of whatever music exists right now from that period, and
I listened to that and looked through whatever written music there
was. I learned about the instruments of the period. But I had to do it
very quickly because, when I was first hired, I had about four weeks

to compose it. I just had to hold my breath and dive in, like I've had to do a lot of times with the movies I've done.

I've read many different opinions on the movie and the score. Some were religious in nature, some were political. Rarely did they review the movie and its music for what it was. Did you have a spiritual connection to the movie?

Absolutely. I'm a lifelong Catholic. I went to Catholic grammar school and was an altar boy. So this is a subject that obviously is my story, my personal belief system. Although, there was a time a few years ago when I had sort of lost my faith. I returned to it because of a number of things that happened in my life.

After the loss of my mom a couple of years ago, I sort of started to re-look at my personal faith and religion in general. It led me back to reading about people of faith through the ages—saints and holy people of all faiths. I was trying to grasp the subject of faith and what that is. And, lo and behold, I slowly but surely regained my own personal faith. When I got the phone call about *The Passion of the Christ* last October, I was sort of at the end of my spiritual journey back to my belief, so doing this movie was absolutely very spiritually personal for me—so much so that it's hard to talk about sometimes. There was a lot of prayer involved, a lot of introspection, and a lot of self-doubt.

I feel it was no mistake that you were chosen for this project.

Yeah, I must say, I believe that there is some truth to what you said in terms of people who were meant to be on this movie. As I've told people, if you were to list twenty composers who would have been appropriate for this movie, I wouldn't have been on that list. I firmly believe that. Mel made that great leap of faith to hire me.

Talk about your interaction with Mel Gibson in this film and how much of a role, if any, he played in defining your sound.

Working with Mel was everything you could imagine. It was incredibly intense. At first it was very difficult because Mel is an extremely nice human being. I think that, if he doesn't like a performance or a piece of music, it's very difficult for him to tell you so. And it was also a new process for him, by the way—he had never had a composer demo every piece of music or invite him in to be such an intimate partner in this thing called "making music." So it was a rocky road at first. But that slowly eased up and it became more and more wonderful. As time went on, he got to know me and I got to know him. A level of trust developed, and, you know, you can't get that overnight. I invited him to be brutally honest to me, which he learned to do.

I would invite him into the studio to work with all these wonderful, different musicians that we utilized, and he would look at me and say, "That's kind of bugging me." And I would look at him and say, "Yeah, you're right" or "What if we tried this?" It was a collaboration. And it literally got to the point where he would run out and tell the musicians something and run back to me and ask, "What do you think?" And I'd say, "It's pretty good, but why don't we try this?" and then we would try something else. That's how the relationship developed, and it was quite exciting. By the end of things, when we were in London recording with the orchestra and the choir, it was more of the same. He would get that look on his face—he would sort of scrunch up his face and he'd say, "I don't know." I got to the point where I could read his body language. And, I think, at the end of the day, we just really had a good time working with each other.

Has he told you outright his feelings about the final collaboration?

He has. Again, he's a very humble man. He's kind of a man's man, I would put it. I think, sometimes, it might be a little hard for him to express verbally what he's feeling. But, right before the film opened, he gave me one of the sweetest phone calls. He very kindly let me know that he felt my contribution was very powerful and that he would love to do it again. And I said I would, too. It was very kind of him to let me know in the way he did.

I noticed that he also performed a little chanting and so on. Was that his idea or was that yours?

It was completely my idea. People forget sometimes what a great actor he is. This guy is a great actor. He is a brilliant actor. He is a brilliant director. He also has a very musical ear and is a singer. He sang on *Pocahontas*, which is that Disney animated film.

Great story: One day when we were in my studio (like we were quite a bit during this process), I said, "Why don't we try some chanting—a Tibetan monk-type of a low, guttural thin?". We were experimenting along those lines when, behind me was Mel, chanting along. He has a very low voice and was doing a very low sort of ethereal, guttural thing. I said, "That sounds really good." He goes, "What?" I asked Mel to go in the recording room and chant along. He goes, "No, you're kidding. No, no, no." I said, "Mel, it's good. Look, I'll make you a deal. I won't let you make a fool of yourself. If I think it's bad, I am going to tell you. And if I think it's good, I'm going to tell you that too." He goes, "You think so?" I said, "Yeah." So he went in and he did a little chanting along. That's what ended up on the soundtrack, and it was quite fun.

You chose an interesting and powerful approach to this score. You have a modern ethnic-style score with a lot of synth percussion elements and sounds. What led you down this road versus an epic symphonic score?

That's an easy one. Mel didn't want to let me go down the big traditional bible-movie road. And I think for good reason. His movie is quite different from most other bible movies. His movie is very visceral. It's in your face. He really wanted the music to be very eclectic, and he wanted it to be situational, which I thought was very interesting. I've never had a director tell me, "John, I want the music to be situational." When he first said that to me, I didn't know what he was talking about. But then, through our discussions, I figured out what he meant. He meant that he didn't want a traditional sort of referential-type score. He wanted the score to be very specific to each moment in the film. He said, "I don't care if one piece of music doesn't relate to the next at all. I really want this to relate to exactly what is going on in the given scene and with the given character." And I think he was absolutely spot-on with that, because we ended up with was a score that's not one thing in particular, which I think is really cool. There's not really one overriding main theme, but there are a couple of themes—there's Mary's theme and there were a couple of motif things. When Mel heard Mary's theme for the first time with the Aramaic vocals, he was crying. He had tears rolling down his face.

What's so cool about the score, for me, is that every piece is sort of its own statement and yet there is an overall feeling to the score, and that is what you mentioned, Christian, that there are common elements. There's a lot of percussion. There are a lot of ethnic and ancient instruments. There are the vocals. These are common threads, and yet there's not an overriding overall theme. That makes it sort of refreshing when I'm listening, when I just have this thing on in my car. It's kind of fresh in a weird way, because of the relation from one cue to the next.

Those in my family whom I have shared your score with have been touched beyond words. I feel the need to share this with you because, in this day and age, it takes a lot of strength to persist in your spiritual beliefs and to allow yourself to remain open and in tune on this journey. The experience is just perfect for me.

Thank you. I think that's the highest compliment I can get, and it humbles me. I don't think I have a large ego in the Hollywood sense. When people I barely know come up to me in tears and want to hug me, I'm touched. People have told me they've listened to the CD in their car and had to pull over because they were weeping. I've heard a lot of special stories like that. And I don't know. It's not a testament to anything I've done. It's just sort of the voice of God speaking through some of this stuff, whether it's the movie, whether it's the photography, whether it's the performances of the actors. I don't know what it is. Call it God. Call it a divine source. Call it whatever.

You've created what I feel is a masterpiece in the history of film music. What does this mean to you?

Wow! I've got to tell you, you're so kind with your comments. If any of that's true, it's just so hard for me to get my mind around yet, and I'll tell you why: When I was writing this music, it was so not about me, meaning the ego me. And it's never happened to me like that before. I want to always write the best music that I can. That's the way I want to keep it. If it speaks to people, then I'm so touched. If, you know, twenty years from now, people look back and they think it was a good score, I'll be very happy with that.

I can look back at my work on *Cutthroat Island*, and, yeah, that was a pretty good score. I can look at *Hocus Pocus* and remember writing it and striving to make every note perfect. But *The Passion of the Christ* is one of those scores where I literally let go and let it be what it was. Luckily, I had a collaborator in Mel who gave me that freedom.

There are all kinds of directors out there, some who will give you freedom, some who will want to agonize over every note. Mel agonized over every note but, then, at interesting moments of insight, he would just go, "Go with it. That's great! We're done. That's good." That's the way it is with him. I've never experienced anyone else who's quite like that, and maybe that's ultimately the genius of the man. And I don't say that lightly. I have no reason to say stuff like that other than that's the way I feel. There is a genius to this man that is very elusive, and I would experience it in different ways.

Getting back to your very sweet comment, if that is the case, I'll be delighted. I'll be delighted if thirty years from now I can be an old guy maybe teaching in a university and find then that it inspired somebody to get into writing music. That would be great. If it would inspire people's lives, that would be great.

Cliff Eidelman's scores are noted for their ability to capture a film's emotional essence, for telling its story as if it emanated from within his own soul. He seems to possess a passionate sense that provides him with the ability to see beyond the picture, beyond what flickers in front of his eyes. This is certainly evident in the enchanting music he wrote for *Untamed Heart* (1993) and *One True Thing* (1998). And his score for *A Simple Twist of Fate* (1994) masterfully expresses each character's inner feelings with music that peers deeply into their lives and souls, offering an emotional vision that only music can provide. Not all of Eidelman's scores, however, set out to focus tightly on such intimate emotional details. He is a multi-talented composer adept at writing highly expressive music for all film genres, a versatility that is clearly shown by his epic score for *Christopher Columbus: The Discovery* (1992) and his moody orchestral sci-fi music for *Star Trek VI: The Undiscovered Country* (1999).

How much of an impact did growing up in L.A. have on you and your relationship to film music?

As a kid, I saw a lot of films. Film music itself probably had a bigger impact than what I was aware of. However, it wasn't a real conscious

impact until I saw *Star Wars* in 1977. That was the first time I was
consciously aware of the effects of film music. I was amazed by the
score, and I was old enough to appreciate a great film score.

What is your musical training?

My first exposure to playing was on the violin. Soon after that, I
became more interested in forming a rock band, so I took guitar lessons. I had a friend who was a drummer and another friend who was
a keyboard player and we formed a band. For years after that, I
wrote original music. We played in a lot of rock-'n'-roll clubs, including The Troubadour, Gazzarri's, The Roxy, and other Hollywood
clubs.

After high school, I went to the Guitar Institute of Technology
for a year to study jazz guitar, because I wanted to become a more-
fluent guitar player and a more well-rounded musician altogether.
This was a really intense trade school where you played guitar ten
hours a day with other people and in different ensembles, learning
jazz and other styles. After graduating there, I went to Santa Monica
College. Right about that time, I started listening to a lot of classical
music. I studied scores for the first time by Beethoven,
Rachmaninoff, Stravinsky . . . and I started losing a little bit of interest in my band, because my band couldn't produce what I was trying to write. With four players you can't really produce the full
orchestration that interested me at that time.

I started writing a ballet while I was attending Santa Monica
College. I finished it and had it performed. I started writing a three-
movement piece for orchestra the following year. While at Santa
Monica College, I studied under Donald Richardson, who was sort of
my mentor. After two years at Santa Monica College, I transferred to
the University of Southern California and studied composition,
orchestration, and conducting for a few more years. At the end, I
received my first film-score commission. That's how I started working in the film industry.

What are your musical influences?

Probably a lot of things that I'm not even aware of, because there are
so many composers I like. It's hard not to have influences from
everywhere.

Every composer strives to develop a unique "sound." Where did yours stem from?

I've always been very conscious of following my own soul for my own voice. When I listen back to the early pieces I wrote when I was in college, I can hear whom I was interested in at that time. As I grew older, I became more aware of just playing from my heart, developing my own expression. Having said that, no matter how much a person tries to make their own music authentically them, listening to other people's music, there's always going to be influences. However, it's very important to me to sound like me and not sound like everybody else.

Star Trek VI is the score that seems to have landed you a firm place as a leading composer in Hollywood. How did you get to work on such an elite project?

First, I had heard through my agent that this film was open and that people were submitting music. I put together music from my earlier scores, like *Magdalene*, which was my first film score, and *Triumph of the Spirit* and other pieces, and my agent sent the tape to the director. It's my understanding that both Nick Meyer and his editor, Ron Roose, whom he is very close with, had the same tape. I guess they were both listening to everyone's music and then talking with each other. It turns out that after they had listened to everybody's tapes, they both had independently decided on my tape. That was the major reason why I was able to get a meeting ultimately.

Was Jerry Goldsmith a part of this at the time?

No. My understanding is that I was able to walk in the door in the first place because this movie was being made for a price, and they were not going to pay the fee that composers like Jerry were commanding. They needed to find somebody willing to do it for a lot less money. That opened the door for people like me to give it a shot.

After I met with Nick Meyer, I went home and, based on his description of the film's opening, I wrote what I thought would be an opening piece of music for it and I recorded it at home. I called him the next day and I told him that I thought I had the opening or main title. He was just about to take off on a trip somewhere, so I asked if I could just run in and show it to him fast. He said, "Yes, come on in." I went to Paramount, sat down with him, put the tape on, and we started listening. I think he related to that piece or understood it. But he said that he was thinking about adapting Holst's *The Planets* as the score for *Star Trek VI*. I was pretty familiar with *The Planets* from studying it in college, so I asked if I could adapt it for him.

He gave me a script. I took the script home and I did a spotting session on it, kind of figuring out where all the music would start and stop, and sent it to Nick. He went through my script and sent back his changes or his ideas about where I spotted it. So you can see that there was a lot of relationship going on, a lot of back-and-forth creative work happening between us without me being hired. Shortly after that, I did get the word that I was hired. But, at that point, I thought I was going to be adapting *The Planets*. As it turns out, I think that the licensing of *The Planets* became too expensive. Once I started realizing that they may not be able to afford the license to *The Planets*, I started developing original material on my own. I had the producer, Ralph Winter, and Nick come over to my apartment and listen to what I was doing. As I played the scenes with my original music, the producer turned to Nick and asked him, "Why are we trying to license *The Planets* when we have this?" That was the end of *The Planets*.

Why didn't it lead to future *Star Trek* movies for you?

That was the last feature with the original cast and that team. When the new generation of movies came along, it was a completely different group with completely different producers, different teams altogether. And they had their ideas about whom they wanted to hire. That's pretty much how that works. I think that the new people who came in were familiar with Jerry Goldsmith, maybe had worked with him before on earlier stuff, so they went to Jerry. I think that, if Nick Meyer or the same group of producers I worked with had gone on to do another *Star Trek*, I would have had a much better shot of doing the next film. Relationships are very important. It is who people know and who they've worked with and all of that.

This led to another epic score, *Christopher Columbus*. This powerful period piece was brilliantly written with emotionally rousing themes that illustrated struggle and victory. What was your approach to this project and what were your influences in the music?

I actually watched the film over and over, and I already had the scenes in my head, so for a lot of it, I just turned off the film and amplified the scenes in my mind. I imagined larger sets and larger battles and just bigger everything. I amplified everything that they had on the screen into a more epic style. I felt like this was a chance for me to write a big, epic, swashbuckling adventure with a whole range of battles and triumphs.

I knew I wanted to use choral elements and full symphony orchestra, and I had five or six weeks to do it. I was pretty much alone, too, because everyone was in a different part of the world: The director was in England, the producers were in France, and the editing was being done somewhere else. It was literally a global thing while I was in Los Angeles writing the score. It was good in a way because I was so much on my own that I was able to write full-on and without any interruption whatsoever.

After this, your music takes a turn with *Untamed Heart*. Your touching and emotionally captivating music for this movie can be "heard" in the heart. Its simple, thematic style will continue through the rest of your career. Was it your conscious choice to start working on more intimate projects?

Well, I had worked with director Tony Bill on a comedy called *Crazy People* and enjoyed it greatly. I knew he was doing a film called *Untamed Heart*, so I read the script—and halfway through reading it, I was in tears. By the time I got to the end, I just got chills. I was just very moved by the story and by the characters. So I called him up and expressed in deep ways that this was my score—I just had to do this one. He was receptive, but not ready to hire me yet. So I decided to start writing music for it as if he had hired me, figuring, "What the hell, I'll take the chance." I wrote pieces to the script, and then invited him over. We started listening to some themes, and after we got through two or three of them, he said turned to me and said, "As long as you've gone this far, why don't you just write the rest of the score?" And that was that. I just continued on in the path I was on.

I love writing chamber music as well as big orchestral music like *Christopher Columbus*. I really love writing intimate music where individual voices in the music represent emotional spines of characters. In the case of *Untamed Heart*, I loved the intimacy of the story and just followed that intimacy into the music.

The emotional style of your music captivates me.

I try to throw myself into it all the way, and for me, it's very hard to move on until I feel chills when I'm playing music up against the picture. I really do have to feel that sense of emotion in those types of pictures before I can feel comfortable to move on.

Are these movies that you are so emotionally tied to ones that you have chosen?

Not all the time. A lot of it, probably most of it, is relationship-based, as I mentioned before. Every once in a while, a project on which you don't know anyone comes along, but you chase after it because you really feel you've got to do it. One such film was *One True Thing*. I had never worked with the directors or the producers, but I really chased after it by writing music, trying to win them over that way, and that was how I was able to work on this film.

I would love another big epic where I can really use the orchestra. I have been dying to do that for a long time, but those projects haven't shown themselves to me. So that's the way it's happened so far.

Yeah, you seem to be pigeonholed as a romantic composer.

Yeah, intimate and romantic. They know I'm the person they can talk to if they're doing a very emotional score. If I have to be pigeonholed, I'm glad it's in the emotional genre. But I would like to get some big, epic, action-oriented films again.

Your next score is *A Simple Twist of Fate*. It is filled with angelic melodies yet with a somber tone. It is hauntingly poetic. What were your intentions in this approach?

The director didn't approach me with any thoughts. He didn't tell me what he wanted or anything. He had heard one of my intimate scores and hired me to do that. I watched a screening of the film with no take on it whatsoever. They just screened it for just me, alone in a room at Disney. By the time I got to the end of the film, something had dawned on me: the whole idea of fate—the things that happened that brought this little girl to the Steve Martin character's doorstep, changing his life forever.

I don't know if you remember, but her mother died. That was a bit of fate knocking at his door. The story had this feeling to me that things were happening for a reason; everything was happening without anyone's personal control; everything was changing everyone's lives. So I suddenly imagined that the score would have ethereal, other-worldly qualities, where it was as if forces beyond their control were at work. I felt the music should carry those forces through the film while continually making the emotional relationships the important thing of the score: the emotional melodies among the characters, the love between the father and daughter, the bonding that took place. Even though I sort of had this conceptual idea—this ethereal quality—in using voices, I kept the earthbound relationship the key force to the score. It sort of combines the ethereal world with the grounded world and sort of molds them together.

I had to watch the film a couple times to figure out this feeling, because the music affects the film in different ways. As you mentioned, there is the interaction of the human and the ethereal. But your score also has a dark edge to it. While viewing the picture, one might feel unsettled. What is the music's darker side revealing?

There was some mystery going on. There was a dark side to it. The girl's real mother had overdosed on drugs in the dead of winter. So there was this very dark element that left this poor little girl in the cold in the dark of night, walking into a new life. But it's almost as if she were walking through a dark cloud to come into light. I felt that, in some way, there was a dark journey she had to take in order for her to come into this new world, this new life, this new family, this new father, and then build from there on the love that they had.

When scoring a film, do you go by the emotion of the scene or do you develop themes for the individual characters?

Both. I try to start in broad strokes. First I try to develop an overall feeling, like maybe a theme comes out of something in the story. Sometimes a theme comes out as the characters start emerging. Then, the broader strokes somehow start to chip at it and you start to create little sculptures of the characters. That's the best way I can think of to visualize how multitudes of themes come out of bigger ideas.

Do you find it tough to be original when scoring movies that have similar themes, similar stories?

No, because every single story is original and has its own voice. No two stories are alike, even if they're in a similar genre. And the core of what you're after is always different. I never find myself on the same exact ground that I was on before. I always feel like I'm walking new ground, because you can never just relax on old tricks, which is what always makes the job so hard. Every job is hard because it's the act of trying to discover something new each time, even within similar veins.

Your career seems to have gone through quiet spells, such as in 2000. What do you do during a year when you may have just one score?

Well, now that I think about it, there were a few other things going on around 2000. I wrote concert piece called *Wedding in the Night Garden*. It's now had a performance by the L.A. Master Chorale and it's most likely going to get another performance by them soon. And in 1996, I wrote *The Tempest*, a concert piece put out by Varese Sarabande. Since 1996, I've been writing songs to eventually compile into an album where I sing and play most of it.

So I'm diversifying into concert music a bit and songs and things of that nature. But the core of what I'm doing is film music. That's the foundation of my living. It's what makes it possible for me to do all these other things. And I would like to be doing more films. I'd love to be doing some bigger films.

I'm surprised that you're not. You put your heart and soul into your work. I feel that you have a finger on the pulse of any project you work on.

Well, I appreciate that. I get a lot of e-mails from people who have said that to me, and I always deeply appreciate that because it confirms that people are responding to what I do. But it's not always that simple. The people making decisions about who does what films are not always the people who are writing me those emails and paying close attention to the music itself.

There are many factors involved in how a person gets a score. It's not always as simple as what people from the outside might think. They might think that a composer did such a great job on so-and-so and wonder why he isn't getting all the movies like that. It's just not that simple. You can see what it took me just to get *Star Trek*. Hopefully, I'll get a critically acclaimed film that does well at the box office or meet a few directors whose careers are blooming and I just do a lot of their films. That tends to be what happens to a lot of composers who get big careers. They gain strong relationships with talented directors and they work on a few critically acclaimed films, and that leads to a lot of stuff. It's a snowball effect.

Robert Folk

Highly talented and prolific composer Robert Folk is best known in
Hollywood for his many well-written scores for comedy films, most
notably the popular *Police Academy* movies (a film series that has
run from 1984 to 2006) and *Ace Ventura: When Nature Calls*
(1995). Folk, however, is adept at writing in all current musical
styles and for all film genres, and his music often weds diverse
streams of popular and classical music. His score for *Lawnmower
Man 2: Beyond Cyberspace* (1996) is dark and powerful; his score
for *Miles From Home* (1988) is lighthearted yet emotionally driven.
A musical chameleon in the best sense, he regularly and skillfully
reinvents his compositional voice to provide each film he scores
with its most compelling music.

Folk is also a first-rate conductor who has conducted prominent
orchestras around the world.

Tell me a little about the beginning of your music career.

I started out in the late-sixties, first playing some guitar and piano.
I got involved with a bunch of rock-'n'-roll bands in the Boston area.
My main ambition was to be a songwriter at that point.

It was really The Beatles that did it for me as far as music goes. That just kind of captured my attention, and once I started heading in that direction, that's all I really focused on. I decided at that point that music was going to be my career, although I took some wandering paths through different types of music and different types of musical arenas.

Besides The Beatles influence, was there music around your house that also influenced you?

You know, my father, although he was not a professional, was a classical violinist. I heard plenty of that. My brother was also a violinist. My sister was a pianist. There was quite a bit of classical music flowing around the house. But I wouldn't call it an artsy family. My father was a career military officer. When he left the military, he worked at the Pentagon for a number of years. Same with my brother. I wouldn't call it your typical musical family, but there was some talent.

Then, being that age, the whole rock-'n'-roll explosion took over the household as far as I was concerned.

Where you aware of film music prior to your career?

I was certainly aware of film music from my teens on. But I was not really aware of the composers who were involved, just the experience of hearing music with film. It was more of an appreciation for the music but with no particular awareness of who was creating it. And I had no thought about ever doing it. How I happened, by accident, to get involved with film composing is a whole story in itself.

Do you remember specific films that inspired you or captured your attention?

I can't really cite one or two or several films that had that much of an impact on me. I know that I was very struck with John Williams' early stuff in the mid-seventies. That's probably the first time that I wondered, "Gee, who is that guy, and what's his background?" Coincidentally, he was a Julliard guy as well and studied with Rosanna Levine.

What led you to work in film music?

It was just a strange twist. I was at Julliard for ten years, writing a lot of concert music. I figured I would always be there. I was a faculty member—and it doesn't really get much better than Lincoln Center in terms of the classical composer's world and the classical-music world in this country. My plan was simply to stay at the school, stay on the faculty, get involved with some of the other Lincoln Center institutions, continue writing concert music, and do the usual combination of commissions, grants, and so on.

Then, a student of mine's father, who was a filmmaker, asked me if I would want to score a film for him. He knew my classical writing; he really enjoyed my work, but had no idea whether I would be appropriate for his movie or whether I knew the first thing about film music. So it was kind of an interesting twist that he should choose me to write a score for him. It was very unexpected. I had no plans to go into film music. I wasn't thinking about it. But the experience of working for him, which led to recording with the Royal Philharmonic in London, was so satisfying and interesting to me that, when I finished that project, I started to think, "Well, gee, this is something I might really want to pursue."

What project was this?

It was a documentary called *The Planets*. It's not a film that's seen by many people, just a small documentary. Nevertheless, they took the music seriously enough to want to record with one of the world's great orchestras. For me that was quite a thrill—being in my mid-twenties and having access to that kind of an orchestra. So when I finally finished up at the school, I decided to move to L.A. That Royal Philharmonic recording, along with some other recordings of my classical music, got me my first project out here. When I arrived here in L.A. in 1980, it took me about five or six weeks to land a feature film with Fox. It was not a very good film, a thriller called *Savage Harvest*, for which they sent me straight back to London, where we hired the National Philharmonic Orchestra.

How do concert music and film music work together? And how do they differ from one another?

They work together because the more diverse your writing background is, the better prepared you are for writing in the film medium because there are so many different film genres that require so many different types of scoring. All the techniques that I acquired in the classical world, and also as a rock-'n'-roll musician, have come into play in various film scores I've written.

The difference between concert music and film music is pretty clear. You're subordinate to a film: You're part of a team. The music is one element. It's not the only element. Of course, when you're writing for film, you're also being influenced by the director's intentions and desires as well as your own. Whereas, if you're writing a concert work, the only thing that matters is the music itself, and you're the only person to consider as to what the motivation of the piece is or what the style of the piece is. There's another difference, too: With film music, you have the whole scheduling aspect. You have very little time to write film music, but you have so much time to write classical music.

Financially, how do they compare?

There's no comparison. You can make an extraordinarily good living in the film world, particularly if you are ranked within the top fifty composers, to pick an arbitrary number. In classical music, you are dependent on grants and commissions. It's a very different way of making a living. I think there are far fewer classical composers who make a significant living than there are film composers. In the classical world, people like John Adams, with that level of commercial success, are pretty rare. There are probably only a dozen guys who are on that circuit.

The *Police Academy* series launched your career in films. What were some of your experiences working on these films?

I started the first one just a few years after I had gotten here. I think I had done two or three films before that picture. They were thriller/dramas. *Police Academy* was such an enormous hit—it has so much commercial visibility—that, of course, in this world I was tagged right away as the guy who wrote comedic scores.

I had really good experiences working on them. We always had really top orchestras here in L.A. to record all the scores. It was challenging music. The whole military tone to them, along with punching up the humor, led to a style where you could really do some virtuoso writing. If you listen to some of that music apart from the film, I think you'll see a lot of integrity in it—a lot of virtuoso writing for the orchestra and, at the same time, a lot of fun. It was also good to have that vehicle to return to every year or two for a while. I think that maybe after the first four of them, they started going down in quality, and we were all affected by that.

It bothers me that we, the enthusiasts, cannot hear this music without seeing the movie over and over. To me, your *Police Academy* scores are classics that I grew up with, and I know many would agree that an official release would be fantastic.

Exactly. From the collector's point of view, at some point it would be nice to put out a CD from that series. I have been approached a couple of times about it. I think it could be done. I think that maybe a deal could be struck with the union at this point. You know, the unions are different in today's world. There might be a way to finance it that would make sense—at lease to put out a thirty-minute CD if not more.

***Lawnmower Man 2: Beyond Cyberspace* has to be one of your most amazing works in terms of depth, creativity, and complexity.**

I really love that score. The disappointing thing about it is that when the film was first dubbed and finished for New Line, we had a phenomenal dub from Todd-AO, where the music was incredibly present and really effectively supported the film the way that both the director and I had intended. Sadly, as can often happen out here, when the movie was turned over to the studio and the executives saw it, they decided to re-cut it. Then they remixed it and re-dubbed it, and not a lot of the music was left by the time the film came out.

It was really very frustrating for me because I'm certain that, if the film had done well and the music had been left alone, it would have allowed me to work more in that genre.

Talk about your use of orchestrational color for this film.

That was another London recording. It was the London Symphonia. London's my favorite town to record in, along with Los Angeles. I would put them on an equal footing.

When I know I'm recording for an orchestra of that caliber, I know there are no restraints on the virtuosity of the music or the orchestrations. With that in mind, I thought of that score as the fusion of a Strauss orchestra with some electronic elements, which were thrown across it. The electronic elements were mostly for motion and energy and the sci-fi subject matter.

I think it has inspired a lot of composers to revisit that sound.

I think so. Like I say, I am more of a student of classical music than of film music, so I'm sure you can find other film scores that are of that making that preceded my score for *Lawnmower Man*. I do think it had some impact on style, though. I certainly have heard a lot of similar approaches to things over the years.

***Ace Ventura: When Nature Calls* is a score with an eclectic mix of sounds. I'm impressed with is your fluent writing for both electronics and orchestra. Which do you find most challenging writing for?**

I live in both those worlds. Having been a rock-'n'-roll kind of a kid, I was always into electronic elements: percussion, drums, and whatnot from the time that I was a teenager. I feel really comfortable in both of those worlds, and sometimes they fuse well.

Ace Ventura was a happy musical landscape for me because there were no budget limitations. It was recorded here, in L.A. When you're using rhythm players, electronic elements, and orchestral players at the same time, you really can't beat Los Angeles because the rhythm players out here are by the far the best that I've heard anywhere. So, in that score, you've got like a dozen of the best rhythm guys in the world playing next to a ninety-piece orchestra. We did it all live, all at the same time, which was really interesting. Dennis Sands is one of the few engineers whom I would have entrusted that kind of recording to, because most people would have recorded that score in sections—the way you would do a record, starting with drums and bass and then adding guitars and then electronic and percussion elements and then the orchestra and finally the choir. But there was something kind of unique and fun about doing it all at once and actually having it come off well, having the final mixes sound really resonant and orchestral but also fluid and groovy.

One of the reasons we made the decision to do *Ace Ventura* all at once over on the Sony orchestral stage was the time element. We had release dates. We didn't have enough time. We just had to get it done in a certain number of hours. The way they set up enough isolation to keep all the rhythm guys sounding good and yet have the orchestra have that big concert-orchestra sound to it was pretty amazing. It's one of my favorite experiences.

Nothing to Lose has a similar fun style, with the jazzy urban beats and electronics.

It's definitely a fusion score that was just born out of the movie, where you've got Martin Lawrence and Tim Robbins, the hip-hopper meeting the baby-boomer straight guy from the suburbs. Then, when they leave L.A. and go out to Arizona, you've got a Southwestern feeling that creeps into the score.

I added six saxophones because I thought that hearing these three tenor and three baritone saxes honking away throughout the score would make everybody smile. It was a huge saxophone sound laid on top of, once again, some of the most amazing groove players anywhere on the planet Earth.

What genre do you find most appealing to write for?

My favorite film that I've worked on is *Miles from Home*, which did not get a lot of exposure. It was a Richard Gere and Kevin Anderson film from the late-eighties. A straight-ahead dramatic picture but with romantic overtones and Americana settings. You know, I would love to do more in that genre given the opportunity.

As every film composer will tell you, whatever your biggest-selling movies are, those are the kinds of scores you are going to do the most of. That's just the way it happens out here. It takes twenty-to-a-hundred-million dollars to make a movie, so they get the guy who has plenty of that stuff on his résumé. Then, every few movies, you get a chance to do something different, which is always more than welcome.

I feel that if you've got a deep musical education and you've crossed a lot of stylistic barriers, as a lot of film composers have, there's no reason why you couldn't pull off any kind of a score. I'm sure that's a universally held feeling among film composers. When you interview people for your book, I'm sure you run into it. I just don't think people understand how diverse we are. The system doesn't get it, and it never will get it. It is what it is. There's no use lamenting it. If you're going to work out here, it's just one of the things you have to accept. But it isn't easy to accept, because we know what we are capable of doing.

What scores do you feel represent your talents best?

If I were to pick a couple, I would say *Lawnmower Man* in the action genre, probably *Ace Ventura* in the comedy genre, *Miles from Home* in the romantic drama. Probably those three films. I also did a small film a couple years ago called *You're Dead*, a British thriller. It was a film that I really enjoyed scoring because it was really a dramatic thriller-action piece, but with a lot of emotion in it. It was another opportunity to reach out into those styles. I think that's a great more-recent example of something that shows my work off well.

Back to my question about your favorite genre . . .

I love melody and theme. For me that is usually a drama or a romance. An example is a film like *Can't Buy Me Love*, where you can write a really strong romantic theme and use it throughout the whole movie. That's always very rewarding for me.

I acknowledge that, in recent years, scores seem to be less and less thematic and more rhythmic. But I think that melody and theme are really important in coming up with a signature for a movie and in coming up with something that is memorable for a movie, so that when you think of that score or film ten or fifteen years later, it just pops into your head. That's an important element in film-scoring, and I hope that it comes back into play a little bit more importantly in the next several years. Although I enjoy the rhythm and percussive kind of scores that you see mostly going on right now, I think that things are going to go back the other way in a couple of years. I think that maybe you'll still have the rhythm and percussive elements, but maybe you'll start to hear more themes again.

The Civil War film *Gods and Generals* (2003) put John Frizzell on the path to wide recognition among film-music fans. However, before 2003, Frizzell was not an unknown and, in the late 1990s, his Hollywood career was certainly in ascension: James Newton Howard took Frizzell under his wing, and together they worked on *The Rich Man's Wife* (1996) and *Dante's Peak* (1997). These scores led to *Alien Resurrection* (1997), for which Frizzell wrote an ethereal score.

Frizzell's music is always heartfelt, regardless of the genre in which he's working: Among his notable scores are the introspective *Crime of the Century* (1996), a film about the Lindbergh kidnapping; the ominous *The Empty Mirror*, a film about Adolph Hitler; and the wild *Beavis and Butt-head Do America* (1996), a popular MTV comedy.

How did you get into the movie-music business?

It's an interesting thing. I've never been in anything else. My father was on the road to becoming a concert pianist before he became an architect. There was so much music around the house—even though he was an architect he was constantly exposing us to tons of music. I started singing as a small child, and I sang at the National Cathedral in Washington, D.C. Then I took some gigs doing chorus work with the Metropolitan Opera Company and the Paris Opera Company. They would do their summer tours on the East Coast, and I spent a couple summers doing that until my voice changed.

I just found that the world of music was something I greatly enjoyed. I studied a lot of music in high school and ended up going to music school at USC; then I went to Manhattan School of Music.

What are your musical influences?

You know, my musical influences are . . . I like such a diverse range of music that I don't think I can say it's one thing that has really driven me toward music in terms of a style. Although it's probably a strange answer, my musical influence is probably the human condition. When I say "the human condition," I mean that I'm fascinated with how music affects the human mind. I think that's what ultimately draws me to music.

Are you inspired by the music of other film composers?

Absolutely. I try to keep up a healthy amount of listening to my peers and to the great composers who have shaped the art of film music. I draw from what they have done to outline the language we use, and I take part in watching the language we use in film music evolve.

What film or films reveal your voice or how you perceive yourself?

I would pick two: *James Dean* and *Gods and Generals*. I love to write very intense music.

What genre interests you most in a composition?

That's an interesting question. The genre that interests me the most is moving people—having them feel human is something that interests me very much. Although, I think if I just did that, I would really long to just entertain and get people very excited.

It's nice to sit down and write melodies and to write thematic material that becomes embedded, hopefully, in the psyche of the viewers and maybe, if you really go a step forward, in the psyche of our culture.

You came onto *Dante's Peak* after James Newton Howard began with the themes. How did all this take place?

James Newton Howard has always been supportive and an enormous help to me in my early career. There was a serious time-crunch on that film, and they needed to get someone in there right away. James said that he would write a theme, and he backed me in being the composer of the score. It was my opportunity to do my first massive action film. James ended up doing five or six cues, something like that, and I think he had two themes that are played in there.

How difficult was it blending your style with James Newton Howard's themes?

Pretty easy. James is a great composer and has been a very big influence on me. Also, so many composers in history have taken themes of other composers and expanded on them. Clearly that was something that was commonly done. I think I did it well.

***Thirteen Ghosts*, with its experimental sounds of the locomotive along with heavy synth textures, is an unusual score for you. Where did you develop these sounds?**

A lot of late nights trying very bizarre experiments in the studio. For some of the sounds I used, I got old car parts and hung them up in my living room and basically just beat on them and then processed those sounds to get some strange, striking, metallic sounds. I purchased an erhu, which is a Chinese bowed-string instrument that's similar to a violin. I had no idea how to play it, and I sat around for a few hours until I was able to get some very horrific sounds coming out of it due to my lack of ability. It's a lot of trial and error, and half the time you come up with a terrible idea that doesn't work. But, during *Thirteen Ghosts*, I found a bunch of things that *did* work. I hope they were innovative. I think one of the most fascinating things with music today is the technology, where we're able to have sounds evolve an enormous amount—they're like a kaleidoscope in the way they're never the same from moment to moment.

The brass cues in *Thirteen Ghosts* seem influenced by Bernard Herrmann.

I think that you can say that they're influenced by him—absolutely. He's one of my great heroes. And I think if you look back into the classical literature, you'll find his influences embedded in there. I believe you can find the real source of the inspiration for most film music back in the classical repertoire.

***Gods and Generals* is the most incredible epic score I have heard in a long while. How did this project come about for you?**

Well, it was interesting situation. Randy Edelman, who did *Gettysburg*, was going to do *Gods and Generals*, but there was a schedule conflict with him because of the film *XXX*. They needed to get the score done, so Randy called me, knowing I would want to score the film and use a couple things he had sketched out in there at my discretion. I met with the director, and we got along very well. It seemed like a good idea, so I sat down and started writing. I was glad to have a canvas as massive as *Gods and Generals* and to be able to get a chance to write this way.

Randy and I have been friends for a while. He is just a great guy and someone whom I am generally in awe of. I was really honored to have him think of me in this situation.

Randy Edelman did a fantastic job with *Gettysburg*, and I would have been curious to see the direction he took with this next Civil War film, which is of a much different nature. However, you ran with this project and excelled in every way.

Well, thank you. I am really very proud of it. I contemplated war and I tried to create something that I hope, upon listening to, will make people not want to have wars. I hope to get more opportunities to do that. I think that I've known about this side of my writing for a long time, and I'm glad people are getting to hear it.

Your music represents more of the soldiers' heart on the field than it did of the battles as a whole. What were you focusing on during the creative process?

The pain and the horror of that conflict, which killed hundreds of thousands of people and practically destroyed our country.

It was really about Ron Maxwell sitting me down and pointing at one guy, who—running through Fredericksburg—gets blown to bits, and Ron saying to me, "Now, John, write about what he's feeling. Don't write about what history thinks about him." I didn't take sides in the conflict; I took the human side. I took the side of anguish, not whether a mother was on the Confederate side or the Union side but that she lost her son. I'm not judging anything. I am just talking about human pain.

I really believe this score will open so many doors for you in the future. The question is, Can this score be topped?

I'm really grateful for what I get to do. I'm from the school where I work really hard and am really tough on myself. I figure, if I just keep working my ass off, I'll get more opportunities where I can create something that moves people.

I love to make people laugh. I loved doing *Beavis and Butt-head*, the movie. I'm very proud of that film because it made people laugh. I think that's a great thing to get to do. I've been getting positive feedback on *Gods and Generals,* and it will be nice to get other opportunities like it. And I want to leave a body of work here on Earth that I can say and that my kids can say, "Hey, that's cool."

Do you take being second in line on a project offensively or as a compliment that you've been referred by another colleague of yours?

Film music is an extremely competitive world, and I love competition. The minute I'm done with a movie, I try to find people to play chess with, so I can destroy them.

I have very close friends who are film composers who I'll call up when I know we're going after the same film and say, "Dude, I'm going to beat you." And if they beat me I get pissed off, but I really enjoy the competition of it. I think you have to have a healthy attitude toward competition to be in a business that is so competitive. I don't look at my competitors as foes. I look at them as competitors and it's a game.

What is your opinion of fans and reviewers? Do you take their comments personally?

You can't. On the Internet, I have seen some of the stuff that people are saying about my score to *Gods and Generals*. It's very ego inflating. But I can't embrace that. I didn't write it for you guys. So it's not about the reviews. You just have to write from your heart and believe in what you are doing. I've had scores that were massively criticized that are some of my favorite works.

Are you searching, then, for others' opinions or is this something directed to you without your control?

At times I've sought it out, and at times, it's kind of self-destructive. You might sort of snoop around the Internet and say, "Oh, my God, how could that person say that about me?" But then you realize that half the information is completely out of context. I think that what's particularly frustrating about reviews is that quite often they're about how a score appears on the CD, with no mention of how it relates to the film. Film music is exactly that—it's film music and it's a part of the whole thing. I tried to create a *Gods and Generals* CD that was a really good listen. But it's still a film score.

I was as guilty as everybody else. If you look at my shelves, I have hundreds of movie scores. At one point in time, prior to working on this book, I was sucked up in the fan-based world of film scores on CDs, making fruitless comments.

You're criticizing the CD. What a thing to do! The CD isn't what the composer sat down to do.

I believe that promoting this notion of getting film-score fans to acknowledge and to think about film scores and not film CDs would really benefit the art of film music. For example, get people talking about why they chose to put this here or there and so on. Maybe that cue got moved at the last minute on the dub stage, or there may be any number of other reasons why it is where it is.

All very true. On the other hand, as enthusiasts or listeners, we tend to become aware of, or become fans of, certain composers because of their music itself—dissociated from films. I listen to James Newton Howard on CD, for example, just as I listen to Arvo Pärt or Antonio Vivaldi. Film music has become so popular outside of films. Perhaps it's the modern opera. Nevertheless, now that I have seen the process behind closed doors and discussed with composers their careers, my outlook has changed, as has my focus in this book. I want to make film-music fans aware of all its elements before they start critiquing it.

Well, that's good, because CDs really are an important legacy. But they're just CDs. Listening to just the CDs is perfectly analogous to going backstage in an opera, looking at the costumes, and then saying, "None of them is any good—they don't fit together." But you're not looking at the whole thing.

You have to consider what our primary function is when you look at the really great film composers. Let's talk for a minute about Elmer Bernstein's score for *To Kill a Mockingbird*. It's probably one of the top five scores of all time. It's also a great CD. Just look at the finesse and the beauty of every note and picture how it relates to every character and how he opens up that main title and what mood it projects against that little box being opened up and how moving it is as part of a whole. That's the art of film music.

What goals do you have for the future, and what can we expect from you?

A baby first. I'm getting married in three weeks.

Musically, I really hope *God and Generals* will bring me to some more films that can take that type of emotional depth. Although I love the fun, exciting things I get to do, I don't want to do just that.

I just finished *Cradle 2 the Grave* with Joel Silver. Joel throws at me enormous challenges that are exciting, awesome, and terrifying. He'll have me try to innovate a whole hip-hop thing into a score and keep pushing me to find new sounds.

Getting back to *Thirteen Ghosts* for a second: Joel really pushed me to get those sounds to come to life that way. "Don't ever bring me the same old stuff. I've heard that one. . . . I've heard that one. . . ." I like getting pushed creatively to bring in something new, and then hear him say, "I haven't heard that. That sounds pretty cool." I start to feed on that. I adore working with Joel Silver because I love to change gears and start something new. I just love the whole process. I'm really drifting from your question.

What do I hope to do? I hope to keep creating, and I hope to keep doing a diversity of projects. I hope to keep getting pushed creatively, and I hope I can stay in touch with the reason I started doing this.

You touch on something that is pretty interesting that I've found in many composers' careers: a relationship with one particular director who pushes for that extra something that he or she knows the composer is able to do.

Joel really pushes me. He really gets me to find new things in myself and get out of bad habits and keep that forward motion in my work. It's really important to have a collaborative environment like that going on in your career. I'm sure I'm going to do many projects with him. You'll see my work evolve and know that I'm pushing myself, but I'm also getting creative input from someone I'm working with.

Another person I love working with is Mark Rydell. He really drives me creatively. I've only done two projects with him, but I'm very proud of the work that I've done in *James Dean* as well as the HBO movie we did, *Crime of the Century*. Mark really teaches me a lot about the idea of acting with music—such as, "What does it say or what does it convey?"—never letting me be passive in my composition.

Did you meet Mark Rydell through James Newton Howard?

I think James said to Mark, "Why don't you listen to Frizzell's work."
Mark gave it a listen and loved it. And away I went. Mentorship is a
great thing. When I hear someone young who I think is really good,
I love to pass that along now.

Philip Glass

Highly influential composer Philip Glass's unique, immediately identifiable voice has spawned many imitators and greatly altered the
landscapes of both film music and concert music. Although many
listeners and critics have considered his music an offshoot of minimalism, one most certainly cannot limit his work, particularly his
current music, to the school of minimalism.

Until recently, most of Glass's work (operas, chamber music,
orchestral music) has been outside of film. However, with increasing
frequency, he has been composing dynamic and dramatic film
scores, including *The Hours* (2002), which flows with emotion; the
dark, haunting *Candyman* (2001); and the cold, introspective *A
Thin Blue Line* (1988). These scores, like most of Glass's film-work,
are beautifully married to picture, yet, Glass's somewhat specific
style may not lend itself as well to less consciously artistic and more
overtly "mainstream" films.

What inspired you to take your music to films?

It depends. I'm interested in certain filmmakers. Starting around
1980, some very interesting people began asking me to write music
for them. There were some very interesting movies that came along

and, since I had worked a lot in the field of theater, dance, and opera, it wasn't much of a problem for me to shift my thinking to a genre that was closely related. At the beginning, I did mostly independent films, in which there wasn't a lot of money involved.

Do you believe that minimalist-style music can work with a variety of storylines?

It doesn't work very much in film. *The Hours*, for example, is a romantic, warm score. I don't think of it any other way, really. I haven't thought of myself as a minimalist composer for twenty-five years anyway, so I never think that way. There are some times when directors want something that is very redundant and reduced, because they don't really want a lot of music, and, in those cases, I have plenty of history and technique in that area of a minimal nature.

How would you describe your sound now?

It's theater music, basically. It's music that helps to tell a story. It uses a contemporary harmonic vocabulary to tell a story and show movement.

When looking at a picture to score, what do you look for?

That's an interesting question because you have to start somewhere. Very often, I start with the director or the music editor, and we decide where the film should have music—we spot the film. Then I have quite a long encounter with the director about what they think the music should be doing. For me, the music has to help to tell the story and not just decorate a scene. I see music as being part of the narrative. So I ask myself, "What is the story trying to tell, and what is the pace?" It's a complicated question because it leads you right into the big area: The function of music in the film and how it's achieved, and it even indicates some of the artistic collaboration that's involved in that endeavor.

You have a signature sound with your music's instrumentation and texture. What has inspired your music's instrumentation, versus using the full range of the orchestra for a film?

Did you see *Taking Lives* or *Secret Window*, which were full orchestras? The answer to your question is thta the larger-scale films allow a bigger budget for the orchestra. That's really the truth to the matter. With the independent films, I had constraints that dictated the forces I had available. The mainstream films allowed me to write for a full orchestra, and I often did. So these things that became a signature were more necessities than choices. They just arrived naturally in that working environment.

There are many Dracula scores covering a full range of styles. Why did you choose a chamber-music approach?

This is a film made from a play that had been in London, touring the UK for about eighteen months. They took this play and filmed it. Everything took place in drawing rooms, bedrooms, maybe the basement of the castle—in other words, we're talking about fairly confined interiors. I felt it needed something that achieved the same depth of emotion but remained in the same scale as the film did, so I chose a string quartet. I remember the carriage ride over the Transylvanian mountains. It takes a second to realize that you're looking at a painted set—the whole thing is staged. So even there I felt that the quartet would be appropriate.

***Kundun* is a Tibetan film. Did your Buddhist faith give you a clear understanding of this culture and the needs of an authentic sound to tell the story?**

First of all, it's a Disney film directed by Martin Scorsese. The actress is Tibetan, but no one behind the camera is Tibetan. There are films made by Tibetans, but this isn't one of them. Martin Scorsese, who is a well-known filmmaker, created the film for a big studio.

Second of all, Buddhist faith is a term that I find rather strange, because I don't think of myself as having some connection to this culture. I don't know if I know what the Buddhist faith is. I have spent a long time with the Buddhist or the Tibetan community, which, as a refugee community, started turning up in this country in the early-seventies. I got to know them that way, and I became very interested in the culture. I would say that I have as much faith in them as I have in anybody. I wouldn't say that it's an abstract thing.

It has more to do with knowing what their conditions were and learning the history of the people. I don't know that I have any special insight into it. I think, for all the time I've spent with it, it still remains a fairly esoteric culture to me, but one that I have a lot of interest in and sympathy with.

You weave the musical languages of different cultures into your work. Do you seek projects purposely to explore these communities?

Yes, I do. When I was in my mid-twenties, I began traveling the world. Not really as a performing musician yet, but mainly to translate the encounters I had into musical language and musical ideas that I felt were very stimulating.

What were your first thoughts when beginning the film *The Hours*?

They were looking for my style of music, but they didn't think I would be interested in film. But, as you know, I've done a lot of work in films. They contacted me and showed me the film, and I was very impressed with it. I connected right away and knew that this is something I could do. I knew exactly what to do. We got along very well. Everything was terrific. You don't get to have that much fun in movies every time you go to bat.

It is interesting that you use the piano as the focal instrument of this score.

I was looking for intimacy, and there is certainly something about intimacy with the piano for me. It's the thing you can have in your home. I contrasted it with the string section to give it depth and variety, but it's basically about the piano. I thought about what instrument would be playing in the room, which might be a strange question in a way, but it sometimes leads to interesting answers.

Your music in this film served as a character itself—one that stood out. Why did you place your music in the foreground?

Well, the reason I did that was that the film needed it. Without the music, you have three stories happening at three different times with three different sets of actors. It was so chaotic in a certain way without any music that it seemed to me that the score had to come in and become like the director and the writer—it had to guide you throughout the story. So it became a bold presence of the film, and I don't think the film would have worked otherwise. I was the third composer they hired. I don't know who the other two were, and I don't know what they did. They had to solve the same problem, and evidently they didn't. I managed to do it.

Your technique or style has influenced so many. Are there particular composers that you are inspired by or look up to?

If you start talking about music I like, I'll sound like an encyclopedia. It's a wonderful art that has been blessed with a tremendous amount of genius and variety, and the more different, the better for me.

Lee Holdridge

Lee Holdridge, like Bruce Broughton, writes colorfully orchestrated, melodically driven orchestral scores that are passionate, imaginative, and diverse and help us explore film and television with our ears and hearts. Although he is perhaps overlooked as one of the fine talents of the feature-film community, the television community—for which he has scored many movies—has honored him with five Emmys and numerous Emmy nominations.

Holdridge is very much in his element with Americana-flavored pictures, such as _Call of the Wild_ (1993) and _Buffalo Girls_ (1995), as well as with such comedy/dramas as _Splash_ (1984) and such epic adventures as _Into Thin Air: Death on Everest_ (1997). One of his best scores—two hours of Celtic-influenced music—was written for the television miniseries _The Mists of Avalon_ (2001).

Your early years were spent in Haiti and Costa Rica. In that time, what exposure did you have to music?

Well, basically, Costa Rica is where I really became aware of music. A lot of this was due to my dad's students. My dad was a famous scientist. A lot of his scientific students played musical instruments, and they liked to get together to play chamber music. I loved listening to that as a kid. I started going to listen to the symphony orchestra in San Jose. I got fascinated by the violin and decided I wanted to learn to play it. So, at age ten, I got my hands on a violin and was able to track down Hugo Mariani, the conductor of the National Symphony Orchestra, whom I took violin lessons from. By the time I was twelve years old, I wanted to be a composer. I used to rewrite my violin exercises and play them for my teacher, and I was driving him crazy with that. I was saying, "It would be better if it goes like this." Then my parents worked it out so that I could go to junior high school and high school in Boston and live with an uncle and aunt there and study music. That's where I met Henry Lasker, whom I studied with. That's how I launched myself. So I thank the conductor of the National Symphony of Costa Rica and my teacher in high school in Boston, Henry Lasker. These are the two men who really influenced my life and launched me on the path of composing.

You seem to be heavily influenced by the classical masters.

Yes, my first exposure to music was all-classical. I did not really listen to much pop music or jazz or anything like that until I got to the States. I mean, I knew Brahms long before I knew Chuck Berry. That was my influence, of course, because of the violin literature I was playing with the chamber orchestras. I loved that music, and that was really what I grew up with first. I think that it has played a really strong influence in my composing life ever since.

Did you ever have aspirations to work in film music? How did it evolve into a career for you?

When I thought of composing, I really only thought of composing orchestral music and music for the concert hall. The film-music idea didn't come until I came to New York in the sixties and was studying music, which exposed me to the richness in a lot of the films that were shown in New York. I used to go to a theater called the Thalia and a theater on 42nd Street, and all they did was show European films or art films. I loved it. I would go to all the film festivals. I loved film as an art form. I was really drawn to directors and their styles and, of course, the music was a big part of it. I was knocked out by certain composers and how they would approach the film—I really saw it as an art form. In academic circles at that time, if you were composing film music, you were looked upon as though you were a prostitute. They had this very snobbish academic sort of old-school European attitude about it. But I met one man, Nick Flagello, who was a great composer and a great teacher, and had actually worked on films as an orchestrator and an arranger, and he talked to me about technique. I just knew that that was the future—it's definitely an art form, and, of course, it has become one of the most important twentieth-century art forms in music.

Your work outside of films, such as your *Scenes of Summer*, has heavy imagery. Although this work speaks for itself, what is your canvas when writing a classical piece versus a motion picture?

It varies. With *Scenes of Summer* I had a little bit of a program idea in the back of my head as I composed the piece. But with a piece like my violin concerto, I didn't; I just simply composed. It varies from piece to piece. With some of my concert works, I will think of something. With some I won't—I just will start with an idea and pursue it. Imagery is important to me, but I definitely could go the road of pursuing an idea, seeing as far as I can go with it.

I imagine that your schedules conflict. Is it difficult to find creative time for your concert works?

No, it's funny, it always sort of works out. I can't explain it. It's never been a conflict. I've always been able to do both very successfully. I might have a break between two films and I may manage to compose something during that time. Ideas come quickly to me. Once I get an idea, and once I get going, composing can move rapidly for me. I sort of get hooked and I can't put it down.

The film scores are very demanding. They take a lot of time, and they take more time now because you have to play things for directors and rewrite things sometimes. You just do it. I just get it done somehow and then find that I can still do the other. It all just seems to fall into place.

You've also composed many television scores. How do these projects differ from a major motion picture, and does either pose bigger challenges for you?

Well, I have the attitude that you write for film and that's it. Whether it's a large screen or small screen, the challenges are: How do you score it? What do you say with the music? What role is the music playing in the scene? In that sense, it's a dramatic art form, however you approach it. You should always think of it that way.

Obviously, in a film, you have an audience in a theater. They're there for a couple of hours. They're not going anywhere. You're aware that you could take advantage of that in terms of taking time to say something. On television, the time is shorter because the programs are limited in their timespan, so you have to say things quickly. But I think the attitude you should go in with is that you are scoring a film, period, and you should just look at what is going to be the best thing for the scene in question.

Almost all of your work is thematic or lyrical, such as the love theme from *Splash*. Do you focus on thematic material as a basis of your scores?

Not always, no. I mean . . . I think, in a lot of cases, yes. Very often the producers who have hired me say, "We want a strong theme, something memorable." So that's an important influence. But it varies. Listen to my score to *Into Thin Air*. It has a lot of orchestral non-thematic material. Although there are a couple of motifs that occur from time to time, there are a lot of cues that have no connection with the theme at all and are just written as incidental music. They're on their own, so to speak.

I think if you listen to a wide variety of my scores, you will definitely hear the strong theme idea, which I love, but you will also hear a lot of stuff that is not thematic, but is written purely as texture.

How do you come about making that decision?

I'm influenced by the film and the director's directions. When you're composing for film, you really start with a blank page every single time, because every film is different. No two are the same, and they're going to take you down different roads. What worked in a scene in one film will not work in a seemingly similar scene in this film because there's something different about it. So you have to start over each time, and you sort of need to empty your mind and refresh it and say, "Okay, what's going to work for this? What seems to feel good?" You just have to sit there and play things against the film and start to get a feeling for what seems to feel right. That's what influences you. It just depends on the scene. Maybe a theme seems intrusive. Maybe something more minimalist might work? It just depends on what you think seems to be hitting the right kind of groove.

In *Tuskegee Airmen*, there is the dramatic underscore and military motifs, but what provide the unique voice is the horn arrangements. There are moments of discord that give you an unsettled feeling, yet they evolve into a beautiful melody.

I love that score. That's a very full, dramatic score. The story so moved me because I thought about these men who, against incredible odds—not only racially, but also in general—just had to excel to such a degree in order to fight for a country that was basically prejudiced against them. Every scene in that movie is based on a true incident that happened to one of the Tuskegee Airmen. These men hung in there and kept going and became brilliant flyers and excelled so much in the war effort, and I wanted to tell that story in the music, too. I wanted to say that there was the military, and there were the emotions: the leaving home, the losing buddies, the conflicts, the fears . . . I even delved into atonal music. In the scenes where they counted their first dogfights, the music becomes very atonal. And I used a lot of polytonal chords in the brass to talk about their conflicts. In the end, they persevered and accomplished a remarkable achievement given the odds that they faced. That story is in the film, but it is also in the score.

Talk about what you mean in terms of polytonal and atonal.

Polytonality is simply juxtaposing two keys against each other. It's a fabulous thing, especially with brass and with strings. You can really jar the listener, because now you're forcing them to listen to completely different keys played simultaneously.

Atonality is a serial technique where, instead of, let's say, writing a C major scale, you create a row of twelve different tones, so there is no tonal center whatsoever, there's no key. What I find it sometimes does in a film score is create a very unsettling feeling. I was trying to recreate the feeling that these guys would feel in their stomachs as they were realizing they were in their first dogfight. I wanted that sense of "Oh, my gosh, what we've known before doesn't exist anymore!"—that feeling of fear mixed with excitement. The director had made a suggestion to me about finding some device to create a change there, and that's what I came up with. I thought it worked great because it just kind of robs you of all reality at the moment.

Old Gringo **is a passionate, epic score that is rich with Mexican melodies beautifully intertwined with Americana color. How much of an impact did this score hold for you, giving you a chance to go back to your roots?**

It was tremendous. I loved working on that score because I did go back to my roots, growing up with a lot of Latin American music around me and a lot of classical Spanish music as well.

I had an interesting time with that film because there were three main characters. I had a theme for each character. You especially get a taste of it in the opening sequence when the three themes are intertwined.

I love doing Westerns. I love that big, sort of panoramic, epic kind of feeling. It's always ideal for a composer because you really get to stretch out, so to speak. With *Old Gringo* I wanted a symphonic Mexican feeling.

Mists of Avalon **is a powerful and profound score that's full of energy and emotion. How challenging was it to produce so much music for one story? Did it require a lot of research?**

Yes, that was quite an epic. The CD contains about seventy minutes of music, but I actually composed two and a half hours for that movie. When putting the CD together, I decided not to put in the battle cues, because we wanted to make it more of a listeners' CD that was focused on moods and the emotional story and the story of the women. I wrote a ton of epic battle music that is very effective and very powerful in the movie.

We skirted around the Celtic issue a little bit. I said, "I don't want to do a Celtic score, I want other things in it." So we reached out a bit; and one of the unique things we used was an Indian stringed instrument called an esraj, which has a beautiful, haunting, otherworldly sound. I thought about and worked on translating some of that sound into orchestral textures and using percussion and voices and the solo voice throughout the score. I thought it worked really well. It just created a great mood throughout the entire film.

I loved working on that score. From the moment when I devised that opening motif, the thing just sailed for me. It's a ton of music, and I orchestrated every single note of it. I never stopped working. I worked seven days a week for, I think, twelve weeks straight, nonstop, until I literally got to the very last note.

On a large production such as this, how do you begin, and what is your process throughout?

The first thing you do is you watch the film two or three times. Then, what I like to do is put the film on and let it run as I start trying things out on my keyboards. It's a mental process: I think about the film. I think about the imagery from it. What's a good sound for this? What's going to work for that? Little by little, I start to find a kind of motif. *Mists of Avalon* started with that little harp motif that starts my prologue. That was the first thing that I saw when I thought about her as she was on the water. That motif sort of came out of that idea of gliding across the water. It was the germ that started the whole thing, and I just built from there.

Once I have an opening idea and once I know where the beginning of a thing is, I find that I can just open the doors and the score kind of builds from there. That's where having the classical background helps, because you know how to take something and develop it and build on it and extend it and vary it. And, I'm telling you, a miniseries where you've got to go for two and a half hours is like writing an opera.

Into Thin Air is a powerhouse score that is regrettably overlooked. Nonetheless, it stirs many emotions in me, from anxiety to fear to solitude. Tell me about your experience with this score and describe your use of sounds—from bells to the rhythmic pulsing brass and percussion—in it.

I wanted that score to be harsher, more edgy, more jagged, you know? It has a lot of percussive elements. I used the Tibetan gongs a lot to create that kind of strange ambience in places. I definitely played around with that in terms of the rocky landscapes and snow and the sense of being lost and not knowing where the horizon is. I wanted the score to kind of jar you a little bit with the sense of, "What are these guys doing to themselves?" They are throwing themselves into this environment that is completely hostile to them, and they are trying to master it. They have all these complex sets of rules they're supposed to follow, but they wind up ignoring them, and nature—in the end—gets them. I wanted the score to have unpredictability. I used a lot of rhythmic and percussive tools to create that effect.

Many of your scores have that Americana feel from Buffalo Girls to Call of the Wild, and they seem to flow from your pen effortlessly. Are you drawn to these stories?

I'm drawn to those stories. My East of Eden miniseries is one of my most epic Americana pieces. I love that score. It's a style that I find myself very much at home in, probably because I love American folk songs.

I also love a lot of early American hymns. Many have been overlooked, but they have some great melodies. Every now and then, I've quoted one in a score. It's a style that I like a lot and I am very drawn to. I never tire of writing in that style. To me it's fresh every time.

What score of yours do you hold nearest to your heart?

It's like asking a parent, "Which child do you like best?" The score you're working on at the moment is the one you love the most because that's the one you're on fire with. When you finish a score, you go on to the next one, which sets you on fire because that's the new score that you're doing at the moment. And when you look back, you realize, "Oh gosh, I've done some wonderful scores," and then you say, "Okay, some may have come out better than others." Sometimes, the circumstance for this might not be of your own making: it may be the film or it may be the situation that you're in or it may be the fact that you were given too many directions in the wrong direction.

Overall, I look at the work that I've done and I feel very good about it. But I feel like a student. I always feel like there's so much I don't know and so much I need to learn. I find something often happens that is very humbling: You write a cue for a movie that you're working on right now, and you say, "Oh boy, this cue is great! This really works, this is fantastic!" Then you take a break. You go out and you get into your car and run an errand. You turn on the radio and on your favorite classical station you hear one of the great masters. Suddenly you hear a piece by Richard Strauss and you say, "Okay, that's how you're supposed to write." So, you're always kind of being brought back down to earth. That's good. I think that's healthy. So I always feel, "Oh gosh, I can do this better. There's got to be a better way." But sometimes you just run out of time. We live with deadlines, and there's a point where you just got to deliver.

Well, I understand your humble point of view, but you are a master at what you do.

I appreciate that. I try.

Are there film composers who inspire you?

Oh, yes, the classical film composers, of course. I'm a big fan of all the great masters, especially Eric Korngold, Franz Waxman, Max Steiner . . . I love all the great composers, Victor Young. They all did, I think, fabulous scores. One of my all-time favorite scores is *The*

Best Years of Our Lives [score by Hugo Friedhofer]. First of all, it's an incredible film, but the way the score works in the film, to me, is unbelievable. It is so magnificently done. In the more contemporary sense, I admire Jerry Goldsmith tremendously. I think he is one of the top film composers of our era because the span of his work is simply amazing. When you consider *A Patch of Blue* and *Chinatown* on one end of the spectrum, and then you go to the other end of the spectrum, to scores like *Patton* or *Planet of the Apes*, you say, "My gosh, look at the work this man has done!" I think he is one of the great icons of film composing.

I admire many different types of scores. I admire the scores that Georges Delerue did for some of the early Truffaut films. I love those scores. They were like chamber scores—sometimes they were scored for like eight instruments or ten instruments. They were wonderful scores, very moody with great ambience. In more contemporary films, I admire some scores by Thomas Newman. I think he's a wonderful composer.

Mark Isham

Mark Isham's music speaks a language all its own. It fuses jazz, classical, and New Age elements with a distinctive use of electronic instruments, resulting in a very personal style. The musical landscapes that his scores depict are impressionistic and sometimes pastoral in their cool romanticism.

Maintaining relationships with directors and producers that extend from one film to the next is an important part of succeeding as a film composer. Isham has had several multi-film collaborations, most notably with Robert Redford and Irwin Winkler. For Redford, he composed the lovely music for _A River Runs Through It_ (1992) and the jazzy score for _Quiz Show_ (1994). For Winkler, he composed techno-influenced music for _The Net_ (1995) and a sentimental score for _Life as a House_ (2001).

The dark, suspenseful side of Isham's music is found in his score for the thriller _Kiss the Girls_ (1997). Recently, once again showing the versatility of his compositional voice, he wrote a lighthearted score for the animated adventure _Racing Stripes_ (2005) and an intense, atmospheric score that profoundly impacts the film _Crash_ (2005).

Jazz and film-music genres often overlap, as in the film scores of Dave Grusin and Terence Blanchard, just to name two. How did you make the transition from a jazz musician to film composer?

Basically, an opportunity presented itself to me. I'd been interested in music far beyond the traditional jazz genre from the very beginning and had been experimenting a lot with electronic music and ambient music. I have a reasonably thorough classical-music background also.

I was involved in a record project with a friend who plays a lot of traditional Chinese instruments—flutes and percussion. We'd written a series of pieces for electronic synthesizers and his instruments, and we wanted to make a New Music record for ECM. We didn't get the opportunity with ECM, but we distributed the music around to various friends after we'd done it, and it fell into the hands of a film director who was very excited by it and approached me based on that music to score my first film, *Never Cry Wolf*. So my film experience didn't really start with the jazz genre. It started off with more of an alternative New Music genre if you will.

It wasn't really until my film with Alan Rudolph [*Trouble in Mind*] that the jazz influence really started to have a place in a film that I was working on. The main thing was that I was not a jazz musician to begin with—I had already spent a lot of time in quite a number of different genres and was very interested in the idea of programmatic music and ambient music. That's probably one of the reasons that film composing came quite readily to me without having been trained in it. So it wasn't a stretch for me to take those ideas and apply them to film. And the first few films I did were very much along those lines.

So you didn't make a conscious career choice to work in film?

No, not at all. It never really occurred to me to try such a thing until somebody approached me and suggested I try it. I said okay, and it took me about four and a half months to score that first film. It was a trial by fire, but I was put together with some very good music editors and orchestrators, producers, and engineers, and they really got me through the whole process. We came out with a very good score.

Then I went about another year before I did any other film music. I
went to being sort of a starving jazz musician and playing with Van
Morrison. Then I came to my senses, as it were, and said to myself,
"Film music was fun, and it paid well. They paid me to produce a
large body of work. Let's look back into that." Then I got myself an
agent and the rest is history.

**You have a signature sound. No matter whether you're scoring a
thriller or a love story, you seem to always have that unique sound.
How did you come about developing your sound? Who and what
were your influences?**

I think my sound had already been developing because I was working in a lot of different genres—writing different types of music and
experimenting with different types of music—and the ideas that I
was working with sort of applied themselves very well to film music.

The basic influences from the jazz world were, of course, Miles
Davis and Weather Report. I think that their influences extend
beyond just their use in the jazz genre. By that I mean, for instance,
Weather Report and Miles, both were great masters of contrast in
music. In other words, they experimented by taking elements from
different genres and laying them on top of each other to create something new. And that's a concept that can be applied across the board,
not just in the jazz world that they stayed in. That general concept
can be used no matter what you're doing. I think it became really
apparent to me when I started to study Brian Eno and figure out a
lot of what his philosophy was. He'd read a lot of John Cage, and
John Cage I think wrote about music better than he composed it. He
had some fascinating ideas, and a lot of this is the concept of music
as a more sculptural art form. In other words, he'd take blocks of
music and juxtapose them and build things out of them, as opposed
to thinking of the compositional process in the traditional Western
way of melody and harmony and counterpoint, things like that.

Brian Eno and David Bowie and David Byrne also were huge
influences on me all through the seventies. And, of course, I had my
classical-music roots: I was a great admirer of some of the late
romantics—in the interesting evolution of harmony—Gustav Mahler
and Samuel Barber. And I was into some of the moderns, [Toru]
Takemitsu and [Krzysztof] Penderecki, just for color and texture.
These were fascinating things to know about.

So you don't really rely on the influence of other film composers?

Well, somewhat over the years I have. I mean, it didn't start that way. In the early days, I was a big fan of Henry Mancini because he sort of crossed worlds. You could go to a big commercial film, like *The Pink Panther*, and all of a sudden there was this great jazz music, and it was the perfect thing for that movie. That had a profound influence on me. That was "Wow!"—the sort of thing that would excite me. Here is somebody who isn't just working with the normal genres. He was willing to sort of stretch things and move things around and try things. That was always interesting to me.

I have certain composers now whom I really admire, obviously. I think Tom Newman has shown a tremendous talent and ability in his career. I think the world of him. I'm a big fan of Elliot Goldenthal. I think he is the real deal. And you can't touch someone like John Williams. I mean, he is perhaps the greatest of all time. It gets very subjective at this point, arguing who John Williams is and his tremendous legacy to the genre.

In terms of direct influences on me, it tends to be certain scores more than certain composers. I will say, "The way the composer handled that sort of situation, I need to remember that. There is an idea that is fruitful. There is an idea that can really be explored." Even though I didn't care much for the movie, I thought Horner's score to *A Beautiful Mind* was wonderful, and it was a unique score for him. I like seeing that, too: You start to think of somebody in a certain way and then, all of a sudden, it's, "Wow!" Listen to that." That's really a special moment for him and a special piece of music. John Williams's *Catch Me If You Can*: I thought, "God, what a great thing for John to have done!" I mean, he found a vocabulary that you wouldn't necessarily have thought was going to come from him, and yet he has proved to be a master of it and did just a fantastic job.

You seem to write from the heart—almost in an improvisational style. How much research do you put into your film music, and how much of it do you find yourself developing on gut feelings?

I tend to do a certain amount of research, but I've never been one for exactness . . . I don't want that to come across in the wrong way. What I really mean is that I tend to be an impressionist when I do my research. I research into an area or genre or sound enough to get what makes it tick, and then apply that to what I do, so that the right colors and flavors come through. I manage to infuse what I want to do with those colors and with those flavors. And I can't help but think that that comes from Weather Report and Miles, because that's exactly what they would do. I mean, Miles never, in his later years, played real hip-hop, but there was a definite influence. You would listen and you would say, "Well, I'm not quite sure what he means." But on the other hand you get that flavor, which he took so much further to make it his own. I think that is part of the jazz experience that I love. I love having to learn about a new way of looking at music, a new point of view in the language of music, and then being able to make it my own so that I feel comfortable creating with it as a new dialect, so to speak.

Improvising, basically?

Yeah, in my jazz experience, improvising is the same basic concept as composition, except you have to get it really good the first time. So, the better improviser you are, the better composer you can be, I think, or at least the faster, more-efficient composer you can be. I've never been the type of composer who agonizes over the exact sixty-fourth note on this leading tone. I have much more of the latter-half-of-the-twentieth-century point of view: The tools of writing are tape machines and computers. You get something going and it has a vibe and it has a groove and it has a . . . It's communicating. The emotion is there, and that's what's really important. Although I understand the rigors of the notes on the page and the score and getting it all sort of lined up for the rules of harmony—and I can use that as a tool—I've never elected to use that as my real creative jumping-off point.

How do you approach a new film? What are your steps to creating a score?

To me, it starts with the sonic vocabulary, to use the metaphor of the score. One of the beauties and challenges of modern composition is that it's limitless now. If you were writing a hundred years ago, you had a finite vocabulary of sound you could choose from. Well, with the advent of electronics and recorded music and everything else in the last hundred years, obviously that's been changing, and we reach a point now in this new century where it's totally infinite.

The first step for me is to pare this down, because if I leave it wide open for myself, as I go, it's liable to just become chaotic. The sounds can so much dictate the type of composition that's going to evolve. The first sort of experimental phase to me is pinning down the sound of the movie. What sonic colors match the story, match the images, match the tempo, the cutting, match the characters, and fundamentally match the emotions of the film? Not to say this won't evolve, or that I'll not throw it out halfway through and start all over.

This is a very positive first step for me that can involve just sitting down for a week and programming or sitting down with five sound designers and saying, "Let's build a new vocabulary here," or sitting down with my orchestrators, and saying, "All right, let's not use a traditional orchestra, let's just write for ten violas and three basses." I just try to get an idea of what vocabulary is going to be needed. And that, for me, just will start the flow. It just always does. It always has. I've never found that to be an ineffective way of starting.

So when you look at a movie, do you look at the story and try to fill in the characters' themes? How do you go about that sort of thing?

I've found over the years that sometimes characters can have themes, but I've not really found them that helpful to me when telling the story. I find that what the story is telling you is more important to identify thematically. Let's say you've got a story of a man and a woman, Sam and Grace, coming together and loving each other, then breaking apart, then coming back together again, and you have Sam's theme and Grace's theme, and when he's on the screen you play him and when she's on the screen you play her, and when they're together, you mix them both together. That's very cute, but it doesn't necessarily help you at all emotionally. What I would probably find more helpful is a theme for loneliness and a theme for the satisfaction of a marriage or a relationship and a theme that represents the fear of commitment or whatever it is that's going to happen in your story.

One of those themes is going to supply the true emotions and the true goals and purposes of the story rather than just telling you she's off-camera, but he may be thinking about her, or that she is about to come to the door. You know what I mean? The pictures are already telling you that information, so the themes can be more about the bigger things-like honor or betrayal or love or trust-the various sorts of things that great storytelling wants to tell us about.

Ken Kugler has been your main orchestrator throughout your career. How important is it to develop such a long-term relationship? How often do you find yourself leaving him, since he knows your style and how you approach things, to fill in the color and texture?

The relationship's quite important. Ken and I have known each other for a very long time, and we've gotten to a point where we don't have to talk that much. Although I think it's very important to always keep the guys as close in and knowing where everything is as much as possible.

We just finished a film that is quite interesting. While I was writing away, all of sudden I had this cool idea of what I wanted to do. I think other people have tried it, but until I actually started down the path, I didn't know that anybody had tried it. I thought I was the first. Anyway, I called up Ken quite early on and asked him what he thought of the idea. He said, "It's a very cool idea. Let me start to do some research."

So he researched players and the way these certain instruments could be recorded and whether we should do this with overdubs or do it live, all the big questions. He probably spent more time researching this concept than he did at the end of the day on the orchestrating. But it was time well spent, and that's where letting him really get involved in the process is really good.

The score that really launched your film career is *A River Runs Through It*. It is a sweet score and one that well deserves its praise. What was the experience like working with Robert Redford? How much input did he have in your work?

Well, Robert is a really fastidious director. He's a perfectionist and an incredibly bright guy who knows how to communicate well about what he wants. He already had a score on that picture that he decided wasn't working. He knew a fair amount of what the movie needed and what didn't work in it. Also, there was this area where it hadn't been done quite right yet. He was very involved. He would come over to the house and bring some CDs and things. He worked very closely with me on demos. At one point, he had to be on the East Coast, so I would send demos to him via messenger, and he would call me while listening to the demos in his car. He really wanted to get it right and I think it all paid off. The score worked really well and people responded really well to it.

Your score for *Quiz Show*, another Redford film, is certainly one of my favorites.

Yeah, I love that score, too. Unfortunately, I don't know if the movie was marketed correctly. It didn't get the audience I think it deserved. I think it's another wonderful movie. Bob makes terrific movies.

Your relationship with Robert Redford's films abruptly halted. Your work on his films was superb, and I can't imagine him feeling any differently. Knowing your capabilities and his sensibilities, were you bothered when he sought other composers?

Yeah, there is a certain level of disappointment because I felt we were doing really good work, and I've never had the opportunity to discuss that with him. He told me that *Quiz Show* was the most enjoyable, productive scoring experience he'd ever had. I was very proud of that. But the truth of the matter is that I've been in the business a long time, and I've worked with a lot of different people who, at some point, just want to try something different. They hear something from somebody, and they say, "You know, that really strikes me. I would love to work with someone who could create something like that." I think nine times out of ten that happens. I've had directors tell me, "Look, working with you was fantastic. I loved it. But I want to try this over here because I just think I hear some-thing there that I know is going to connect." That's the decision that they make, and it's an absolutely totally valid decision, obviously.

Blade **was a movie that I would not expect to see you attached to, yet you pulled it off seemingly effortlessly. Is there a dark side of you that needs to come out every once in a while?**

Well, to me, a movie like *Blade* really isn't that dark because it has that comic-book element about it. It's sort of three feet above the real darkness. It's sort of tongue-in-cheek dark. You can be bombastic and big and gothic. I actually enjoy projects like that. I think they're a lot of fun. But there are certain movies that are—to my mind—really dark, and I'm not necessarily sure I would get involved in them.

Well, *The Hitcher* **was a pretty dark film.**

Yeah, but again, I think different things push different buttons in different people. That was an early film for me. It's about confronting evil. There is something to be said for that. It's not something that's easy to do in life. Whether that movie is good storytelling is a subjective opinion. Robert [Harmon, *The Hitcher*'s director] is just an old friend of mine. We've always hit it off. I enjoy working with him and I've done a lot of his films.

Jeff Rona has worked with you on a few occasions, probably the most well-known being *Chicago Hope,* **for which you composed a great theme and Jeff ran with the score. Why does a composer such as you, or James Newton Howard with** *ER,* **come onto the scene and then another composer takes over the show?**

It's just a question of what you want to do in your life. Television was something that I wasn't very interested in doing because it didn't seem like an opportunity to write music in a way that would be satisfying.

I had an album coming out and I wanted to take some time off to be able to do some touring, when it suddenly occurred to me that if I had a theme that was in circulation on TV, there would be a certain amount of consistent income from that without having to be home writing all year long. Then, when David Kelley was the one behind the project my agent brought to me, and I looked at who Kelley was and what he was doing, I said, "Well, let's take a look at this." That was basically how I entered the world of television. It was mostly because of David Kelley. I thought he was a tremendous talent and the show was going to be something interesting.

How did Jeff Rona come into the picture?

I've known Jeff for many years. He's a talented fellow. I wanted someone I trusted to take over, and he was a good choice.

Irwin Winkler is a director you have worked with on a few notable occasions. How does this sort of experience differ from working for the first time with a filmmaker?

Yeah, I have a couple of guys: Irwin, of course Alan Rudolph. I've done over ten pictures, I think, with Alan. I've done a couple with Irwin.

It just gets easier. You know them and you know where their tastes are going to be, and I think you're a little more relaxed in saying what you think in a quick, efficient manner. You know how the communication goes between you. A friendship has started and it's fun.

What's interesting is that of the three movies I've done with Irwin, the last, *Life as a House*, is probably the best score and maybe Irwin's best movie, too. You know, when you start to get everything rolling like that, when the relationship is good and the material is good and the movie is going well, the results get better and better. Those are the experiences you are looking for.

What about a new director?

I've worked with a lot of new directors. I just worked with a first-time director, Wayne Kramer, who I think is going to be one of the all-time greats. We've just done a movie called *The Cooler*. Wayne's a writer/director and he's the real deal. He's unbelievably talented. His first film got big raves at Sundance. Lionsgate is putting it out in November, close to Academy consideration time because it's really good. What's especially great about Wayne is that he's a huge music fan in general. He knows more about film music than I do. It's just a pleasure to work with someone who has such a love for the music and such respect for what the music offers, and then is so knowledgeable. I mean, his temp scores are just tremendous because he knows and loves that process of just finding the right music.

You seem to have a more positive view toward temp tracks than most of your colleagues.

Well, they're great tools. The trick is not to abuse the tool. I guess the complaints you hear from composers are that the director loved the temp score so much that they wouldn't take anything else but it. That's happened to me, and most of the time I've been able to handle that. What I usually do is get the director to critique it. They say they love it, and I say, "Great, I'm glad you love it. Now that's a flute in the beginning. Do love the flute? Would a clarinet be better?" The next thing you know, "Well, it would be much better with a clarinet, and I really wish it would go down here when it goes up here." You've got a whole slew of things that you can do to make it better and different. But having said that, I've also gotten caught in that trap myself and not necessarily been able to get out of it elegantly.

I think it is a skill to know what music does and be able to duplicate it in a different way. Of course, that is one of the big things a film composer has to do that most other musicians never have to think about. There is somewhat of an objective result from a piece of music used in a certain way, and that same objective result needs to occur with a different piece of music. To a certain degree, it's the responsibility of a director, too, to be willing to look at something newly and know whether the overall same objective result is being achieved, even with a different piece of music.

What confuses me about the temp track is that it's not used as a language so that directors can simply convey their thoughts.

Well, directors use them differently. A lot of it has to do with the directorial style in post-production. I know some directors who put more time into the temp score than they do into the score. It's the sort of thing they can control. They can sit down with the music editor and say, "Move that two beats over" or "Put a swell there . . ." The next thing you know, they have it exactly like they want it. That process with the composer is more difficult for them, but it shouldn't be. If that's the level of detail they want in a score, then they owe it to themselves to allow the time for that level of detail in the final score. Just find a general vibe, then go to work with the composer to find more of the details.

I don't want to get stuck on this subject, but I feel that if you get a composer in on the project early and put that composer's own original music to the movie before it gets test-screened and so fourth, then you have complete originality and style from the composer who was hired to suit the film in the first place.

Well, I've just done that. I've just finished a film with Philip Kaufman that I worked on for close to eight months. At the last screening, I think eighty percent of the music was mine. And everyone kept saying, "That's great! Whose music is that?" They were told, "That's the score." And everyone said, "Even better!"

Was that easier for you?

I don't know in the end. It was certainly the way that Philip wanted to do it, and it was fun doing it with him in that regard. It was a lot of work. I've probably achieved equally good work coming in right toward the end, replacing a temp score. I don't know which is more effective. It's just another way of working.

What is your prized project thus far?

There's a wide variety of different things that sticks out to me. I think of *A River Runs Through It* because I did the whole thing in less than a month and yet it turned out to be a strong piece of work and got recognized. I also have fond memories of strange scores, like the score to *Cool World*, which was like a huge orchestra and a big jazz band and drum loops. It was sort of a monstrous production. It was the first time I ever tried anything of that scale. And to pull it off and have it all work was pretty exciting. I also think of the exact opposite, a movie with no money and just a concept for the score, *Romeo Is Bleeding*, for which basically they had nothing, but they temped it all with *Basic Instinct*. I said, "You've got to be kidding. That's like 1.3 million dollars you're listening to. But I have an idea. Let me try some things." I think it was one of the most creative and interesting scores I've ever done.

Jan A. P. Kaczmarek

In 2004, Jan Kaczmarek composed Oscar-winning music for the film *Finding Neverland*. His score, which combined full orchestra with voices and nearly mystical moments of solo piano, beautifully portrayed the film's mix of fantasy and reality.

Prior to *Finding Neverland*, Polish-born Kaczmarek's intense, passionate music had graced such powerful yet lesser-known (in the U.S.) films as the ethereal *The Third Miracle* (1999) and the Polish-made epic *Quo Vadis?* (2001). Not until 2002, when he scored director Adrian Lyne's *Unfaithful*, did Kaczmarek receive widespread recognition in the United States. In his music for *Unfaithful*, the piano is the featured instrument, weaving the emotional strands of pain and sorrow and deceit throughthis story of love, lust, and betrayal.

What kind of exposure to music did you have growing up?

As a child I studied piano in a small local school. My mother was very serious about this and made sure I started at an early age and that I continued. Music as taught in Eastern Europe was based on extreme discipline. It was very hard labor with very few rewards. I somehow became completely discouraged. I felt that music would never be my profession. It took me two years to recover. In high school, I started writing music and I came back to music on my own terms, studying privately and also just writing from a newly discovered passion.

How did your interest develop into film music?

First, I was completely fascinated by theater. In Poland, theater is very strong. It was as strong as the movies at that time, and so was music. In Polish theater there was less dialogue and more visual information than in American theater. The scores became a driving force. I look at it as more of a movie of some kind with very little dialogue but with extremely powerful vision in terms of design and movement. It wasn't until I came to America that I understood film better and I was able to form an idea of my passion toward it.

So how did you get into the Hollywood scene?

When I came to the United States in 1989, I started with theater. It was a natural place for me to look. But then I discovered there is a limited amount of satisfaction a composer can get in a dramatic theater, so I started looking into film. It was very difficult coming from Europe without major works in film. It is very difficult here to work on a meaningful picture because people ask if I am someone who comes from a different culture. So, basically, a level of risk is perceived. So I slowly built my reputation through small projects. A decisive moment happened in 1995 when I met Agnieszka Holland while she was doing the film *Total Eclipse*. We met a bit earlier when she was editing *Secret Garden*. I presented a demo because I really wanted to write music for *Total Eclipse*. She liked my approach very much and she wanted to do it.

Where do you get your musical inspiration?

Life. A composer almost needs to be a psychologist, which means I very carefully listen to and observe people, learning from their emotions and ways of thinking.

When you enter the film, the music is a very sophisticated tool that defines emotion and meaning for the picture, and if you have a profound knowledge of psychology and emotion and the culture, and what things mean, you can influence the picture in a very strong way, just by applying this knowledge. Sometimes, if you are a sensitive man, intuition helps. But intuition is not enough. If you are not deeply into people and people's emotions and motivations, sooner or later, if you do a dramatic film in which you deal with these things, then you are in trouble, because you don't understand what actually happens below the surface. On the surface, all is clear and able to be understood, but so much happens that is not on the surface, and music is supposed to support those emotions. That's what creates a good movie. When you see something happen between, let's say, two actors on the surface and the music plays about something else, which is hidden—hidden thoughts or hidden emotions—that music creates a much deeper and much more interesting film.

Which current composers inspire you?

You may not hear it in my music much, but Philip Glass is one of very few people who has heavily influenced me, but not directly, because I'm not a minimalist composer in the sense of style. But there is something in his way of thinking.

How do you approach writing a score?

Sometimes it starts when I get the script. Sometimes I am hired before the photography starts, and then I read the script and I have first ideas and first responses to the picture So the script needs to be inspiring enough that I feel that I can contribute something of value, too.

Sometimes I go to the set, and this is also part of the inspiration. It's important. It's on a human level. It's important because you meet people. You feel connected to this group of people. But always the most important part comes when I see the first cut. I watch it and I have an emotional reaction. This is the first thing. I need to have an emotional connection to the picture. I don't employ my intellect yet. I need to feel the essence of the picture. And this is very spontaneous: Sometimes I sit at the piano or my keyboard, and then, under the influence of the first emotion, I write a theme or two.

Then comes the next stage, when usually the director, the music editor, and myself choose the places where the music will be in the picture. Sometimes this works out before because sometimes when

I am coming to the picture late, they already have a temp track. Nevertheless, I then build a structure. I look at the film thematically, deciding where to place themes for different people or different aspects of the picture. You have two basic modes of thinking about scoring a movie: The first is thematic, and the second is when you depart from one point and you go with the picture, which can be very exciting.

You have such a gorgeous style of writing for piano. The piano often warms up your scores with life and passion. Is this a favorite instrument to write for?

I'm basically in a phase. Our lives are connected in cycles. And in my cycle, the piano is very important. Recently, I used it very much. At first, I was a bit afraid of using the piano because there is so much piano in the history of music that it always creates a danger of repeating things. I hope I have found a different way to think about the piano. I don't know how long I will have this belief that I can bring interesting things from the piano. But if there's a picture of a gentle kind or things happen between two people that require a gentle touch, then the piano seems to be very appropriate. In Poland, I did *Quo Vadis?*, which is a huge Roman Empire epic. There's no place for piano there. It required a big epic score with some ethnic voices in it, so the piano would've been very inappropriate.

What other instruments do you favor?

In the big tradition of Eastern Europe, I love strings. If properly used, strings bring certain emotions that you cannot generate with anything else. They have passion and mystery and . . . I am in love with different things. Sometimes oboe seems to be a very bright moment and brings this kind of light. I'm interested in ethnic instruments very much, so if there's an opportunity to use them, I use them.

You have several top-notch scores, but I want to highlight a couple that stand out for me. First, tell me about your creative ethnic approach to *The Third Miracle*, which is a little different from your other scores.

Well, the subject was very different. It was about a priest who was losing his faith. It was a journey to prove or disprove the miracle that
happened in the life of the woman who was supposed to become a
saint. A very spiritual topic. It was very inspiring. You don't want to
go into church music because it would not show the truth here. The
truth was that he was at the edge, fighting with the doubt in himself.
The music should be the spiritual aspect of this from a different perspective. So I wrote my own Ave Maria, which is very ethnic and
which worked very well, carrying most of the emotions without being
too obvious. I use a number of rare instruments, rare for film music.

Do you still record in Poland?

Yes, I record in three places: here in Los Angeles, in London, and in
Poland. Where I record depends on the project. Each place has different qualities and different ways in which people work.

I enjoy tremendously going to Warsaw because it is always an
occasion to connect with my friends in my native country. I admire
the quality of musicianship there. I'm very surprised that so few people record in Warsaw. Unfortunately, nobody has invested in or pro-
moted the studios and the orchestras in Warsaw. I see Prague in the
Czech Republic being such a popular place. In Warsaw, we have two
orchestras. But there's no real organization that promotes it and
makes it comfortable for strangers who go there. When I go there,
obviously, I know the place, the people, and I have my own organization, which is very efficient. I can have excellent quality—not just
excellent musicianship but also excellent recording. I wish that
there were somebody who could really put together this thing and
create a stable environment for people from here or people from
Europe to go and record in Warsaw. The food is great in Warsaw. It
changed after Socialism collapsed and very soon people opened
incredible restaurants. Recently, Adrian Lyne came with me to
Poland for the opening of *Unfaithful*, and he was absolutely seduced
by the food and the people and what happens there.

**How are you received in Poland? Do they follow your work? Are
they able to follow it?**

It's called Art Society of Film People that follows things. They are interested and really appreciate my work here. I have a strong following there. But it's not easy to buy my albums. You can buy them in every Western European country with no effort, but find them in Poland only recently, except *Quo Vadis?*, which was a big hit there. All my American works are very difficult to get. The most difficult is *Third Miracle*, about which I heard unpleasant news a week ago from my agent. The record company decided not to print it anymore, which bothers me. I don't know why people do this, because it is such a minimum effort to print anything. I like this music so much, and it should be in distribution because I know people years from now will want to buy these things. This is music that should not get old easily, I hope.

Although you use similar techniques in *Total Eclipse* and *Lost Souls*, you add some powerful and haunting synth textures in *Lost Souls*. Is this a comfortable change for you?

Oh yes, very much. Again, this is my response to a different subject, a different kind of picture. *Lost Souls* is a film about dark forces at work. We deal with the idea of Satan and very dark emotions. Obviously, it is different from *Total Eclipse*.

I like a combination of live orchestra and some electronic sounds because it creates a new quality. This is refreshing to me to jump into something different like this because I used a lot of electronics before I immigrated here. I was one of the pioneers in Poland of using this sort of sound. I feel very confident in the world of electronics. But there's no need to use it when the picture doesn't call for it. *Lost Souls* certainly called for it. By using electronics, you escape from this spirit of the historical score for a thriller or a horror movie. All big scores of the fifties have a certain character. Today we score horror films or thrillers in much more subtle ways. If you are going for a strong gesture, then you use electronics, which kind of send it into a different place. It has a fresh value. Through electronics, you can revise the sound of the orchestra. You can make it less defined, not so obvious.

Unfaithful really gets inside the soul. You bring the story to life with such beautiful melodies. What made you use the piano as the focal instrument in this score?

I compose in three places: at my piano, at my computer setup, with the keyboard where I have all possible sampled sounds and a simulated orchestra, and also I just go outside with no instrument and I walk and disconnect myself.

Quite often I start my work with the piano. When I write something or play something, it's very natural for me to record emotions that I remember and, quite often, the first emotions are the most important. You work, you work, you work, and then you come back to your first original discovery, which is quite often at the piano

When I sit at the piano for too long I lose the emotions. Then I go to my synthesizers. I sit at the synthesizers and use the samples, which are very advanced and almost sound like the real thing. But that has limitations because you cannot escape certain sounds that you already have. Then I go to the piano, which is very refreshing. Then I go outside—and the best ideas always happen when I am disconnected from everything, and I don't have a medium except my imagination. But then I need to come back.

I don't know if you're familiar with *Fatal Attraction,* but Adrian Lyne went along the same path in his work with Maurice Jarre— using the piano as a heavy part of the movie. Did he have any say in that with you?

He never defined anything. He was very active, very involved in the process, which was one of the most exciting and creative that I've been involved with, but he never set the conditions. He never said, "Jan, I want this to be a piano score" or "Listen to this." He never compared the music with Jarre's or Morricone's. He went with the bigger names in the profession in these earlier films, so I was very honored to be invited to score *Unfaithful*.

Very few composers use a melodic approach to their music anymore. I feel yours is a breath of fresh air.

Thank you so much. I am glad you pointed that out, because I hope it is being noticed. It is my deep belief that melody is neglected, and melody has such a great power. But also it's a very risky business. When I write a melody, I am always asking myself, "When will I be accused of plagiarism?" You know, no matter how deeply you believe and how original you are in your own mind, you are always at risk for writing a melody that happened somewhere else on the planet without your knowing about it. No matter how pure you are in your intentions and your emotions, there's always that mathematical risk.

I ask myself why American composers or contemporary composers don't write melodies. I think this may be a part of it. But this is only part of it, because the second part of it you have to remember is that there was an entire music education of the sixties, seventies, and eighties was based on the no-melody approach—at least in contemporary music, melody was a big no. In the nineties, people rediscovered melodies. But you don't have too many people who can write melodies because, when you are limited in your mind, when you associate melody with something that is forbidden, it is very difficult to suddenly come back to it and to find the truth in it. I think there is tremendous truth in a good melody, and I look for it always. I give up on the melody only if it is really not possible. At certain scenes, you cannot go into melody because then it becomes too specific, and music tends to stand out too much. But, if I can use melody, I always go for it. I deeply believe in the tremendous spiritual power and emotional power of melody.

Are you happy with where film music has progressed today?

Yes. People complain, and I sometimes catch myself complaining, too, but let's be realistic: Never in the history of music have you had only masterpieces being written. Most of the music is good or decent, but very rarely do you have things that are outstanding—and film music is no different.

This is an interesting period for music. You know why? Because it opens up so much room for many things. Besides the synthesizers and electronics, you have a lot of ethnic instruments from around the globe, and this is great because it's very refreshing to use elements that would never meet otherwise. You can combine instruments from different places around the globe without effort. You never meet Iranian singers with a symphony orchestra. The instruments would never geographically meet with the symphony orchestra. The world is divided into cultural zones. The beauty of today's music is that it allows for this kind of collaboration, for this kind of creative encounter. I think this is the biggest trend of today's film music. Who needs to be praised for the introduction of a lot of ethnic styles is Peter Gabriel, who brought a tremendous amount of ethnic music to *The Last Temptation of Christ*. This was actually the beginning. He was the father of this ethnic way.

What about temp tracks?

The temp track is a tremendous obstacle to creativity. But it is a tool that helps communication, which is the positive aspect of it. But when filmmakers use the temp track, sometimes they are extremely afraid to do the music differently when it comes time for the original score. They push composers quite often to copy the temp track, which results in a lack of creativity. People are presented with the same temp tracks, and they respond in very similar ways. So it requires courage to take a different approach and to take risks to present a different approach from the temp track and be able to carry it through and convince others that it is better. This is one of the biggest challenges of contemporary writing.

You seem to produce one or two scores a year. Is this a choice that you have made or would you want more-frequent assignments?

Sometimes I do three or maybe four. But when you do three or four, they can work only if those movies are different. That is why I really pay so much attention to writing different kinds of scores. It's very important not to go in one direction and be perceived as a composer who writes only suspense or only period things. Because once you are in a category, it is very difficult to score anything else.

What can we anticipate from you in the future? Will you be continuing to write for films or are there other musical places you'll explore?

I want to explore a little bit more, but I really enjoy film music.

I am developing a place in Poland for the young artists to kind of help them in transition. I want to create an environment there in a very beautiful place, a big old park and a big nineteenth-century building. I will be bringing people from here, not just people linked to music, but also writers. Generally, the place is going to be devoted to music and film, including screenwriting and producing and directing seminars. I can have this experience of influencing young minds and helping both worlds to meet, because there is a tremendous amount of talent and passion in Eastern Europe, but there is a lack of understanding of how the business functions here, and also how you apply your talent.

Here, you understand the terms of compromise better. It is a great art to combine the integrity of your talent with compromise, which the industry brings upon you. So it requires a certain kind of training. You must train your mind to keep writing interesting stuff, not only as a composer, but as a writer or anybody involved in the filmmaking process. You need to understand that film is a medium that needs to communicate to people because it's such an expensive undertaking. And people who invest in films expect that their investments will be returned. For European artists, this is difficult to understand, and they neglect the part of being understood. Let's take an example of screen-writing: People here go through a number of drafts, sometimes too many, but there is this absolute consensus that you need to improve it until it becomes strong enough to become a picture. In Eastern Europe, people just write one draft and they believe it is fine. So this is my passion, and I want to spend more time in Europe now. It's also refreshing to keep traveling. Inspiration is the word. To be inspired we should be moving all the time mentally and physically as well. That is how it works.

Rolfe Kent

Rolfe Kent's clever character-driven score to director Alexander Payne's *About Schmidt* (2002) fits the film's eccentric characters to a "T," deeply, though unobtrusively, exploring their minds while breathing great liveliness into their bizarre personalities.

British-born Kent has maintained a successful ongoing relationship with director Payne, working also on Payne's films *Election* (1999) and the Golden Globe-nominated *Sideways* (2004), for which Kent provided a jazz-based score.

Although Rolfe is a relatively new addition to Hollywood, his star is in ascension, having already built an array of fine credits, including James Mangold's period dramedy, *Kate & Leopold* (2001), and the romantic comedy *40 Days and 40 Nights* (2002).

Tell me about the young Rolfe.

My music career probably started in my early teens. I didn't study music, but I was always playing on pianos at my high school. One of the music teachers encouraged me to put my music on paper. He got people to play it at school. So that's really where it began.

And now you are a film composer.

It led to film music because I loved film music. Perhaps it was the glamor of film, I don't know, but the idea of being involved in film is certainly a very attractive idea, especially because music—classical music—has very little significance for me because I didn't grow up in a musical family. We didn't hear music very much. So most types of music meant very little to me, whereas film music meant a lot to me because it had associations—images from films, stuff filling your head when you heard the music from those films. Films and musicals appealed to me very greatly as a child because they had these associations, because they meant something. They were about something. So, I was about eleven when I thought, "Okay, I really like writing music and playing music, and I really like what happens when you hear film music away from the film—it fills your mind with images. So that's what I want to do. I want to write film music."

Do any particular scores from that period stand out in your memory?

No. There's a mixture of stuff: *The Jungle Book*, *Mary Poppins*, James Bond, *Lawrence of Arabia* . . . All these movies had very memorable music elements and memorable film images as well.

Composers are often typecast from the beginning of their careers. This happened with you in romantic comedies. I would think that this is a tough gig because of the limited vocabulary, but you've managed to stay away from the clichés and have developed a technique that is unique. What are your feelings on this?

There are worse things than to be typecast.

Hollywood likes to make things more manageable by simply thinking that any creative individual does only one thing. It doesn't seem like a downside at first, because at first it's great to be getting the work. It's great to be invited to participate in that process. But the creative downside of being asked to do a similar type of job again is that it becomes harder and harder to work out satisfying ways to say the same kinds of things. In other words, you establish a musical vocabulary for comedies that is uniquely yours. But you tire of that vocabulary pretty easily because after you've done two or three films, then, "Oh, now what am I going to do?"

So, for me, there have been two challenges. One is to make sure that comedy becomes only *part* of what I do and not *all* of what I do. And the other is to find different ways of scoring these things. For example, I approached the score to *Legally Blonde* in a completely different way from what I had ever done before because I really needed to feel like I was making progress, that I was moving somewhere new, starting from a very different angle. I think that's an ongoing thing. Even if you are into typecasting, if you are into just doing one thing, it still seems vital to find new ways to do things and new musical vocabularies.

Are there genres that particularly interest you now or that you hope to break into soon?

You said that comedies don't provide a very broad canvas for music. The music is not likely to be noticed by the audience because it doesn't have very much room in which to work. I would very much like to be working on some films that have more room. *About Schmidt* actually has a lot of room for the music. There's an opportunity for the music to be heard and to do some serious work. So that was very satisfying. I would like to get more dramatic films, because the canvas is very exciting to me.

You've formed a strong composer-director relationship with Alexander Payne.

I have a number of relationships with directors. My relationship with Alexander Payne is the most high-profile.

An established composer-director relationship makes it much easier to work and to know the terms upon which you are involved together. The way I work with Alexander has a very unique character to it. Because I know the relationship is in existence, I can get involved much earlier than I might in some other project, where they're waiting to the last moment to decide who they're going to have score the film. I'm involved in scoring the film while the film is still being edited, so there's a lot of organic movement, both in the score and in the film, all the way up to the film's completion. It's a very creative environment to be in. Alexander is a very creative director and very open to ideas.

I hear in your work a strong reference to characters more than the scenes or overall atmosphere.

I don't know. I think every film is different. I've always varied my approach. I watch the film and talk to the director, and I "listen" to film. By "listen," I mean I live with it and I think about it and I experiment to see what direction is going to work. What does the film really need? The truth is, some films do not need music, and some films need a lot of music to help tell the story. So I try to work out what it is that the film is really asking for, what will help it really live on the screen. I don't know if I'm actually character-driven or simply personality-driven. I think that my contribution has a lot to do with putting personality into music. So it becomes very personal because it's very much about finding qualities and reactions in myself and figuring out how to contribute them to the film.

Your voice is often the orchestra without a lot of focus on modern technology.

I love acoustic sounds. I have a lot of time for synthetic sounds, but acoustic sounds seem to captivate my interest in ways that synthetic sounds can only occasionally achieve. I don't think there's ever a substitution that I care for. I don't really like the results from using synthetic sounds *instead* of real acoustic performances. But there are synthetic sounds that are very interesting and very useful because they're nothing like any real acoustic sound. They're very cool sounds that are just unique on their own. Drum loops I think are terrific.

I do demos and my demos are done synthetically, but I don't intend them to end up in the film. They are always replaced with a real live orchestra or band.

Among the things that make your music blossom with color is your versatile use of sounds and ethnic instrumentation. How do you come up with these ideas?

Again, it's my fascination with acoustic sounds and what certain sounds do. As a very small child, if someone had a piano, I would go and just bash on the piano. I was fascinated by its timbre, its sound qualities, what it does acoustically, what it does around your head. The same applies to all instruments that I come upon. They have unique qualities that do certain things—they emote in certain ways.

I think it's very easy to be very boring with sounds. But it's also not very difficult to find sounds that have great depth and quality and interest. I don't need to use particular ethnic sounds or sounds from any particular culture, but I'm fascinated by the qualities that they contribute. And that's what draws me to certain things. Certainly Russian instrumentation, or Greek or Chinese, have certain qualities and effects that really interest me. I go for interesting sounds simply because I'm fascinated by them.

Kate & Leopold, bouncing between two time periods, was a step in a different direction for you. Was this challenging?

Well, it was done very quickly. I think we got it done in five weeks. It was a very intense five-week period of long hours. The director, Jim Mangold, was very closely involved, coming over to my little studio two or three times a week to hear what I was doing and give me some direction. He was very clear as to what he wanted—that we had different time periods and different emotional things going on. And he had very clear ideas about how to deal with those time periods. He felt he was making a sort of fifties' movie or sixties' movie along the line of a Rock Hudson and Doris Day kind of innocent romance. So the contemporary portions of the music would have a slightly dated Mancini quality. And that's what I attempted to do. The period stuff, which was set back in the nineteenth century, would have a much more classical approach.

I originally wrote the main theme as a classical waltz, and it became this Gershwin-esque love melody, which seemed to translate very well. I fell in love with the tune. Maybe I should be embarrassed to say that, since I wrote it, but once I translated it from this very classical waltz, which you hear only at the very end of the film, into this Gershwin kind of jazz string arrangement, it achieved a seductive quality that was enormously satisfying to me.

You use the tuba as a comedic tool in *Town & Country*. Why did you choose this instrument?

I did a cue in demo form in *Town & Country* and the director just loved the tuba sound. That was really the reason there was so much tuba in *Town & Country*. It is a good sound. It has a really great flavor to it. I get nervous when sounds are that effective because I worry that no one will want me to use any other sounds again.

We're so used to bass sounds coming from certain instruments, yet there are loads of different instruments that play bass sounds. There's bass saxophone. One of my favorite instruments of the moment is the rumba box, which is a Caribbean instrument. It's really just a giant thumb piano, but it's a bass instrument and it sounds terrific. I'm always on the lookout for other ways to do the same thing, to move from tuba, for example, to using bass clarinet or contrabassoon makes perfect sense to me, but they have different personalities. It's a question of whether that personality matches the job you need to do.

What are your thoughts of a score being listened to outside of a film? Do you keep that in mind when you're writing the score?

It's like job number two. Job number one is to make the score work for the film so that the film moves in the way it was intended until the vision of the director is realized. And job number two is to write music that is so good that people will want to hear it outside of the film. So it's the second priority, but it's definitely something that I like the idea of, because the music is one of the very few elements involved in the film that can be taken away from the film and appreciated independently.

Do you ever take an interest in the listeners' opinions?

I'm interested in what people have to say. But frankly, I'm not very aware about many people reviewing my scores. So there hasn't been a lot to think about.

Randall's theme, which is a character-driven theme in *About Schmidt*, shows up in many cues and changes the tempo of emotion. Talk about the overall chemistry of this score.

It was a very tricky one. The film may be very clear about what it is now, but it wasn't clear about what it was when we started on it. Instead of taking a short period of time, it actually took a good three months. At least half of that was just searching for music or ideas that would resonate with the film.

The temp score never worked and was never used as a basis for anything. So it was very much up to me to unlock the character of Schmidt and find a way of making him seem resonant, making him someone we identified with, someone we understood and even cared for. Even though he's not a particularly likeable character, nonetheless, he is a human being and he has things that we understand and identify with. So I spent a long time trying to figure out how to do that for him and, of course, for the other characters, the other elements in the film, Randall being one of them.

Randall is not a sophisticated character. Randall has the tuba and, in a way, that was the most two-dimensional piece of music. It was really playing him as a humorous character. But the rest of the film had a much more sophisticated approach from Alexander and, hopefully, from me.

This score was a slowly evolving process, and the great discipline that Alexander imposed on me was to keep things simple. They should be melodic, but they shouldn't be fussy or complicated. So the score actually is very simple-sounding. There is not much in the way of counterpoint or any of that kind of thing. It's very narrative and fairly straightforward. Throughout this score, when I was really thinking about how to nail it, I would never manage to find a melody. But when I stopped thinking about it and started just playing and playing around with ideas, the good ideas came out.

Mood is a huge factor in this score, and it takes so many different turns that I often couldn't figure out if it was supposed to be a comedy or a drama. The Russian-style march was forceful, but yet it has a funny tone to it. Tell me more about your reason for using the various styles you used.

The Russian sequence was all about momentum. That's evident just looking at the picture. He has got so much anger and momentum going on that it was really just a question of sticking with it and supporting it and making it as big and energetic as it needed to be. He is, at that particular point, both angry and, from our point of view, a figure of fun. We're clearly not entirely on his side as we watch him go ballistic, but it's kind of ridiculous. So the music had to take it seriously enough that you've got the energy and the momentum there. But the music didn't really want to be comic; it wanted to be serious in such a way that you would see the ridiculousness of it. I think the pompous Russian quality highlighted its ridiculousness.

Actually, the music is what told me whether to laugh or not.

Right, the function of the music that I come up with is generally not to make the joke, but to set up the environment where you understand that it is a joke and that you have license to find things funny. Alexander's films certainly tend to be very satirical. There is the possibility that you could take things seriously, the things that when they look bad, feel bad. And if he wants you to regard it as satire— see the humor in it—then that's something the music can contribute. It can give you a different point of view, a different perspective, so that you see it the way Alexander is looking at it, not just for what it is on its own.

I am so moved by your passion in *About Schmidt*'s dramatic cues. You write romance and comedy very well, but what I take from your music is the style of almost an operatic tragedy, such as when Warren's wife dies or during the last letter to Ndugu. Is this style your coming out or becoming more natural?

At the moment, it's something that I'm very keen on. The breadth of emotion in this film I respond to very deeply. I'd say the answer is yes. It's funny: I always thought I was very emotional in my music, except in Alexander's films, because he generally doesn't want emotion, he wants a distance. When we started *About Schmidt*, he said the funniest thing. He said, "Rolfe, I know you're very dry in your music, but I want you to be emotional here." And I was like, "It's not me that's dry, it's you that's dry. I'm dying to do emotion." It was very funny that he had thought that. I don't know how he comes to these conclusions; I've always thought that emotional music comes very readily to me.

Which one of your scores are you most fond of?

About Schmidt. I think it is the most complete score I've written.

Have you set any goals for your career's journey?

I want to keep doing work of quality and variety. I suppose one ambition at the moment is that I want the witty material to be part of what I do, not *all* that I do. I do a variety of different kinds of films, but the ones that do well so far have tended to be on the wittier end of things. I'd like to achieve some more balance in what I do.

Cliff Martinez

Cliff Martinez's music is anything but simple, although one might detect a hint of the influence of minimalism in his scores, which have the ability to pull filmgoers into altogether new realms, new ambiences. His music often arcs across a film, flowing from scene to scene with great internal continuity. His eight collaborations with director Steven Soderbergh have allowed him to speak in his unique voice while bringing to each movie a different style of expression.

From his pulsating, electronic scores that propel _Narc_ (2002) and Soderbergh's _Traffic_ (2000) to his less dense, eerily spiritual music for Soderbergh's _Solaris_ (2002), Martinez has repeatedly proven to be a talented film composer who chooses to use predominantly synthesizers to express his very contemporary musical voice.

How did you enter into the film music world?

I played drums in rock-'n'-roll bands for about ten years and became fascinated with the music technology in the eighties. I had a drum machine, a sampler, and one of the first hardware sequencers ever built. This was around the time I was in the band Red Hot Chili Peppers, and there was no place for that kind of technology in that band. They weren't interested in it.

I just started creating a bunch of strange music using samples of kitchen utensils and so on, but I couldn't find an outlet for that kind of stuff until I was channel-surfing one day and saw *Pee-Wee's Playhouse* and thought that it would be a perfect outlet for this music, which I thought was new and wonderful at the time. I happened to know the director of the show. I contacted him and sent him tapes of the music I was making. And my first scoring job became an episode of *Pee-Wee's Playhouse*. I started in TV, and after that came my first feature film, Steven Soderbergh's *Sex, Lies, and Videotape*.

A lot of your music is atmospheric and with a dominant use of synthesizers.

My style has been influenced by Steven Soderbergh because most of my early film projects were directed by him. Steven has generally preferred a very stark, minimalist style. I think I have a natural tendency toward that sound anyway, but I would have to say that the films and the people I work with have had a very strong influence on my sound.

You use the orchestra occasionally, but is it less of an interest to you?

I've used the orchestra for films, but most of the films I've done are small independent films with limited budgets that preclude the use of an orchestra. I would like to use more orchestral elements in my scores. I have, however, been fortunate a couple of times.

Solaris is my only orchestral score that I would really call "atmospheric," which was what Steven was looking for. He wanted an atmospheric ambience that was also organic and orchestral in nature.

How did your relationship with Steven Soderbergh begin?

I was doing a scene in the film *Alien Nation* for a friend of mine who was primarily a sound designer. Steven, who was his roommate, happened to walk in and heard what I was doing. He liked what I was doing and asked me if I would be interested in scoring his first film, *Sex, Lies, and Videotape*. I agreed.

Your music is somewhat outspoken. Does this provide challenges when you want to expand into different genres or A-list films?

Aside from *Traffic* and *Solaris*, which were really big studio films. I suppose that's a problem. Typecasting exists for film composers as it does for actors. With my scores being electronic and unconventional, I haven't received a lot of calls for big studio pictures. The few that I have done are through Steven.

I'm beginning to work with other directors now. I have a film coming out from Lakeshore Pictures this year called *Wicker Park*. I'm gradually working my way up, trying to become more of a name-brand, but it's taking a long time.

Some composers don't really get exposed because they're typecast, like you said.

That's true. Partly it's the politics and partly it's if you have a certain style that they know you for. I don't know exactly where my music fits, but it probably isn't viewed as a commercial style.

Do you have a dream project that you would like to do?

No, not a particular film. After *Solaris*, I wouldn't mind doing one that is more of a conventional science-fiction picture. I'd also like to do a comedy or a big action-explosion summer movie. I would just like to tackle some of the other categories I haven't had a chance to do. *Solaris* was great fun because it was outer-space music, something that I'd never done. That was exciting.

Your *Solaris* score is an unusual approach for this style of movie. The music was translucent while encompassing all the emotions of the film at the same time.

Well, I guess that's something that I've had some practice with, having worked with Steven. He has always wanted the music to stay out of the way somewhat and not be overly emotional or dramatic, to be atmospheric without being obvious in its emotional tone.

The problem I had was making a purely atmospheric score with little emotion. It's hard to create music that has ambiguous meaning.

Perhaps a lot of the emotion to the score of *Solaris* is unintended. I tried to be emotionally neutral.

It was a mutual decision that the music in *Solaris* would be a little bit more emotional than Steven would typically prefer. It was filmed with much more ambiguity than Steven's films have been, so we thought that the music needed to be more direct. So it was just somewhat more traditional in that regard. I suppose making it more emotional than usual was the easy part. It is always difficult to create music that is stripped of all that.

Traffic seems to be your most complex work in terms of the separate elements in the movie.

I guess it was complex in the sense that there were about four or five separate storylines. When I looked at it in the script stage, it seemed very fragmented and that it would need the score to pull the film together. However, when I saw the rough cut of the film, I didn't have that perception at all. It was tied together very well despite the different storylines. Steven had this clever device of color-coding the different scenes. Mexico had an amber color and Washington blue . . . There were things about the way it was assembled that pulled all these different stories together nicely. So the music didn't have to function that way.

The challenge was to create compelling, interesting, dramatic music minimally. For example, Steven used a temp track that was one note for two minutes. It was really hard to design music that was a single note for two minutes and that had something to say without being monotonous. The challenge was to create very austere, minimalist music that served the dramatic needs of the film. It was music that was interesting as a stand-alone experience as well.

You have the ability to mesmerize the listener with a surreal landscape of sounds without using many themes. How do you go about developing a score like this?

Usually, the rough cut is where the process begins. If I get a script, it will give me some ideas, but those ideas are usually wrong the minute I see the film. Usually, everything changes as soon as I begin to put music against a picture. That's when I have a good idea of what works and what doesn't.

The filmmakers have an influence on the process. Generally, there's a temp score. This tells the composer where the director wants the music, and it gives an idea of the style they are looking for. All of those things steer the project initially. And then, I devise my own concepts. This is largely intuitive. It just comes from watching the film and being inspired by it and trying to figure out what the music can do to contribute to it. I usually look at what's weak about the film that the music might be able to improve.

You've worked a lot with Soderbergh. Does he now offer much direction to your music for his films?

Steven doesn't say a lot. During *Solaris* and *Traffic*, we probably had no more than four conversations total over a three-month period. He does, however, narrowly define the kind of grammar he wants used. With *Solaris* and *Traffic*, he assembled a pretty complete temp score. It told me the spotting of the music and what style he was looking for. After that, he trusts me to create the music within those parameters. He only steps in if I get off track. Sometimes it's frustrating not to have much contact with the director, but I guess after working with him for fourteen years now, he trusts me to a degree.

Is there a score that you would call your prized work?

Well, my favorite up to today is *Solaris*, because of the scale of the project. It was exciting to be able to hear ninety people play my music. Unfortunately, it was one of the films that died a swift miserable death at the box office. Nonetheless, the scoring of it was one of my peak scoring experiences.

Were movies a big part of your life growing up? Did you know about the industry at that time?

I didn't. I always went to the movies, but I never paid that much attention to the music. I got into electronic music and, then, this is where my own tastes took me. I didn't want to write pop songs. I wanted to write unusual music, and it seemed like the only outlet for that was film. Film was the only place where you heard jazz, world music, and modern twentieth-century symphonic styles.

Are there film composers now that you admire or listen to?

I have respect for anybody who is making film music, because it's not easy work, especially when it has to be done very quickly. I like Thomas Newman. He's one of the greats. I also like Carter Burwell and Harry Gregson-Williams, along with the big-shots, John Williams and Jerry Goldsmith. Of the older guys, I like Bernard Herrmann. I think he was the original minimalist. I really admire his music.

It's amazing how just about every composer I've interviewed has mentioned Herrmann. He's such a huge influence.

Definitely. He's one of the real artists within the film-music hall of fame. He was associated with some great films, *Vertigo* and *Citizen Kane*, and his work on its own is amazing stuff.

John Ottman

John Ottman's broad filmmaking talents are daunting. He both edited the film and composed the music for the now-classic *Usual Suspects* (1995), *Apt Pupil* (1998), *Urban Legends: Final Cut* (2000), a film that he also directed, and *X2* (2003). Seemingly immune to the inherent pressures of balancing his multiple roles, he successfully dons the various hats and creates his movies with panache.

Looking at Ottman's long list of music credits, one notices that many of the films that he has scored have a dark, moody, ominous atmosphere about them, a quality that Ottman's music captures and heightens very successfully with sultry themes, eerie-sounding arpeggio patterns, and his great command of colorful orchestration techniques. With every picture he scores (and he has scored every imaginable genre of film), his music is very well-tailored to the specific film, yet his colorful sound pallet and impeccable composing techniques remain consistent from project to project.

How did film music enter your life?

It was sort of a hobby, really. I started having fun doing it while I worked a full-time job at a hotel. Just for the hell of it, I would experiment on my friends' student films and re-score them because, usually, the music on their films was awful. I found out I had a knack for it. Then I started scoring Aampco Parking and Kwikset employee-training videos for a couple friends of mine who own a production company. I found out how cool it was to make a couple hundred bucks to write some music. I thought, "Gee, it would be so neat if I could get paid to do this for my job." That's how it all started.

When Bryan [Singer] did his first feature film [*Public Access*], I was the editor on it, and the composer dropped out in the eleventh hour. I had been dabbling with music for these little videos and student films and I said, "You know, I can score this movie. As the editor, I know this character better than anybody." "Well I don't know if you can do dark music. You've just been writing all this happy kind of music," he replied. And I go, "No, no I really can do dark." And that was the first time we discovered the symbiosis—me doing both jobs. Now the joke is that most of what I've been hired to score for the last few years are dark films!

Film music is a difficult task in itself, yet you manage to be involved in editing and directing as well. What makes you take on all these tasks, and do you prefer one over the other?

I don't prefer one over the other. It sort of depends where I'm at in my life. If I stick with one thing for too long, I start to get antsy and want to move on to something else. Then I realize how good I had it on the other job! So I move back to that. I guess I'm never happy. The glass is always half empty for me.

Both directing *and* scoring have their advantages. It's nice to be the director because you're the high man on the totem pole and don't have people to answer to except for the executives. As the composer, you sometimes feel like the grunt because you're not always in control. But, at the same time, you have a hell of a lot less to worry about when you're the composer. You're just doing one job on the film and not having to supervise every job. But directing and scoring was a very strange situation. I'm somewhat used to be being schizophrenic and having to compartmentalize between jobs, having been an editor and a composer on the same movie. But, when you're the director, it's very strange, because directing is a highly insecure job.

You're desperate to have test audiences like your movie, and if you put together a temp score that everyone likes, it becomes a security blanket. I was fighting within myself to compose something different from the temp score because it was working so well. As the director, I was sort of my own worst enemy, loving the temp score, but as the composer, I felt like I really needed to part from it and do better. So that was a very strange position to be in.

You recently both edited and scored *X2*. How was it for you working in what seems to be an impossible situation?

Well, I wouldn't recommend doing both jobs on a movie like that to anyone. What's the phrase? Don't try this at home? But it was one of those situations where Bryan [Singer] and I go way back, and he really missed me doing both tasks for him on *X-Men*. I wouldn't exactly say it was blackmail, but he pretty much implied that if I were the editor, he probably was going to like what I wrote a lot better. I felt it was worth getting through the scoring process alive by being the editor. So I did it for the sake of the score, and, of course, so I could make it the best movie I could to score!

It's hard to believe I got through that. It's nearly an impossible thing because there's a huge overlap between the editing and the writing of the score. When you're the same guy, it's very hard time-wise and also for the brain, because I would be writing the score for a couple hours and then be called down to the editing room to have a screening for the executives. And when we screened for the executives, I was hearing the temp score. So then I'd come back and continue writing the music, trying hard to disassociate myself from one concept or the other.

What was your take on Michael Kamen's *X-Men* score? Your *X2* score didn't make reference to it, except its main theme a bit.

I only saw that movie once. I'm not really familiar with Kamen's score. I went into *X2* as a world I was going to define for the first time. I wanted to make it my own world, and no one wanted me to adhere to what was done before anyhow.

The only piece of music that I really knew of his is the theme, and I wanted to make sure that my theme had the same attitude; but

I wanted to add some sort of humanity to it and expand upon that aspect in the score. I like to keep alive those earlier traditions of scoring—having strong character motifs, basically writing from characters. *X2* was so fun for me because there were so many characters to write for.

I just interviewed a composer who disagrees with character writing. He stated that film music should be written for the scene and the emotion. It's funny to hear opposing views on something that seems be a main function in scoring.

That's funny. I have the total opposite approach, which doesn't mean that characters have to have individual themes, but, at the very least, the film needs some sort of familiar signature musically—*a theme!*—to give it cohesion and greater understanding.

I read the script, then I look at the footage. I will write the film's overture, which basically has a lot of the themes—including character themes if appropriate—from which I am going to draw. If I haven't created that well to draw from, then it's more difficult to write the score than just scoring for the moment. Even if I'm doing an action scene, I have to sort of know what's at the root of this action scene: Which characters are in jeopardy? What is the scene really about? I tend to be far more motivated if I know where the music's coming from character-wise. The music is the soul of the movie. The more you pull out for the audience without hitting them over the head and without holding their hand too much, the better you help tell the story. It's a fine line, of course, and it doesn't mean that you write for every single character.

I think approaching films that way is a dying art form. To me, the best scores are ones from which you can somehow take away the gist of a story being told without having seen the film. That's very hard to do. It takes a lot more time for a composer to do that, but it's worth it in the end.

What influences have helped you to develop your style?

I don't know. I guess just growing up having been a *Star Trek* fan and, as a result, getting into Jerry Goldsmith and rediscovering his older scores. Then, John Williams, of course.

I became a big fan and film-score collector. I was just an odd kid growing up in San Jose. I only listened to film scores and classical music. I guess they just rubbed off on me and the way I score movies. And when I would go to the symphony and watch performances of my favorite pieces, like Dvořák's Ninth Symphony, which I knew by heart, I would sit there and say, "Oh, that's an oboe doing that, "Oh, that's a clarinet doing that." That's how I learned orchestration—by watching.

How difficult is it writing for a film versus composing a piece without a film's restrictions?

I would say it's a little more difficult writing a piece without some visual direction. And that's sort of a double-edged sword because, sometimes when you're writing something, you wish to hell the picture didn't do what it did, so you could expand upon something. You find a really cool moment to write but the moment's too short. It's frustrating; you really want to do more. Nevertheless, the picture really helps me write. If I just had a blank screen in front of me it would be more difficult. However that's what I have to do when I write my little overtures to my movies.

But, as you write, you discover things, too. I'll write the overture, but then as I start scoring the movie I'll start discovering things: "Oh, I should change the theme to be this way." Or I'll discover new themes and go back into that piece and reintegrate or modify the themes I had written.

Is film-music composition a natural talent—in the sense that one either is or isn't in tune with the picture and having one's music fit this medium—or is this something that can be taught?

I think both. I think basically it's an innate thing, just like anything creative, but you can learn to expand upon those things you already have, your innate talent. But I don't think someone who has no sense for writing music can take a music class and become a really good composer. I think there has to be something you were born with.

What about a Dvorak or a Mozart—putting them in front of a film screen? They possessed genius, but writing for a motion picture is an altogether different art that makes me wonder if it requires an extra something inside the composer to do.

I think all the best composers are storytellers already, especially composers who wrote symphonies. But, having said that, I think there are two different breeds of composers. You can have music theory, but you may be clueless when it actually comes to writing for a scene in a movie. To write for a movie, you really have to have that popcorn mentality in a way. You have to think film. That's why a lot of people who have ten times more musical training than I do may be lacking in terms of tackling the drama in a scene, which is where a film composer has to tap into his filmmaker side.

Your first big film was *Usual Suspects*. You scored and edited this complex story with Bryan Singer. Tell me about this experience. How did it come to be?

It came about because of our first movie, *Public Access*. That actually won at the Sundance Film Festival in 1993, but it wasn't released. Based upon that movie, Bryan put the deal together for *Usual Suspects*. It was in his contract that I both edit the picture and write the score. If it hadn't been in his contract, they never would have gone for that because no one had really done that before, especially a guy who had never written a score for an orchestra. But they were sort of trapped into it and were a bit ambivalent about the prospect, as was I. In fact, I remember early on, before we started the film, the producers met me for lunch. They sat me down, looked me in the eye, and said, "You're sure you can do this, right?" "Gulp, sure." I went home with my heart beating because I had no idea if I could pull it off. You know, I learned a lot writing for the orchestra, which was a trial-and-error process.

What is your formal music training?

I played the clarinet for eight years, and that was really the extent of my musical training aside from what I told you—watching symphonies. Then, in the eighties, when MIDI came along, I was able to sort of get out what was in my head, to use the keyboard as a pencil on a staff. I used to write songs with a pencil and paper when I played the clarinet, but I got very rusty. I guess Danny Elfman and I were sort of similar in that way. He was a trailblazer who took all the shit for not being classically trained before I came along. No longer in any meeting for a movie does anyone ask you, "Oh, what is your musical training?" I think he's responsible for that, because they actually used to be concerned with that. He came along and actually put that to bed. No one really cares about that anymore. They care about the bottom line: what kind of music you produce and how well you score a film.

What you say is inspiring, I'm a film-music enthusiast, the odd one in school who appreciated a different world. Like you, I played the clarinet and sang in high school. My aspiration is to be a film composer. You give me and others like me the feeling that whatever you believe can be achieved, no matter what hurdles you have to jump, as long as you are committed.

Absolutely. With today's technology, if you have a musical sense, and you have the motivation and the stomach to read a lot of manuals and understand the goddamned technology, you can do it.

As long as you've got a musical sense and you can hear the music in your head, there's no reason why you can't do it. You have to learn a lot, obviously. Working with the orchestra more and more, you learn more and more, like the ranges of the instruments and not to do idiotic things. Like if you have one hundred pieces playing in the orchestra and then write a line for an oboe and hope to ever hear it . . . I guess that's one of the biggest things I learned in my early scores: what were and weren't realistic dynamics.

Usual Suspects **was a remarkable score that seemed to launch your career in the horror/thriller genre quite rapidly. Being typecast must be frustrating. What are your feelings on this?**

Yeah, I think it's frustrating for any composer or anyone in the industry who gets typecast after being successful with a certain thing. You'll always want to be given the opportunity to write something that shows that you can flourish in other styles. Actually, I have had the opportunities, but the problem is that those opportunities were films that bombed; so the work went unnoticed. Even though *Snow White* was a dark movie, as was *Incognito*, both were movies where I got to write some sweeping music that wasn't necessarily completely dark. But, of course, no one saw those movies.

You can write the symphony of your career, but if no one saw the film it doesn't really matter. That's the way Hollywood is. They aren't solely going to sell you on your talent. God knows, they're going to sell you on the success of your last movie. It's all about numbers. Some film composers actually have the film profits shown on their résumés. That's the way some producers will look at a list. Half the time they don't know anything about film music. All they know is "This person did a movie that made 200 million dollars. This must be the guy we need." Even though, for all they know, the score for that movie may suck. But that's the way it is. It's a security thing. If producers see a film that made a lot of money, they want every facet that was involved with that movie.

The Cable Guy is an outrageously fun score to listen to. Did Ben Stiller let you run a little wild with your ides?

The funny thing with *Cable Guy* is that Ben had never done a film with a film composer before. He had always done films with source music. He was under the misconception that the film composer is on from day one of shooting. Well, I wanted to have it work out right between us, so I agreed to be on the film from the first day of shooting; and I was on the movie forever. The irony is that I think I wrote three hours of music for that film, but in the end, my score was like twenty-four minutes long because there were so many songs in the film; plus the film got cut down.

But the good thing about it was that I was able to temp the movie with my own renderings without having to copy any temp score. That was the fun part. It's important to be able to go to a scoring session and not have everyone surprised by what you did. Just for my own security and sleeping the night before the session, I believe in knowing that everyone's on the same page. With *X2*, I wanted to make sure I formed a coalition, so to speak: I had the producers over here to hear all the mockups of the cues. That way, I knew that everyone liked the score and knew what they were going to get; so when we got to the scoring stage, there would be no situation where someone hears a cue and asks, "What the hell is this?"

In your scores, I hear hints of a passion wanting to escape.

There's passion just screaming to get out. It's very hard to do some scores where you have to hold back and be reserved for the sake of the movie. The theme I wrote for Jean Gray is very emotional—it's the love theme. I hope that can show people what I can do in that vein. The funny thing is, again, executives who look at my résumé are not going to see *X2* as a romantic movie. They're going to see it as an action movie. Despite the fact that I wrote a lot of humanity-based music, they won't look at that because they'll just look at the title. And, hell, I'll take the big adventure films! But my dream score is a *Dances with Wolves* kind of movie. I would love to fill that John Barry voice. All the scores I have seem to be complicated. They're exhausting to write—so many goddamned notes. It would be nice just to do a series of whole notes and call it a day!

I really enjoyed *Trapped*. What I liked most were your subtle piano themes. They almost give this thriller a romantic touch. Do you use different instruments to convey different messages?

Yeah, that's sort of the thing I do. I love writing piano pieces because it's easy to play both sides of the coin with a piano. You can be romantic and dark at the same time. I could have done an overtly evil theme for the bad guy, but I wanted to write something a little more romantic.

I like to imply some sort of backstory with the score. Perhaps there's some deeper reason why people are evil. There's a romantic notion to taking on evil. Even Keyser Söze's theme in *The Usual Suspects* isn't plainly sinister but quite stirring.

Trapped was a different-sounding score for me only because we had no budget. There were like fifteen people in the entire orchestra, so the score was about ninety percent synthesized. But something unique came out of it because we were so limited.

Growing up, did you ever see yourself becoming a well-known composer?

No, it was the last thing I thought I would ever be doing. My intent when I grew up was to be a film director who could hire my idol, Jerry Goldsmith to be my film composer. I never expected to have the same film-music agent as Jerry Goldsmith. It's really quite bizarre. Even now I still laugh. I think it's kind of crazy that I'm doing this. But I love it.

Have you ever met him?

Yes, I did at the yearly BMI dinner. My agent sat me down next to him when his wife left to go to the bathroom. So I knew I had about one minute to fill him in on my entire life. I think his head was spinning by the time his wife got back. I think I spoke too fast. This guy was probably like, "What was that?" To me, sitting down next to Jerry Goldsmith was like sitting down next to Jesus Christ. It was very difficult to speak to him, but, yes, I did get to meet him.

Ironically, he had a scoring session for a film at the same time I was recording *X2*, but we booked our orchestra way in advance of his, so I had all his horn players. The irony: I stole my idol's French horns.

What do you feel are your strengths and weaknesses when you come to the table with your ideas? What separates you from other composers?

I tend to be orchestra-based. I would say that if I were given a very synthesizer-heavy, drum-loop kind of score, I could do it in a unique way, but that sort of music is not really my bag. It's funny because my agent said, "You gotta get music like that on your demo reel. You know whether it's really right for the movie you ultimately get hired on or not, but it just turns them on that you do stuff like that." A funny story: My agent also told John Debney the same thing. So John Debney took a cue from *Cutthroat Island* and put a bunch of synthesized drums under it. The cue he chose happened to be in a very constant time signature, so he was able to do that and put it on his demo. It sounds really cool. In my music I couldn't really find anything like that because I tend to change time signatures all over the place.

Do directors torture you with Bernard Herrmann and Christopher Young temp tracks?

I think many get haunted by Christopher Young temp tracks. Many of his cues work very well on a number of different scenarios. One of his cues can work in an interesting way for three or four different kinds of scenes. His music always seems to bring something introspective to a temp. I love Chris's music! And he's a really nice guy! It's actually a compliment that his music can work in so many different ways.

I hear some stylistic similarities in your darker scores.

Well, I think we're both influenced by the same guys. When you hear Chris's earlier work, you definitely hear a Goldsmith influence. I think, in the beginning, we were both Goldsmith wannabes, but then discovered our own styles, our own paths, and became secure with our own techniques. I feel more comfortable in my own skin now. I think it's been the same with him for a while. There are definite Chris Young-isms in the scoring world, and I think I've forged Ottman-isms, too.

Which of your scores are you most fond of?

I would probably say *Incognito*, only because it was a movie that was sort of a composer's wet dream because there's no dialogue or sound effects in these long, extended sequences. So the score didn't have to tuck itself under dialog. It was basically a movie that featured the score. It was basically expository music—almost like being commissioned to write a symphony.

How difficult is it to be original?

I think you just have to not be afraid to have confidence in yourself. Simply let your fingers work on the keyboard and just do what flows freely out of your head. Use The Force! Inevitably something unique is going to come. If you're too paranoid about it and try to refer to

too many other people's work, you're going to start to copy something, you're going to come up with something less original. I found
that if I just sit at the keyboard and doodle and just have the confidence in myself that "Gee, this might actually be better than what
they're thinking," it always will be better. And I can sleep at night
knowing what I wrote was really part of me. Sometimes it depends on
your state of mind. Sometimes I'll come back the next morning, listen to a part of a cue, and push the delete button!

Basil Poledouris

Upon hearing the name Basil Poledouris, what often first come to mind is his muscular, forceful, pulsating scores for such films as John Milius's epic *Conan the Barbarian* (1982) and Paul Verhoeven's *RoboCop* (1987) and *Starship Troopers* (1997). But Poledouris's talents must not be pigeonholed. He has repeatedly proven himself to be highly adept at composing to the emotional pulse of any film, regardless of its genre. A good example of his more-intimate musical persona can be heard in his score for the highly emotional *It's My Party* (1996); his lighter musical persona can be heard in his music for the family classic *Lassie* (1994) and the popular animated film *The Jungle Book* (1994); and his lush, expansive musical persona can be heard in his score for the celebrated Western *Lonesome Dove* (1989), a television miniseries for which he received an Emmy.

Coming to film-scoring with a great understanding of all areas of filmmaking, a field he studied while attending USC with John Milius and George Lucas, Poledouris has used his broad knowledge of the medium to help him create some of the most prodigious moments in the history of film music.

What was music to you when you were growing up, and how did you come to film music?

Music had always been part of our family. I started formal piano studies when I was seven and had been pretty convinced that I was going to be a concert pianist. I followed that track until I got to college. I went to USC, where I decided that I really wasn't interested in being a concert pianist but was interested in conducting and the orchestra. The sounds of the orchestra just totally intrigued me because of the power and the textures.

Then lots of things opened up. I wandered into the cinema department at USC at a particularly volatile time, you know, the mid-sixties, when everything seemed to be changing and in flux. It just seemed that the movie camera and the art of cinema itself had a little more to say to my generation than classical music. So that's how I got interested in film, which my degrees are in. When it came time to look for music for the movies that I was making, I really couldn't find anything that I thought was appropriate, so I started writing it. That's basically how I started.

I guess I wrote my first real film score in 1966. Then I started scoring movies for fellow classmates—most notably for John Milius. He and I became good friends while we were at USC. We were both surfers, so we would ditch class and go surfing and then talk about movies. I think I was the first person who turned a John Milius script into a movie. That's where that association started. Once John got out into the real world, he wrote scripts for AIP, American International Pictures. And from that, he started his directing career and invited me to do *Big Wednesday*, which was my first large feature film. Prior to that time, I had done a lot of educational industrial documentary kinds of movies. Then I decided that I didn't really want to be a film director and went back into music. I studied composition privately and took some classes at a state university in Los Angeles.

Coming from both composing and directing, what are your views on temp tracks?

I think it's a crutch. I think it's an unnecessary tool that's used too early in the making of the motion picture. It doesn't allow the film to develop its own life. It imposes something that has come from the outside world. Usually it's a film score because there are serious differences between film composition and just pure musical composition. For the most part, it has nothing to do with the internal organism, or the organization and the rhythm, of what the film could be.

Previewing a film before it's finished has become the standard process. But when I did *Big Wednesday*, we would *finish* the film first and *then* preview it. Then, based on the reaction of the audience, we'd go back in and re-edit the film. I would re-score the film and we would do it again. And that was sort of the way it was done. Most films were done like that. I mean, the filmmaker got to make the film that he or she wanted to present to an audience, and then, based upon that audience's reaction and the way the studio assessed the reaction, they'd make changes.

What also happens with temp music is that the directors sometimes fall in love with a particular melodic notion or the way the orchestra builds. There are so many elements that make up a musical composition and its execution that it's very difficult even for a musician to discern what exactly it is that somebody might find intriguing about a piece of temp music. Is it the fact that the melody is played on a trumpet or is it the melody's construction itself? You know what I mean? So, although you're not quite sure what it is they like about a piece of temp music in the first place, particularly if it's completely inappropriate music, you kind of end up trying to parody it.

I was just working recently on a picture that was a period piece in which it seemed like every action scene had temp music that sounded to me like it was science-fiction. It didn't seem that anybody else picked up on the fact that, even though the film was set in the 1800s, there were these incredibly modernistic harmonies and orchestration devices that would be more appropriate for *Star Wars* or *Matrix*.

My feeling about the temp track is that it's hideous. It's a hideous imposition upon somebody who really is interested in bringing a creative vitality to the film for the film's sake. It really is.

I just went to see *The Hours*, which is a beautifully done movie all around, but I have one criticism, and I am curious to know your thoughts about it. We've talked about temp scores and music placement. In this case, I felt that the music placement might have been over-abundant. The music, by Philip Glass, was beautifully composed, with movement and emotion, but it was a bit overwhelming at times. Who ultimately makes these placement choices?

That's interesting that you say that. I watched *The Hours* a couple of weeks ago and I thought the music was very appropriate and kind of wove everything together quite nicely for those three time periods and all. But I had this funny feeling that if I were to watch it again, the music would exhaust me. There were a couple of times when I felt, "Damn, do we really need this here?"

There was this constant churning and this agitation going on within the characters. I think that may have been the request that they made. But it was also very strongly Philip's style. I think it worked. I'm not putting the score down at all. He probably has a strong influence over what ends up in the film because of who he is. Same with John Williams, who has a strong influence on the way the music ends up in the picture. Maybe not. I don't know anymore.

In answer to your question, it's really hard to know what is the composer's choice these days. When I first started out, there was no question: The composer was the musical director of the film and made all of the musical choices in concert with the director, of course, and sometimes the producer. Directors didn't assume that they had either the expertise or the knowledge, and some of them frankly didn't have the concern. They hired Elmer Bernstein because they wanted Elmer Bernstein to score their movie. They hired us for our expertise and our dramatic sense and our familiarity with film. These days it's really hard to know. Is it the editor's choice because that's where the temp track was? Is it the director's choice because he or she took the cue from the first reel and stuck it in ten times throughout the rest of the movie?

You are one of the most versatile composers in the industry. Talk about your approaches to, and the influences on, your various styles.

I'm not going to say that I'm schizophrenic or have multiple personalities, but when people ask me what I listen to, I tell them, "Well, in the morning, I like to listen to Bach or Leonard Cohen, and in the afternoon I like to listen to Ministry of Sound and Nine Inch Nails. It just depends."

I think the answer to your question, in terms of film scores, is whatever is appropriate for the movie itself. I don't have the need to impose my style on a movie. The style should grow from the formal requirements of the film. It's like we were talking earlier about the period piece set in the 1800s. I don't think that should sound like the latest DJ music. That's a little inappropriate to me, so I try to find out what it is about the film—in the film's writing or direction or color or style of the film itself—that dictates the musical style. I don't know how this happens with me—that's the magic part—and I don't really want to know, because I think if I ever figure it out, then I probably wouldn't be interested in doing it anymore.

I want to touch quickly on *Conan the Barbarian*. What sort of research took place for this broad and powerful landscape of different sounds?

Conan had a temp track, and it was an amazing one. It was mostly classical music because it was of a different era. It was kind of like what Rózsa used to do with the Roman epics. He created "the sound of Rome." We don't know what Rome sounded like. They had long trumpets and lutes, but no one really knows any more about it than they know the sound of music of ancient Greece.

Well, *Conan* was supposed to be ten thousand years before history, and John Milius always had the notion that the score should play like an opera in that there are motifs. He likes a very strong emphasis on melodic ideas. That's always been John's request and requirement for film scores. So, okay, the simplest melodic form seems to be the folk song. Since the earliest folk songs were before history, no one wrote them down. So I went to Celtic songs and drew in thoughts, not that I did a whole lot of research. If you look at Celtic music, it had to have been an outgrowth of Druid influences. So I read a little bit about what they thought the music of the Druids was. And, since the number three is very strong in all mythologies and religions, I thought, "Well, I'll repeat the thing three times." I also had the idea that it should be sung, because they transmitted their history to future generations through song.

I used very primitive kinds of harmonies—open fifths and octaves, which were the beginnings of harmony. I kind of tried to deconstruct something like a modern folk song and put it back into time. The orchestra was big because of the operatic style and the size of the movie. Arnold's *big,* for Christ's sake! I couldn't do it with a lute and drum. I mean, I guess you could have, but all those factors kind of come into it.

What does the Latin choir represent?

I think it gives it an antiquity. John originally wanted it in German. I resisted that notion only because it seems like German is kind of a modern language. I guess, ideally, if I were really going to pump that concept, I would have created my own language and have them sing in it, but they don't speak that language, they speak English. Latin seemed to work, and choirs know how to sing in Latin.

I've been lucky with the science-fiction stuff that I've done as well as the mythological films. You're creating a world. You're creating an environment that the audience is invited to participate in. That's why I feel my primary responsibility is being true to a style or true to a period or being true to a vision that the director has.

You've added amazing color to Paul Verhoeven's science-fiction movies. I'm curious why you didn't go on to score any of his others, such as *Basic Instinct*.

I was unavailable after we did *RoboCop*. Paul has said in the past that, if he's got a movie with a tremendous amount of heart or emotion, he likes to work with me, and if it's more of an intellectually based kind of idea, he likes to work with Jerry. I think *Basic Instinct* was a really terrific score. Jerry did a great job!

Once you develop a relationship with a director, how does this affect you or in general?

Oh, I think it would have bothered me ten or fifteen years ago, but it's no problem.

You know, it's really easy to pigeonhole people in Hollywood no matter what their discipline is. If a costume designer does a really contemporary, outrageous, punk kind of thing, you're not going to consider them to be the costume designer for *Les Misérables*, when, in fact, they might be totally right for it. I think we all suffer from pigeonholing. That's one reason why I have always embraced doing films with different styles.

For a long time I was the action guy. Even though I had done *The Blue Lagoon* and several very delicate films, I was the blood-and-guts and thunder-and-glory guy. It's tough to be pigeonholed, but on the other hand, if it's done by somebody you admire and respect the way I do Paul, then fine. He knows what he wants. I'm not going to contest him. He's much too strong of a director. He has a vision. If more people made movies like Paul Verhoeven, we'd have a hell of a lot better movies going on out there. So if Paul Verhoeven wants to use whomever, then he should.

I respect directors. You have to understand that, after studying to become one, I realized that I really didn't have that kind of discipline and dedication. They're amazing people. I mean, there are thousands and thousands of little details to have to deal with and keep under control and keep from being overwhelmed by. It's like a big circus. Milius always compared directing to being a general in an army. I think he's absolutely right. You have to have leadership qualities to pull sixty or seventy people together to a single vision and then go fight with the studio and the money people.

What was your approach to scoring *Les Misérables*? It certainly was far away from the Broadway musical based on the same story.

I hate to admit this, but I think I am one of the few people on this planet who never saw the show. I've never been a fan of musicals, or opera for that matter. I think that was one reason why they hired me.

It was a replacement score, so I didn't have the kind of lead-time that I usually get. Knowing that I'm going to be scoring a film, I do research, particularly when the movie's based on a book that is so well-known. I think the time from I was set to do the movie until I finished it was maybe eight weeks. I read the book—which is a big, brilliant, wonderful book—as I was writing.

Billy August is an amazing director, and he understands what he wants. I knew the period, and the style was basically Berlioz. So that was the kind of harmonic setting that I knew the film should stay in. Billy agreed with that. The main thing I think that he was after was a sense of movement. I know the studio wanted that. Then he wanted an idea that represented the repression that the characters felt. I mean, the character Jean is put in jail for nineteen years, I think, for stealing a loaf of bread. That's outrageous. It's kind of a hard concept to follow today, when people can kill and get out in thirty days or not go to jail at all. So, musically, I tried to create the sense that there's this kind of darkness. There's a lid on the music that never really opens up until the last shot of the movie. There's this muted quality to the score itself. It never really becomes free.

What was the reason for presenting it in movements, like a symphony, on the CD?

They wanted to have a simultaneous release of the album and the film, which is smart marketing. The score hadn't been written yet. I probably still had three weeks of writing and recording left to do, but the record had to be compiled for the artwork. It was a marketing demand that I had to meet.

So, instead of giving track titles and that sort of thing, I said, "Screw it. The film basically moves in four acts, so I'll find some music and throw it together." That's not the way I would have liked to have done it, frankly, because I think it plays way too long in certain sections.

Without being boxed into making decisions before I really knew what this score was, I said, "Hell, I'll just do about ten minutes here and about twenty minutes there and maybe this will be fifteen." So I basically cut it into those sweeps. It was a way of my hanging on to a little bit of control over what goes on the album without having to be so specific: What if I hated a cue that I thought I was going to put on the album?

For Love of the Game is a departure from most of your other scores. There is the Americana side and the dramatic emotions in which you hit every nail on the head. What kind of spirit did you gain from the story?

I loved it. First of all, I really like Kevin Costner's stuff. I think he's really a strong actor and a good guy. I think he represents a lot of things about America, Gary Cooper things, particularly in *For Love of the Game*, where there's that silent-man kind of strength. He's an old-fashioned guy. He doesn't believe in trading. His commitment to—and love of—the game is strong. It's not that he's on the cover of *Sports Illustrated* and can make millions of dollars just by jumping from one team to the next.

It was a particularly intriguing script because I was sort of in the same place in my career, not that I was trying to figure out if I wanted to marry somebody, but just in terms of summing it up in a way. It had lots of really interesting themes going for me. It was highly romantic.

Baseball brought in all of the Americana. It was something that Sam Raimi and I talked about a lot. What is baseball? It's an American institution. So the score should have almost a folk feel. That's what the acoustic guitars are about. And then you also have the process of what it really is like to be a pitcher, when he starts doing that breathing through his mouth. Can you imagine how exhausted that pitcher must be? And the fact is that it's based in reality. I mean, there are guys who pitch no-hitter games, and they do have to zone out like that. They shut out the crowds. I think that's the thing that's really cool. We all have to do that at certain points when we're under incredible stress.

I think it really is one of your greater works.

Thank you. I'm very fond of it. I got to do a lot of things in it, too. There are some hints at rock-'n'-roll. There's some big orchestra stuff when he's pitching that last game. Sam wanted the choir. He said, "Let's kick this last cue way over the top." I said, "Gee, we've already got a hundred-piece orchestra sawing away. What else do you want?"

He goes, "What about a choir?" I never would have thought of sticking a choir in that film. Sam's cool. I loved working with Sam. Also, I've got to tell you, *Evil Dead 2* is one of my favorite movies. It's so funny and really well done. It's very stylish. Sam's going to be a terrific director.

You have great variation from project to project. Is this your choice or does this just happen?

It's a choice in that I always tend to refuse certain kinds of projects. And if it's the kind of thing I've done before, then I'm not that passionate or excited about doing it again unless I can bring something new and different to it.

The filmmakers have to want me to be involved in the first place. The only thing I can affect is that I can turn down things that I don't want to do.

What kinds of projects don't appeal to you?

Slasher films. That's probably it. They scare the hell out of me. I know full well there's pyrotechnics and blood, prosthetics and stuff like that, but it messes with me. I don't like it. On the other hand, in *Conan*, we chop off people's heads, so . . .

But that was history.

Yeah, exactly. And it's stylized. How else are you going to kill somebody? Sneaking around in the dark, scaring women and doing hideous things? In *Conan* they're up-front warriors. That I can deal with.

What about *Flesh & Blood*?

I loved doing that movie. That movie's got balls. And it was a rare thing. It was the first time I'd seen a Hollywood film, with the exception of Milius's stuff, that wasn't timid. It was really strong stuff. It had strong and ambiguous characters. There wasn't a good guy and a bad guy. Those guys are both good and both bad. It's all gray stuff.

I like that. There's a complication to it that appeals to me a great deal. Also, I'd never done a medieval thing.

What aspects of your career or certain films moments have impacted you most?

They're all representations of where I was at the time I wrote them. It's very difficult for me to separate them from what's going on in my life when I write. What I'm saying is that I try to plug into my film scores the emotions that are going on in my life at the time.

A lot of the stuff in *Lassie* and in *Jungle Book* is from experiences with my own children. What is it that they would find interesting about the piece of music that I would write for the particular scene? Would it be charming, would it be enchanting, would it be magical for them?

Lonesome Dove **and** *Lassie* **are just gorgeous, openly expressive scores.**

Lonesome Dove was a joy to write. They are two films that were absolutely easy. They were almost effortless to write.

What is the happiest thing about pursuing a career as a film composer?

There are many positive things. You get to explore yourself when you're given an assignment. It's a challenge, and you have to wrestle with yourself and your insecurities and your fears. It gives you the opportunity to overcome them in the production of something. That's a very personal thing.

The other great thing about being a film composer is that you get to work with some of the most wonderful musicians in the world. I don't think if I'd have gone through the concert route that I would ever have been able to work with the London Symphony Orchestra or the London Philharmonic or the Beijing Symphony.

It gives you a kind of musical legitimacy because it's a commercial medium. You have access to the finest studios. There's usually the money to finance that sort of thing. It's work that has been accomplished. It's real stuff. It doesn't just exist in my head or on a piece of paper. It's produced and it's out there. That's pretty amazing to me. Something that I've written has been heard by so many people! And people respond to it. It has a vision that can be tangible to people versus a classical piece that doesn't have a vision with it.

Are there other places you want to take your music to?

Yes, I'm very interested in doing that. But I'm certainly not going to refuse films that I'm attracted to. What I've done is I've sort of cut back on going after the typical Hollywood film, whatever that is. It's a mentality more than it is a specific thing. I'm not really interested in working with people just because they've got something they think is going to make a fortune, which is not a bad thing for some people who want to do it, but it doesn't attract me particularly. I draw on the material. If the material interests me, and it provides the opportunity for me to expand my musical vocabulary and my dramatic vocabulary, then I'm very interested.

From what I've seen, because I think I've scored seventy pictures, or something like that, there's a lot of repeating. These days we tend to make the same film over and over and over again. I'm constantly looking for the new film that provides me with the opportunity to do new things and, yes, I'm expanding my musical interests. I've never written for the concert stage before. I'm kind of interested in doing that, working with various ethnic instruments in conjunction with the orchestra.

I think the state of the orchestra in the United States is in pretty bad shape. I was recently looking at a list of the concerts offered by the Seattle Symphony. It was boring stuff for the most part. They need some new material—a little combination of commercial Hollywood music and with the traditional classical music, some kind of a synthesis of those two things. I'm not going to save the orchestra single-handedly, but I think some new material wouldn't hurt it.

I have seen credits for the animated film *Paul Bunyon*. What is the story with this project?

I am certainly going to be involved in writing the thematic material for it. I don't think I am actually going to be scoring it myself, just because with animation it's a huge commitment of time and energy, and I'm frankly not sure if I want to be involved with a film for that long. My longest involvement on a film was *Conan*. I spent twelve months on it. *Starship Troopers* was the second longest. I spent nine months. I tend to like long involvements, but an animated film can go into two years sometimes, and I never write two films at once. I don't have that kind of multi-track mind where I can multi-task. I like to stay in the world that I am writing for. To stay in an animated movie for two years might be a little more than I am willing to do.

Jocelyn Pook

Jocelyn Pook's music is mesmerizing and evocative. It speaks with a cosmopolitan voice as it weaves musical soundworlds of the past with ethnic and ambient vibrations of the present. It is also a uniquely stylized voice that beautifully interacts with and breathes life into the films in which it has been used, and those films become hard to imagine without her music.

One of Pook's most notable scores was written for Stanley Kubrick's last film, *Eyes Wide Shut* (1999). This project perfectly wed her haunting music, which also provided the film's heartbeat, to the skewed reality of Kubrick's picture, which some filmgoers found unsettling in its direct and intense eroticism. Another particularly interesting Pook score is the one she wrote for director Michael Radford's *William Shakespeare's The Merchant of Venice* (2004). Here, her music hearkens back to the Renaissance era of the play's origin.

Pook also maintains an active musical life outside of her film scoring, frequently collaborating with dancers and a variety of popular and not-so-popular musical artists.

Where did you grow up, and at what point did music become an integral part of your life?

I was born in Birmingham and grew up in London. Soon after I was born, my parents separated and I came to London with my mother, brother, and sister. My father was a violinist, but I didn't know him very well in my childhood, and he died when I was thirteen. So I had that in my background—the fact that my father was a violinist. My sister and my brother played the piano and another instrument each, and I started playing piano when I was five or six and I later learned violin at school when I was nine. So I kind of grew up in a musical family.

When you were young, did you have aspirations of taking your music to the big screen?

No. I did actually do some composition when I was a child, but I didn't consider myself the kind of person who would be a composer. When I went to music college, the Guildhall School of Music and Drama, in London, I just studied as a performer. I took viola as my main instrument. I didn't study composition. It just didn't occur to me to go on that path at that time. It all happened later. Sometime after I left college, I ended up in a very interesting theater project as a performer, and got quite bitten by that world. It was sort of an experimental world—the visual/experimental kind of theater. I was exposed to a whole new cultural world and saw other ways of composing at this time. I was learning through experience.

Prior to your own work in movies, did you have much of an interest in, or understanding of, the combination of music and movies?

I would say that I was affected by music in other mediums, such as the music of Philip Glass, Michael Nyman, and Gavin Bryars. Particularly the minimalist style or, basically, the New Music being done in the eighties. I wouldn't say I had my sights set on film music. It was just an amazing thing, starting to compose my own pieces, and many of those were for theater and dance.

Would you talk about your work with Peter Gabriel?

I met him as a player originally. He used to have these Real World recording weeks in the summer where he would invite musicians from all over the world down to his studio. We would all be contributing on pieces together, but there were really unusual combinations of people and instruments. It was really an amazing experience to be a part of that. Then I worked with him later as an arranger on one of his albums along with another release, *OVO*, in 2000.

How did you become involved in Stanley Kubrick's *Eyes Wide Shut*? What were your first thoughts about this film?

It was one of those chance happenings. He heard my music because a choreographer who was working on the film had my album and was playing it in a rehearsal. Stanley thought that the piece she was playing was really appropriate, so he rung me up. Actually, first of all, he sent a car over so I could give him some more music, and then the next day, the car came back for me. It was quite an incredible thing. By then, I had done quite a lot of theater and dance and had started to do some TV drama also. But I hadn't done a feature film before.

I was really thrown in at the deep end. But, to begin with, he had only hired me to do the masked-ball scene. So that's what I started working on. I didn't know anything about the film apart from that scene, but because it was a self-contained part of the film, I could work like that. It was much later on when I got called back to do the rest of the score for the film.

What was tricky at first was that they didn't want me to see the film. They just wanted me to work on bits that needed music in isolation. It was really quite an interesting exercise because I realized there was absolutely no way I could do that without knowing how loaded certain things might be. You just didn't know how to pitch the music. Finally, they relented and let me see the film. I have to say that it was really enjoyable working with Stanley on that film. Obviously, I was a bit daunted at first, but he was very warm and encouraging.

What was their reason for having you score parts of the film without seeing the whole film?

Well, because they were nervous about the film getting into the wrong hands. There was a lot of interest in that film before it came out. Stanley understandably didn't want it to be seen until it was ready to be seen.

Eyes Wide Shut **is an intense and bizarre story that almost works as an opera from the orgy scene to the masked ball. Your music becomes the foreground of these scenes. What were your inspirations when starting these scenes of the movie?**

I was told about the basic situation, the narrative of the scene, and the atmosphere. They hadn't shot it when I started working on it. I saw pictures of the masks and descriptions that gave me a good idea of the atmosphere. I did a lot of sketches. I played around with quite a few different approaches, particularly for the orgy scene. At that time, I think the original orgy scene was going to be a bit more erotic rather than nightmarish. What we ended up working with was based on something I had done before. I remember the brief for the orgy scene was "sexy music." That's incredibly vague, whereas for the masked-ball scene, there was much more to go on. He was quite keen on the voice idea and the kind of ritualistic idea.

I have huge admiration for Stanley. I like the fact that he would take such a risk. I think that's very admirable and really unusual. I didn't even have an agent, and he couldn't care less. He had complete belief in me, actually, and knew exactly what he wanted. It was incredibly good for my confidence.

Before we talk about your next film, I want to discuss the unique palette of color that you use in your music. How did you discover this?

I absorb a lot from many places. My background started in classical music, and later I was influenced by the minimalist movement combined with listening to artists like Laurie Anderson and Brian Eno. People mention a religious tone, and this may partly be the influence of medieval and early church music, which I love, coming through. Many other things, like playing in the Eastern European band 3 Mustaphas 3 and hearing Holger Czukay's "Persian Love Song," have had a huge influence, too. So I guess my music is a melting pot of many interests.

Michael Radford's *The Merchant of Venice* is richly filled with a Renaissance flavor but intertwined with a modern ethnic voice. Did you find yourself researching a lot of this music, or did the film itself create the setting and atmosphere for you?

I knew a bit about early music, but obviously there was much more to learn. I did start off by doing some research and listening to lots of music from that period and trying to get to know the instruments. What was interesting was learning all the instruments from the period and their qualities. Early on in that film, I had to work on the scenes that were being shot with musicians. Because of that, I had to decide what instruments they would be playing. I had grand ideas with big ensembles, but the budget was restrictive. Nevertheless, the film was just a gift. The picture was just so visually rich and atmospheric. There was just so much to respond to. It was also incredible to have such amazing musicians bringing the music alive.

I found it interesting that you used the Edgar Allen Poe poem "Bridal Ballad." Why not use something Shakespearean?

Well, I looked at a lot of Shakespearean ideas, but I like the dark atmosphere of the Edgar Allen Poe. I know it was a strange choice. Setting the poem came so easily, and it just felt like the right thing. Sometimes you work with a text and it just doesn't flow very easily. It is one of those hit-or-miss things. The rest of the text I set for the film was from the period, though. I also felt that it was allowable to use the Poe setting for the end credits of the picture; had it been for the middle, I wouldn't have done so.

Talk about how you begin what ends up being a fully orchestrated piece.

Most of the time I sit at the piano and discover what the feeling is I'm trying to achieve. It's a mixture of that and playing ideas that come up on the piano. Usually that's how I start.

Do you have instruments and colors in mind while you compose, or are they layered on after a basic map is drawn out?

I start with a small idea. It may be a melody, a group of chords, or even just a drone. It is always something very simple and small like that. I also work quite a bit on the computer these days, and I can bring up sounds that aren't too dissimilar from some of the live sounds I need. I often try things out this way.

Rachel Portman

Rachel Portman is one of the very few women film composers to have found great career success in the movie industry. She is also the first female composer to have received a Best Music Oscar, which she won for *Emma* (1996).

Portman's music can tug at the filmgoer's heartstrings while carefully distilling a film's emotional essence. From her introspective score for *Ethan Frome* (1993) to her soul-felt music for *Great Moments in Aviation* (1993) to her inspiring score to Robert Redford's *The Legend of Bagger Vance* (2000), Portman's music always enriches a movie's emotional depth as it gently pulls in listeners as if it intends to consume them in a great yet lovely sea swell.

Used People **launched your career in the States. Was writing for film your goal in composition?**

I had done theatrical films in England before then, but I hadn't done an American feature. You sort of have to break slowly into these things before people trust you to let you work on their film.

Writing music for films is what I love to do really. I love music that tells stories. I love finding colors and dramatizing and energizing a film. A film sometimes needs energizing in the score. Writing music for movies is a wonderful job.

You are one of the very few female composers to attain huge success in film music. Did your career choice pose any specific challenges for you, and, if so, what kept you motivated to continue forward?

I've never had any problems. I can barely think of any moments when I've been treated differently. I was lucky because the schools and the university I went to gave me a lot of experience for coping in a man's world. I did my A-levels, which in England means from the age of fifteen to seventeen, at a school where there were hardly any girls. This school, which was extremely good academically, was experimenting with allowing in a few girls, like two in each section of about seventy other children. So I never felt myself any different in a way. The same thing happened when I went to university. I went to an all-male college, where there were very few girls. People were always asking, "How are the girls doing?" So you had to work very hard to compete.

I never batted an eyelash about being female. I never felt self-conscious. I've always thought of myself as a composer, not as a female composer. I think if you project that, people tend not see otherwise.

Why do you think that our culture segregates men and women in career fields like film directing and film music?

There aren't as many women in most areas of film. It's strange. It seems to be changing slower than I thought. I mean it's definitely a historical thing in terms of women. You read in the paper every day that women aren't as big earners as men in the city. They don't take the top jobs and all of those kinds of things. Slowly, women are infiltrating into areas in film. There are a lot of women film editors. Also, historically in classical music there are hardly any women either. It's strange.

Your classical approach to scoring films is a breath of fresh air in this world of technology. You have done a couple scores that have used synth textures, but obviously you are more sought-after for your orchestral style? Is this your choice?

The world of technology, as you put it, is a world that just doesn't really speak to me creatively. I'm interested in live music and acoustic instruments. To me, they live and breathe and bring life to the music in a score. How you can make an "instrument" made up of potentially eighty or ninety players work as one thing is a constant source of fascination for me. You can never exhaust the different colors that you can conjure up with orchestration. That's the music that I write. That is my voice and I don't mind if I'm not considered for some things because of that, because I would be considered for others that would interest me more.

Orchestra is your voice, with which you seem to speak so effortlessly. When you sit at the piano, composing, do you hear the instrumentation in your head or is it part of the discovery process as you fit the music to the film?

I do hear the instrumentation, although I don't hear it in its entirety. Often the instrumentation sort of comes together as I'm writing, and then I always leave the orchestration until later. Orchestration is such a detailed thing. It's so tricky. Even though I've probably got a good idea in my head, I don't focus specifically on that until the writing's in place.

You tend to favor clarinets and flutes and a couple of other instruments.

They mean different things emotionally to me. Depending on the melodic line they're playing, the voice of a clarinet is more appropriate than the voice of a soprano saxophone or an oboe or a flute or a string section or just violas.

Which composers influenced or inspired you as you found your own voice?

Ravel and Bach, who is probably my all-time favorite companion in music. I don't know why. I just find that his music gives me huge sense of self and serenity that I sometimes need. And it can make you feel centered again, if you are rushing around or stressed. So he's the person I come back to. I think I was slowly influenced by Ravel as I was growing up, and Debussy to a certain extent. But in terms of film composition, I've never formally studied film music or film composers. I don't tend to buy scores.

You began by orchestrating your own music. At what point did you realize that you needed a second hand, and how difficult was it to share some of the responsibility?

It's very difficult to share. I feel like it's still my orchestration, though. I don't feel like it's anybody else's voice in there. I still write out a very comprehensive map of the orchestrations with the orchestrator I work with. And I've worked with the same wonderful orchestrator, Jeff Atmajian, for many years now. He completely knows my shorthand, which enables me to put it down very quickly.

It was interesting to write the opera because I orchestrated every single note of that again, and it was wonderful to do it. There's something very caring and loving about the orchestration. It takes a lot of time because, for each instrument, you have to put in the expression, all the crescendos and decrescendos and the manner in which they're going to play. Whereas when I work with Jeff, if I've specified that a melody is going to be on the oboe, for example, I don't need to write those things out because I know that Jeff can tell from the way I've played it on the piano. He listens very carefully. He'll be able to give them the expression and the dynamics that I didn't have time to do. He'll have a piano sketch of it too, and he'll have the film. He can tell the expression that I want. He can put that in.

In general, what would a composer look for in an orchestrator?

It depends what you're looking for. I want somebody who is meticulous, who doesn't make mistakes. I don't want somebody to change anything. I've worked with orchestrators who want to put their own brushstrokes on something, and that's a disaster for me, because I want somebody to follow exactly what I would have done myself. I sound like a monster saying that, but what I mean is otherwise. I know there are other composers out there who are perhaps not so controlling or perhaps aren't so sure of their own orchestrations. Maybe they're not sure how to write for the orchestra what they intend to convey. In which case, they would rely more heavily on an orchestrator.

With *Emma* you became the first Oscar-winning female composer. What was it like for you personally to receive this recognition?

It was a huge shock and really good fun to get to go to all the parties. It was all I could dream, really. It's not something I ever think about as the badge of pride, and I don't think it means that you did the best scoring either. But it does endorse, most definitely. It is something that makes people think, "Well, she must be all right!" if they haven't heard of me.

You worked with Lasse Hallström on *The Cider House Rules* and *Chocolat* and received two more Oscar nominations. What memories do you have of these two scores and working with Lasse?

Working on those films were very good experiences for me. I really enjoyed the challenges. I really liked working with Lasse. It's not easy to read his mind. It's not easy to understand what he's after, but I think his films are very clear in what he means. It's part of my job to determine what people are really looking for. And if that means searching for a while, that's fine.

I loved *The Cider House Rules*. It's a special film and I loved working on it. It was a long journey because we wrote quite a lot of it and then went back and worked on themes again. A lot of it stayed and I wrote a whole lot more. It was a big commitment.

The fact that I'd worked on *The Cider House Rules* made working on *Chocolat* much easier. I had three and a half weeks for *Chocolat*. It was just about to come out and I was doing a re-score on it. There was hardly any time. That music just popped into my head, though, and it spoke so clearly, and it was so much fun to do as well. To me, it isn't as great a film as *The Cider House Rules*, but Lasse said to me when he made *Chocolat*, "This film is like a soufflé.

It needs to rise. A good soufflé needs to be extremely delicious but very light." I thought that was a wonderful thing to say.

One of your scores that has impacted me dearly is _The Legend of Bagger Vance_. Robert Redford's films seem to have an aura about them in all aspects. The music he gets from different composers also has this magic. What were your experiences working with Robert Redford? How large of a role did he play in your music?

I really adored working with him. He is a fascinating man and a great storyteller and a very seriously good human being. He spent a long time talking to me about that film and about golf and about letting go of one's great desire to do something really well and how you reach to a different place. What was wonderful about him was that he was always available to talk to me about any scene or any moment or what was happening in the main characters' minds. He was terribly eloquent about it, which gave me a lot of food and a lot of material to work from. The other really good thing about Redford: He talked to me about what he wanted in words and adjectives that described what he was feeling, which is the best way for a composer to work.

As opposed to a temp score?

As opposed to, "Oh, I love the cello!" which is a nondescript killer. He asked me to interpret musically what he felt emotionally, which was great.

The Human Stain has to be one of your most emotionally power-ful and captivating pieces. When writing for such heavy emotions, or any emotions for that matter, do you find the sound within your-self, or do you rely strictly on what is on the screen?

The Human Stain was a strange kind of experience. I'd talked to Robert Benton a bit about the film, but we hadn't really discussed the music when I said to him that I thought it would be really good if the music just had its own abstract voice that didn't really bear any relation to the film. The music would sort of be in its own place in the movie.

I watched that opening with the car driving and I just wrote this piece. There was no reason for it. I mean, I wasn't trying to do anything specific. We hadn't talked about it. I played it to him and he said, "That's it. That's what I want." Then that became the thread that went right through the whole film. It's weird because it just sort of popped into my head, utterly unconnected to the film. To me, it isn't in a traditional dramatic sense. It's sort of this dreamlike trance.

Do you think it's based on your personal emotions?

I don't know. It's sad, but it's not trying to be too sad or too emotional. It's full of pain. It's also slightly secretive and hidden. It also had this prepared piano in there. It's got this broken thing going through it very subtly, like these slightly broken notes, which you can just hear sometimes, that just stop it from being perfect. The other thing that was great was that I used a lot of strings in it, a lot more than I normally would, so it feels like waves. It's heavy and hovering. The weight of strings is enormous. It's like a big swell in the sea that's fairly calm. It goes up, then it comes down. It recedes and then comes up again. The strings play very quietly. Nobody plays loudly in that score.

It's amazing that you use this analogy, because I recognized this. I listen to it when I am drawing or painting. It's almost a tool that instills a picture or an emotion of the ebb and flow of the tides.

Yes, it's just like that. That's what I wanted to do with it. That is what I mean about orchestration being fun. The written idea for *The Human Stain* is incredibly simple, but the execution of it—the way it's played—is very living and breathing. It has its own life. If you played that with everybody wearing headphones and playing it to a click, it would kill it.

Your latest score, *The Manchurian Candidate* (the 2004 remake of the 1962 film), is a leap into a new realm for your music. Director Jonathan Demme, no stranger to the ambient and minimalist approach to film music, pulls out a different sound from you, versus most of your other work, which is melodic and constantly moving. Was this score challenging for you?

Beloved [directed by Jonathan Demme] was probably the most fulfilling experience I've had working on a film. He said that he didn't want me to use any traditional instruments at all and that he wanted me to look to Africa. So I researched a lot and I found all these players and put together this score with this weirdest, oddest group of handmade and African instruments and a lot of singing. It really freed me up from writing for orchestra. It was very good for me to do that. It was also a very emotional score for me, and I love that. Jonathan pushed me into other areas. I worked on that film for nearly a year. That's a long time these days.

On *Manchurian Candidate* it was a totally different thing. It was harder to find the voice, much harder. Jonathan is always looking for something very specific. It's, again, my job to find that. A film like *Manchurian Candidate* could be scored a hundred different ways. It's a thriller. The music could either roll up its sleeves and get really busy, making you feel really frightened, or it could stand back and just be a layer that keeps you sort of uneasy the whole way through, but also sort of binds the piece together. That film was a very complex, complicated journey and a really wonderful experience, too. I haven't done many thrillers, so it was fascinating for me to do it. I really enjoyed the challenge. I love doing new things. I love going into areas where I haven't been before. That makes me very keen to work on new projects. If, for example, I were constantly writing romantic comedies, I'd be feeling very sad by now.

Which would happen if you were typecast.

Well, after I did *Benny & Joon*, every quirky romantic comedy seemed to come my way. I'm very glad I don't work in that genre only anymore.

You have composed an opera. Can you tell me about this and if there will be a CD release?

Yes, it's called *The Little Prince*. It's a full-blown opera. It premiered at the Houston Grand Opera [in 2003]. It's going to New York City and Boston next year. Sony is putting out a CD of it. It's being filmed by WNET for the BBC, which is great because operas normally do not get filmed. I think it should be available in the shops in the next few months certainly.

It's very close to the book. It's a very emotional and very moving story. I wanted to write an opera that you could take a child to but also enjoy as an adult, because there are very few of those. The opera has a boy in the lead role, and it also has a children's chorus in it. It has adults in it, too. It's a really fun thing to perform, because the grownups get a huge amount out of working with children, and the children have an amazing experience of working in an opera. It's great.

In music or in life as a whole, what has been your greatest achievement?

It's either having three children or, I should think, the opera, just because it's such a huge piece. It's like writing a book. I think *Beloved* would be my greatest film-music achievement in my mind. That or *The Human Stain*. I'm not sure.

When we think of modern animation music, the first composers who comes to mind might be John Powell and Harry Gregson-Williams, who collaborated on *Antz* (1998), *Chicken Run* (2000), and *Shrek* (2001), helping to create a new era of animated adventure.

Very early in his career, Powell seemed to be following in the footsteps of Hans Zimmer, for whom he worked at Media Ventures, but since then, Powell has created a fresh new cinema sound that is all his own. His entertaining and spellbinding music is intense and energetic and reflects certain interests he maintains in ethnic music and the latest electronic-music technologies.

With his scores for the intimate *I Am Sam* (2001), the mysterious *Bourne Identity* (2002), and the suspenseful *Paycheck* (2003), Powell built a unique palette of complex textures that at any given moment may be drivingly rhythmic, eerily ambient, or traditionally melodic.

Where did you get your start in the film industry?

It's interesting because, in the fifties and sixties, my father was a tuba player with The Royal Philharmonic Orchestra, in which he actually performed a lot of film scores. I remember at about age three being taken along to the recording of Ron Goodwin's score for *Battle of Britain*. This influence led me to desire playing the violin as a child, but I remember my father saying, "Don't be a player, be a composer. There's a lot more money in it." I was very insulted by that at the time. I assumed he meant that I wasn't going to make it as a violinist, which he was absolutely right about, of course. I studied violin, viola, some percussion, as well as played guitar and keyboards in bands anyway. I went to Trinity College of Music and studied composition for four years, and then electronic music and percussion. Later, after unsuccessfully producing a band, I got into doing jingles—advertising music—for a while until I became bored with it. Long story short, I had met Hans Zimmer in the midst of all this, which later brought me to L.A.

With all this influence of composition for moving images, did you see yourself here today at an early age? Was this a dream you set out to accomplish?

I think it was a lifelong dream, but I didn't realize it until I was actually doing it. Thinking back to the time when I saw Elmer Bernstein's *The Magnificent Seven* and *The Great Escape*, I remember thinking that the way the music supported these images was incredible. It made everything so exciting as a combined art form, which profoundly affected me at an early age. So I think even though it wasn't in the front of my mind until I went to music college, I had this feeling that I would love to be doing films.

Here you are with a strong music background, writing music for commercials. How did this take you to L.A. and working with Hans?

I had known Hans for a while, working at the same company together, writing jingles. At that time, what was great fun was trying to write pieces that excited him. Hans is really interested in people with a sound that differs from his, although a lot of stuff that comes out of Media Ventures fits into his style, but it's for commercial reasons. Basically, I just tried to write pieces that got him going somewhere.

I was at Media Ventures for only about two and a half years. At a certain point I wasn't seeing my wife at all. I was in a room with no windows, just working all the time. It got to be too much. That's why I worked at home for a while, even when I was associated with Media Ventures.

Many listeners have enjoyed your collaborations with Harry Gregson-Williams. Was this an enjoyable experience for you, and what did you gain from it in your own work?

I love Harry. I think he's an incredible composer and an amazing human being, but he's very different from me. What was interesting and wonderful and maddening about working with Harry was that we are so different. It was very mind-broadening to see how some-body else who comes from a quite similar background approaches things from such a different angle. It's a very difficult experience writing a film score with somebody else.

I think *Antz* was very much a revelation for the both of us. We would sit down and write the themes together and then divide up the work on a cue-by-cue basis. If one of us wrote a cue that was com-pletely hated by all the filmmakers, the other person would try it. This works so well because there is nothing worse than doing a cue that doesn't work and having to completely revise your first impres-sion that you felt worked best for the scene. To have somebody else step in and go, "Okay, I'll have a go at it now," is great. By *Chicken Run* we became a bit more of a well-oiled machine. *Shrek*, however, was a tricky film because there were so many songs in it that the score played a much lesser role than it had in the other two films. Where do we fit in in the greater scheme of things when they have six or seven songs?

All three films were different, educational, and very trying at times just because music is a very difficult thing to talk about and, you know, you're talking about music with somebody else who has a very individual style. There were a lot of negotiations and some struggles to try and work out how we were going to combine our efforts the best. It's not an easy thing, but it was very rewarding.

You have so many approaches to your scoring, but your style always seems to be somewhat "tribal"-influenced with your beats and sounds, as in, for example, *Endurance*. Where do you find your sources of inspiration?

I have always loved world music, but I really got into it when I was in Trinity College of Music. They had a big library of records at that time. I remember sitting in the record library, which was right down in the deepest bowels of the basement, going through these crazy records that had probably been donated. Learning these other rhythms of the world was fascinating. Eventually I'd just go and search out $500 worth of CDs a week. I had about 5,000 CDs, and I'd try and listen to them as much as I could.

What led you to your instrumentation for *I Am Sam*?

I felt that it had to be very delicate and small, so I bought some ukuleles and did a demo with them as well as guitars and a bit of piano, keeping it simple. The players made a big influence on that score, especially Heitor Pereira, George Doering—each of whom is as good a guitarist as there has ever been, and each of whom is very different in style. I found that I could write some really simple things that these two guys could make come alive.

It's certainly a unique sound that worked very well.

If it had just been strings, it would have been another cliché.

You experiment with sounds. In *Forces of Nature*, for example, you use the sounds of a telephone dialing and all sorts of unique beats. How did this came about in your music?

Ultimately, I probably am a little bit embarrassed by those cues now. I probably would have done them differently today. It was just a way of trying again not be cliché, which maybe it wasn't, but it was definitely too obvious.

Looking at Jerry Bruckheimer's and John Woo's productions, for example, how much are composers who have been associated with Hans Zimmer expected to work in his voice? Are these cases where Zimmer, if couldn't be involved with a project, would present it to you or whomever with guidelines?

It's not Hans. Using the same [sampled] sound library has a lot to do with it. But it's mainly commerce.

In *Face/Off*, I tried to put in enough of my own voice that I didn't just sound like Hans, but it's an 80-million-dollar film, and the first film I'd ever done. I think I would have been stupid to sound like Jerry Goldsmith or John Williams or anybody else really. Clearly, they wanted Hans—they wanted his kind of approach, so I gave it to them. I tried to give them enough of that so I could also experiment a bit with my own voice. So it's kind of a combo, and I'm sure some people think that it sounds just like Hans. A bit of it had to, because that's what was going to work. In other bits, hopefully, it feels a little bit more personal to me.

I posed these same questions to another composer who was pretty offended by them.

Some are touchier about it than I am about it. But, yeah, there's an approach to cues that I think came around with some of the composers who were connected with Media Ventures, for which Hans definitely led the way. I think some of it works extremely well and some of it is beginning to get very old. Hans has been doing scores recently that don't sound anything like his earlier work. People don't realize how little he likes everyone working in that style. But, at the same time, it's a business.

You've got all of the same sounds that Hans has been using for the last ten years. The trick is to find a better alternative, but when you're early in your career and you're in the midst of trying to keep your best chance going, you're not necessarily going to have the time or the will to experiment. So that's why the younger composers will go with what's kind of an accepted sound.

But you pick up training you can't get anywhere else. You get these experiences, and things rub off from people that you normally wouldn't get to meet. So there are all these dynamics that are very difficult to explain. It's a commercial business and yet it is also a great artistic experience.

You have a truly creative and authentic voice.

Well, I think this is just me trying to pursue the kind of music I like. Hans is definitely embedded in there in an inspirational sense. The first time I saw *Driving Miss Daisy*, I thought, "This was a really unusual score that was really well done, really cool." I thought, "Man, this guy's got balls!"

In the end, though, I'm very confused. Stylistically, I love lots of stuff. It all goes in and mangles up and, hopefully, comes out in some interesting way. I've always believed that style is the mistakes you make trying to steal other people's ideas. You start sounding original when you let yourself make these mistakes that are your own oddities. So I just try to make music that helps to tell stories, and I just love a variety of music styles. I would describe myself as a "music slut."

David Raksin

I had the golden opportunity to sit down and talk with legendary composer and pioneering film-music teacher David Raksin shortly before his death in 2004. He immediately impressed me as a sweet, warm, and inviting man. Our time together was extremely limited; however, I will always cherish my memories of meeting with this film-music giant.

Although he scored more than 100 films and numerous television shows, Raksin is most readily remembered as the composer of the haunting theme for the classic film _Laura_ (1944), a theme that, with the addition of lyrics by Johnny Mercer, quickly became a jazz and pop standard. Among other classic films that he scored are _Forever Amber_ (1947), _The Secret Life of Walter Mitty_ (1947), _Force of Evil_ (1948), _The Bad and the Beautiful_ (1952), _The Big Combo_ (1955), _Two Weeks in Another Town_ (1962), and the television series _Wagon Train_ (1957) and _Ben Casey_ (1961).

As a professor of music at USC, Raksin pioneered the teaching of film-scoring as a discipline unto itself and greatly influenced generations of film composers who studied with him.

When you were young, film music was just coming to life. What influenced you to become a film composer?

Well, many things, including the fact that my father conducted for silent films. On Saturdays, I'd sit in the pit next to him while he conducted. It was a marvelous experience. It was a unique way of getting some real understanding of the power of music joined to film. People tell me that as a boy I spoke of writing music for films. Eventually, when the time came, I got my wish.

Can you describe how your early career as a film composer unfolded? How did you get started, basically?

I was working in New York when I got a call to come out to California, where I went to work with Alfred Newman. Actually, my boss was Charlie Chaplin, who was working on the music for *Modern Times*. He didn't know how to notate music, how to write it down, and he didn't know how to develop ideas—but he did have ideas—and my job was to work with him.

Well, I didn't seem to have the same idea of what my position was as he did in the beginning, so he fired me after about a week and a half. Al Newman got a look at the sketches I was making of Charlie's tunes, and he said to Charlie, "Are you crazy!? I can't let this guy go. You should see what he's doing with the little melodies and things like that." They asked me if I would come back. I said I only would if I could have an understanding with Charlie. So I had a meeting with Charlie, just the two of us. And I explained to him that I did not see myself as a stooge or anything like that. He listened to me very carefully and said, "Fine, let's go." So that began about four and a half months of very intensive work on the score. That's how I got my start. A better start than that? There is no such thing.

Let's jump right to your memorable and beautiful score to *Laura*.

When I went to work on *Laura*, I was living on a farm and my studio—a special room with a piano and stuff like that—was in a barn. In those days, to divert my mind from intense concentration on a score to the point where it was all-cerebral, I used to put a book of poems or a photograph or something like that on the piano. In this case, I put a letter that I had received on the piano. It was from my wife, who was then living in New York, working in a show. I was reading this thing and playing when, all of a sudden, I started off on this melody that later turned out to be "Laura." It's as simple as that.

At the time, how was this music received?

Judging from what I remember of those days, I think it was probably ahead of it's time, a little bit different.

How was your rapport with the directors or filmmakers?

Oh, it was almost always very good. But some of them didn't understand that I didn't see myself as an extension of their own thinking. I had a mind of my own and I had a talent of my own, and I thought that my job was to make that available to them in the best way possible. That is what I endeavored to do. Sometimes we differed, but more often than not, we did not.

Do today's film composers differ much from film composers of the past?

I think the best composers always do the same thing: They go look at the picture and they make up their minds what they need to do, and then they try to do that. We tried to do that.

How do today's films differ from those of the past?

With some exceptions, I think that films today don't really try to delve deeply into things.

And today's film music?

We worried a lot about the innards of the music and how they related to the story and how they brought out various things in the story. I think people still try to do that.

Today, people make a big deal of how different it is. I guess it is, but I don't see it as an awful lot different. I think there's a less probing sensitivity in the scores today. Part of that is because of the people who commission the scores and can pass on whether or not they work for their pictures.

You've had the privilege of knowing some of the other great establishers of the art of film music, such as Max Steiner and Alfred Newman. How were your relationships with these composers?

I worked with Al Newman a lot. Steiner wanted me to work with him, but I decided I didn't want to do that because I figured I'd get buried in that and wind up with a career full of music by some other guy. But I was very friendly with both of them. I knew Max very well, and I like him. I knew Al very well. We were very good friends, and he conducted a lot of my earlier scores.

We all love a good story, and you must have a thousand of amusing Hollywood tales. Would you care to share one?

I once was asked to come into a picture, quite a good film, by some friends of mine who were the producers. The director of this film was a talented guy, but he was one of those New York guys who had to make sure that you knew that you weren't as good as you should be, in case you're at risk of that. He said, "I don't want one of those Hollywood scores. I'd like something more modern, like *Wozzeck*." [Alban Berg's popular and influential 1922 opera] I said to myself, "My God, he didn't say *Wozzeck*!? I'm in heaven!" So I said to him, "Why don't you and your wife come out to my house? We'll have dinner and we can talk away from the studio." So he and his wife come out there—I had a farm in Northridge at the time. The ladies are off talking somewhere and he and I are standing in the living room. There's some music playing on the phonograph and he and I are talking when he suddenly turns to me and asks, "What's that crap you've got on the phonograph?" I said, "That's *Wozzeck*!"

What prompted you stop composing for films?

I didn't really stop. The work just sort of flew away. After a while, I wasn't working very much. I realized that my standing in the industry was not as great as it was in the past, because there were younger guys coming up, and that suited me just fine.

Graeme Revell

As do most great film composers, Graeme Revell possesses an identifiable voice that runs through the many successful scores he has written for every imaginable genre of film. From the gothic, supernatural
The Crow (1996) to the Latin-flavored *Out of Time* (2003), Graeme
combines multi-cultural influences with electronics and sultry, often
dark, orchestrations. And many of his scores have a haunting and
even glassy edge to them, as evidenced by his music for the mysterious *The Negotiator* (1998) and the eerie thriller *The Hand That Rocks
The Cradle* (1992).

**What did films and film music mean to you when you were grow-
ing up?**

I didn't really take much notice, except I was a very big fan of musicals as a kid. In New Zealand, seeing films all the time was not a big
part of the culture. It's much more of an outdoors lifestyle there. I
probably only saw one or two movies per year until I was about
eighteen. My favorite musicals were *Oliver*, *The Sound of Music*, and
West Side Story. Then, I suppose, I started to notice the Maurice
Jarre scores. I got an interest that way. The other person whose
music I noticed very much early on was Bernard Herrmann. As a

young adult, I became more of a film fan. I suppose I was a foreign-film guy initially—Tarkovsky, Buñuel, Godard, Wenders, Roeg, and Kubrick, among others.

Film music came to you in a rather unusual way. How did your career begin?

For years, I had been working as a fringe electronic musician/performance artist in my group SPK. I'd expressed a number of times in interviews that I would really like to be involved in film, but I didn't receive any offers, so I decided to write an album in 1982, which initially was called *Music for Impossible Film*. I eventually retitled it to *Songs of Byzantine Flowers*. It took about another five years before the opportunity to write for film came along.

I was sitting in my publisher's office when George Miller called up wanting a little piece of rap music or hip-hop music for *Dead Calm*. I overheard this and said that I could do that. They said, "Okay, how long will take?" I said, "About five minutes." It actually took an hour, but they liked it and it worked really well. They were having trouble with their composer, so they asked me, "What else can you do?" My publisher gave them a record of mine, and they really liked it and that's how it came about. I was extremely lucky.

I would say that your sound is tribal and rhythmic and dramatic. It also has an edge of darkness mixed into it, giving it mystery. What are your inspirations for your music?

I have a great passion for all kinds of music that other people wouldn't think go together. It's fun, and I love finding new types of music from around the world that I haven't encountered. I found early on that tribal and techno rhythms drive action scenes in a very visceral way, and I've layered textural elements on top to punctuate important moments and cuts. When I began film-scoring, the attention to detail in the editing by composers was at a much lower level. With modern scoring techniques and frame-accuracy through computer-control of sequencing, so many more moments can become exciting.

How did your work lead you to the U.S.?

After *Dead Calm*, the man who was to become my agent and friend, Richard Kraft, called. He had heard my score and started calling every person with my last name he could find in the Southern Hemisphere. I think I was his sixth or seventh call. It was the middle of the night in Australia, so I thought it was some friend in America just playing a prank, you know? But he was for real. I came to the States and haven't had a day off since. Pretty cool. I really had a lot of great fortune getting into this industry.

Film music is a tricky art form. What sort of skills does it require, and how did you know it was meant for you?

From my point of view, I suppose, I'm very eclectic. I wouldn't have been a very successful rock musician even if I tried to be because my attention span for particular kinds of music is very limited. In other words, I like to change a lot. So film music is the ideal art form for me because from one six- to eight-week period to the next I can be scoring anything. I could be scoring horror music with an electronic component or some tribalism or rock-'n'-roll, but the next job will be something like I just finished with Carl Franklin, which is a Latin music score. Next month I might move on to some big classical piece. It's just such a wonderful opportunity that I knew would suit my temperament extremely well.

As far as the skill set involved, it's really quite enormous. But, for me, it comes down to two things: understanding drama and how a script works and reacts with all the rises and falls and the characters involved, and, at the same time, remaining as musical as I can be. Ultimately, it's music and drama.

Many people will talk about the political skills necessary to try and fulfill several people's agendas or visions at the same time when some of the team—the studio, the producer, or director—don't really see eye to eye. That's another trick. I always say that, instead of arguing in an academic way about how something *should* be, let me write the music or let me write two pieces of music for that scene and let's look at it. One finds there's a surprising commonality at the end of the day. Music works as it works. And if it doesn't, it just doesn't. Most people agree on that when they see it.

How do you score a film? What's your process?

I feel like an artist, and I have this palette beside me, which in my case is sound. I tend to know what that palette of sounds is going to be when I start out. Then it's a matter of mapping out the drama and figuring out how many themes I need and beginning thematic writing. In my case, the thematic writing often is not just a series of notes. It's more of a series of colors, or textures as some people call them, as well as notes.

I just go from there, building up blocks of thematic material. With romance or drama films where two characters become intertwined, I particularly like the idea of designing something that can intertwine at some point in the picture, and not have motifs for every different character, which is a style that I think is gone a little bit. We now have to think, particularly on the kinds of films that I work a lot on—fantasy and action films—about the attitude we're trying to promote. In other words, you would never score a love theme for two eighteen-year-olds with the kind of instrumentation that you would use to score a love theme for two thirty-year-olds. That wouldn't work. It has to be much more song-like for the younger demographic, something more contemporary, whereas you might use the strings or some more common orchestral instrument or guitar for an older audience. I always take that very much into account. After that, it's a matter of the usual path of composition. Scoring to picture using sequencers. Playbacks to the creative team to get approvals. And, finally, enhancements using real instruments and orchestra.

What's your feeling about the orchestra versus the synth sound?

To me, they both go together. I had a conversation the other night with some people at an awards dinner. We were talking about certain scores that had been thrown out. I said, "There's a common element among them." And they said, "What's that? They all sound different." And I said, "Well, on the one hand you've got somebody scoring a film who is very good orchestrally, but doesn't have a clue about synthesizers or electronics or rock-'n'-roll. In two other cases, you have guys who've come mostly from the electronic or rock-'n'-roll field who were asked to deliver that plus the orchestra, but they're not capable of it." In a lot of the big blockbuster movies, it's very necessary to have both sets of skills and to understand how they go together, which I think is the most important advance in film scoring in the last ten years. Hopefully I've had a major influence in showing that they're not two different worlds anymore. They really are the same world.

There are melodies and passion that you can't deliver with a synthesizer, and there are interesting, previously unheard sound textures that you just can't deliver with the orchestra, that you can only deliver with the synthesizers. There's also that cutting drive of electronically generated percussion that an orchestra just can't do because you don't have the timing, the crispness, or the impact from acoustic instruments.

The Crow, the first and its sequel, seemed to elevate your career to a higher level. Would you talk about your experiences with them?

What inspired them, I suppose, is my great love of world music. They were probably the first movies I'd worked on that were purely comic-book fantasy and set somewhere in the future. Now we're in Detroit, ten years into the future. So what's the music in Detroit ten years into the future? I don't know, it could be anything. What is so wonderful about those kinds of films and the scoring opportunities is that you're not locked into a genre at all.

The scripts also really inspired me. They were just revenge fantasies. Here was a guy who lost, in one case, his girlfriend and, in the other case, his son. In revenge, there's not really a sufficient motivation for you to like a character very much. My idea was to make him much more human—to keep reminding the audience of the intense sorrow behind what was happening.

The thing that was really upsetting and astonishing about *The Crow* was the real-life death of Brandon Lee. The film became a real tragedy in my mind when I was scoring it. I felt like I was almost writing a mini requiem for Brandon. I spent a lot of time and a lot of passion on that, and I think that it worked out. Hopefully, I did him justice.

The Craft also has a dark storyline, yet your approach to the score was quite different. Describe your use of tribal and Middle-Eastern influences.

It's sort of two things. There's a lot of atonal/ambient orchestral stuff, which I did because they wanted an orchestral score without any budget at all. I think that was the first time when I went out of town and just recorded blocks of atonal-style textures with an orchestra. I only had one day. And I just wrote down all sorts of Penderecki-type ideas and recombined them into the score later on using samplers and tapes and so on. Then, because they were involved with magic in the story, I decided to go to Indian and Middle-Eastern music a little bit.

A score that I love is *The Hand That Rocks the Cradle*. You did a superb job of creating suspense with dark motifs that are almost romantic in a perverse sort of way. What were your thoughts on this film?

Thank you. Well, when I met Curtis Hanson [director of *The Hand That Rocks the Cradle*], he asked me if I had any objections to using a Gilbert and Sullivan song as part of the theme. He wanted to have it playing in the family situations to throw the audience off to what's happening in the background, to make the audience think that these people were completely innocent and gullible. I said yes to the idea, but expressed reservations because of the 3/4 time of the original, which sounded very nineteenth-century. So I asked him if I could turn it into 4/4 time, so that it was less like a lullaby. That was fine. That was an interesting task.

The only thing that I would say about the scoring experience is that it was my first very real encounter with temp music. Up until that point, I had never encountered it—we didn't use it in Australia at all.

Was the temp music a Jerry Goldsmith score by any chance?

Yeah. There were two—a Jerry Goldsmith score and a Howard Shore score.

I'm not all that proud of that score. I was a little too young and inexperienced to know how to reference something and yet not actually copy it, you know? It was certainly a learning experience. It was something that I feel like I didn't do really well that time, but from then on, I didn't have any trouble with that sort of thing.

I always ask that they don't temp a movie that they've asked me to work on with my own music. Even though they feel that it's actually being respectful to me and that it works, in my opinion a composer gets more badly trapped by his own music than he does by somebody else's. You've already done it. How can you change it?

You're well-known for heavily textured, dark, or action-oriented scores. Do you feel you have been left out of another side of scoring that you want to be considered for?

Very much so. I suppose every composer answers that in the affirmative. I've tried very hard to take films, often for no money at all, that give me an opportunity to shine in those areas. I guess I'm thinking in terms of films like *Human Nature*. I really had to try hard to get that because nobody really believed that I had the sensibility for it.

What I really like about films like *Human Nature* is that they're the ones I actually enjoy watching the most. And so they're the ones I think I would enjoy working on the most. I really love Spike's work and I love Charlie Kaufman and the Coen brothers. Having mentioned all of those people, there's one lucky composer out there, isn't there?

What are your goals as a film composer?

Mostly, to try to broaden the frame of the genres that I'm able to work on.

Jeff Rona

If you musically blended equal parts Hans Zimmer and Mark Isham and an unknown X-Factor, you might get the mystical beauty of Jeff Rona's music for *White Squall* (1996). With this score, Rona's first solo effort for a major motion picture, he captured the film's heart with a hypnotic, ethnic-music-influenced voice. But Rona had been composing film music for quite some time prior to this score, working as a ghostwriter and working with the two aforementioned talents, Zimmer and Isham, who would ultimately play a role in his rise to success.

Rona has written highly engaging music for a long list of noted films, including *Black Hawk Down* (2001), *The Thin Red Line* (1998), and *The Fan* (1996), and such television shows as *Chicago Hope* and *Homicide: Life on the Street*. He also is the author of the insightful book *Reel World*, in which he shares his vast experiences in depth. (*Reel World* is not just a book about Rona—it covers every aspect of the film-scoring process, thus providing a great tool for anyone interested in persuing a film-music career.)

Have you always been interested in film music?

It was never a particular interest to me growing up.

How did your career evolve?

I played the flute when I was in school. I started to do a little bit of writing only because the only thing worth doing was playing in the jazz band. I was thinking of being a jazz musician. There are no flute parts in big bands, so I would actually have the conductor's score and would make up my own parts. And this led me to writing my own things. Then I started playing with synthesizers and got very into sound design and synthesizer playing.

When I was at college, I came in to practice one morning in the music building and found that somebody had the night before posted a "Composer Wanted for Student Film" notice with those little strips of paper with a phone number at the end. It was on one of the bulletin boards spread out around the buildings to hold announcements of upcoming concerts and what have you. Assuming I was the first person there, because I got there very early in the morning, I went around the building and took all these ads down. So I was the only person who called, and I got the gig!

It was a wonderful and eye-opening experience. That probably turned me toward thinking that this is something I might want to do, though I didn't get into it more formally for quite some time. First, I became a studio synthesist "gun for hire." I also was a part of Jon Hassell's ensemble, which included album work and some touring, and I worked with a lot of record producers. But, by far, most of my projects were for film composers. I learned so much. Eventually they asked me, "Jeff, would you like to try ghostwriting some things?" I'd been writing concert music, working with dance companies, writing modern ballet, theater, and some more avant-garde things—concert music, you know, mostly useless crap. The opportunity to try my hand at doing a cue here and there got me going, and I've been doing it ever since.

So where did your actual film career start?

When someone actually paid me to write something! As I said, it started off with bits and pieces of ghostwriting, working without credit on films for other composers who were behind schedule or too busy. They'd say, "Look, I don't really have time. Could you do this?" So it started where I'd do a cue here and there—those were the first bits and pieces of my filmwork. It was fun most of the time. It was all the joy of writing music for picture, but none of the responsibility: Your name doesn't go on it, and you're not in the room with the director when he says, "That's the worst piece of crap I've ever heard!" But, in fact, I got to sit in on a lot of those meetings, a fly on the wall. They were as important as the work in a lot of ways. I was seeing the politics of film music with people who had been through those minefields before. Those days were my film-music education as well as my start as a working composer.

From a few cues here and there, I got more and more calls to write. Before I could put my name to the scores, there were some films and TV shows that were scored entirely by me anonymously. Around that time I met Hans Zimmer, and I did some synth programming and sound design for him. He was just getting popular and very busy, and he called on me to write a few additional music cues, but not as a ghost, for a Barry Levinson movie called *Toys*. That led to me scoring Barry's next project, a television series called *Homicide: Life on the Street*. From there I began steady scoring for both film and television.

White Squall has a unique approach. It almost seemed New Age in style to me. Was this intentional?

White Squall was my first large feature film. I was a huge fan of director Ridley Scott, who had a pretty open mind about the music, and he helped steer me in the right direction. Celtic folk music had a significant influence on that score, though it was by no means an ethnic score. There was a lot more going on there. The main theme of the score is harmonically very simple and very open in its orchestration. But if you listen carefully, it doesn't fit into the category of New Age music, which I'm not too fond of myself. It's more layered and textural.

You became a composer for the hit television show *Chicago Hope*. How did this happen?

Mark Isham and I are friends, and I had worked with Mark on a couple of his films, *The Net* and *Fire in the Sky*. We hit it off, and I really admired his craft and methods. Although he's much more into jazz than I am, we still found ourselves seeing a lot of things the same musically. Mark was asked to write a theme for a new pilot from producer David E. Kelley called *Chicago Hope*. David had liked something Mark had done. Mark approached me and said, "Look, I'm going to write this theme and pilot, but why don't you help me with it? Maybe you could just keep going with doing the series." I had just finished working with Barry Levinson and wanted to do another television project, so I ended up working on that show for the first few seasons. I did some films during that same time.

In the projects you worked on with Mark Isham, such as *The Net*, how much of a role did you play?

Like other projects that I've done with Mark, *The Net* started off with Mark saying that I come up with really interesting palettes of sound, electronically. I have a particular style with the way I program sounds. He said he was doing this thriller, but he's not as technically savvy as I am, so maybe I would help him put together some cool sounds. And then he just ran into the time crunch that comes up frequently with composers. He said, "Here are a couple of cues." He had already written some themes, so we started with that, and then I wrote some pieces for a big orchestra and an all-female choir.

Going back to your work with Hans Zimmer, tell me about your work on *The Power of One*.

On *The Power of One*, I just helped do some arrangements. There were some very complicated scenes. For example, there was a prison camp scene in which the prisoners start singing a song—and this song has to become scored. Then Morgan Freeman gets the crap beat out of him while they're still singing. It turned out to be beyond complicated. It was poorly planned. It was a simple scene, but it required, at the time, some of the tools we have now to time-stretch and fit singing recordings to pictures. So it was me, just doing unnatural acts to the audio to make it musical. It was not a very creative thing. It was just arranging.

I believe that you played a larger role in *The Mothman Prophecies*, although you are not credited as the composer. Talk about this picture.

By this time, I was no longer assisting other composers on their films, but doing my own projects, plus a few collaborative scores, such as *Exit Wounds* with hip-hop producer Grease, *Shelter Island* with Michael Brook, and *A Thousand Roads* with Lisa Gerrard. I also contributed music—as additional music—to such films as *Traffic*, *Gladiator*, *The Thin Red Line*, *Black Hawk Down*, and *Mission: Impossible 2*. In these cases, I wrote my own thematic ideas that became elements of those scores.

In the case of *Mothman*, Mark Pellington, the director, had already hired the writing team of tomandandy for the score. He had worked with them on his previous film, *Arlington Road*. But some of my music had made it into the temp. Claude Letessier, a friend of mine, was the sound designer on the film, and he had a very heavy role in the overall architecture of the soundtrack, sound effects, and music. Everything to do with sound passed through him in a really unusual way, with him integrating music and effects together and manipulating everything rather abstractly. Pellington had really responded to some of these pieces that I had written and licensed them into the score. In the end, they used around eighteen cues of mine in the film, including the opening title music and the whole ending sequence of the movie. Actually, tomandandy took a whack at replacing some of my music and they just couldn't, because their approach is somewhat different from mine. There's a couple of their cues in the movie that quote my pieces, if you know what I mean. I think they did a terrific job on their score.

So why weren't you credited for that?

My name is at the end of the movie as "additional music" because the music was licensed and not written as a "work for hire"—it was music I had already written for myself, plus a few I adapted for the film. At the end of any movie, the licensed music is put in a separate section of the credits, just as the songs are credited. Since I am the publisher of my music in *Mothman*, it must be credited as such legally. So I appear several times in the credits, plus several of those pieces were used many times.

Net Force is another score in which you take a technological approach.

Net Force was a television movie based on a Tom Clancy novel. Rob Lieberman is a talented director, and he let me do my thing. The plot was a lot of pseudo-American patriotic drivel, but that's Tom Clancy. It gave me a chance to push harder on some of my electronica work. I worked with Rob again on the theme and pilot for the series *The Dead Zone*, and we did a very high-end television project called *Earthsea*, which was done with full orchestra, choir, and a lot of Middle-Eastern and Celtic players. So I've gotten to cover some range with Rob.

What is your most prized work?

I usually love whatever I've done most recently and tend to forget about the rest. I'm very proud of the *Homicide* series because we completely broke the mold of how television music is made and sounds. What we did was like nothing that existed up to then, and I really enjoyed being given the invitation to innovate and work with a brilliant guy like Barry. I'm very proud of the work I did on *White Squall*. It was the first time I was able to do my own thing with an orchestra. Ridley is an amazing director. I'm also very proud of the music I contributed on the film *Traffic*. I think a lot of my soul is in that film in one way or another. I liked the music I did for *Black Hawk Down*. There's a good chunk of my music in that score. That film was scored as a group effort. Producer Howard Koch hired me on his first television film, *The Riverman*, and I got to do a very contemporary, moody score for him. I only had a few days to do that score, but it came out very well.

If you had to choose a score or composer that influenced you most, who would you say it was?

That would be really tough. Music is so deep and varied and personal. I have a lot of influences and inspirations.

In college, my roommate was a rabid film-music collector who had a huge collection of film scores. He introduced me to film music. One score I loved in particular, because I was so into synthesizers at the time, was the score by Jerry Goldsmith for *Logan's Run*. It had orchestra and very cool, weird, old-style synthesizers. I was so blown away by that. It had elements of the avant-garde, but still had elements of deep emotion and excitement. I also loved Jerry's score to *Alien*.

A bit later, I saw *Never Cry Wolf*, Mark Isham's first film score. It was a very different approach to film music—simplicity. Now, if you want to talk about New Age, that's the one. But I had never heard a film score done so sparsely. I just adored that.

There are other composers I really admire and whose work has inspired me. Zimmer on some things, Tom Newman, John Williams, Mychael Danna, Philip Glass, Danny Elfman, Zbigniew Preisner, and anyone who finds a way to maintain a truly original voice in the cause of scoring films. I am probably as influenced as anybody by Bernard Herrmann and his use of repetition as a method for creating tension. He's the father of minimalism, yet it never shows on the surface. He showed that if you came up with something really good, you could repeat it and it would just grow in your mind. He could keep a theme going for five minutes, yet it always remained brilliant and full of tension. His score to *Taxi Driver*—my god! I hear every composer relate his or her work to Bernard Herrmann. One way or another it always comes back to him. He was, back in his day, the forties and fifties, the guy who broke away from the romantic classical music—the Waxman- and Korngold-style scores. He wrote truly modern music. In fact, it was somewhat avant-garde at the time. He was the first guy to dismiss the overwhelming lexicon of musical thought for film in his day. He turned the tide of film music to allow it to do more modern, interesting things. *The Day the Earth Stood Still* is another stunning score of his.

You've also written a book on being a composer, *The Reel World*. What was the purpose of writing that book?

In addition to my work as a composer, I've always been deeply involved in the technology of music-making and sound. I have been the "go-to" guy for a lot of my friends and other composers. Some time back, I was asked to write a column on film music for *Keyboard Magazine*, a very popular musicians' magazine. It became a semi-regular column in which I would relate my personal experiences, almost like a diary of my musical life in the trenches of film music. I would talk about how things would go well, as well as how things would sometimes go badly. After having written numerous articles on the art, craft, business, technology, and politics of the field, my publisher approached me with the idea of doing a book. We gathered up all my columns and went through them picking out the best ones. Because they spanned about five years, I realized that my thoughts and opinions changed over time, as did the technology that made the work possible, so I ended up using the topics I'd written about as a springboard, threw all the articles away and started all over. I wrote the book nearly from scratch, and I interviewed several of my composer friends—Mark Isham, Hans Zimmer, James Newton Howard, John Williams, Carter Burwell—as well as some recording engineers, my agent, a top music editor, and the head of music at a major studio. It has every perspective.

You played an important role in developing MIDI. What is it, and what were your contributions?

After I quit college to pursue music, I did a variety of music jobs: I was a staff arranger for a major music publisher, a synth programmer, an accompanist for a dance company, and much more. But I was always really into music technology. At one point, I worked for a few years for one of the major electronic instrument makers. I helped them develop new electronic-instruments and wrote music software—a very new field at the time. I've never been trained technically in software writing. In fact, I only got Ds and Fs in math, but I needed a job and, for some reason, I had an aptitude for writing software code. So I lied about my background and got a job doing it.

I happened to be working at this company the year that a group of talented and forward-thinking engineers from different synthesizer companies came up with the idea of a universal method that would allow any electronic instrument to plug into any other electronic instrument. This would allow the instruments to be interconnected in order to layer sounds together and to perform them into new recorders called "sequencers" and have them play back your performance perfectly.

All the things we take for granted now didn't exist yet. And it's not that far back! Back then, there were competing technologies that weren't compatible with one another. So I got involved with that group of amazing engineers to develop this idea of a universal, industry-wide method—MIDI [an acronym for "Musical Instrument Digital Interface]. They had started the technical aspect before I got onto the scene. When I got involved, they had the idea, but needed to figure out how the whole competitive business could function together as a single group. I became the person who brought the entire world of musical instrument development together for a number of years in order to facilitate the communication, cooperation, and development of all aspects of MIDI. I spearheaded everything to get Japanese, European, and American engineers to work together to define where MIDI needed to go and solve any conflicts or problems from the early days to its rapid worldwide acceptance and success. I created the structure of how the worldwide developer community could interact in a way where everybody felt that they could do what they wanted to do. It protected everyone's investment in technological growth and product marketing, which are vital elements to making a standard a standard. I think we were incredibly successful. Even after I quit programming to work as a composer and musician, I kept doing this because it was important, vital work.

Where do you plan on taking your career? What are your goals?

I am doing my own films and television projects now. I am also collaborating on some scores with Lisa Gerrard. I continue to develop myself musically. I make every score a challenge to do things better. I have a lot of musical ideas that I'm just trying to bring into better focus. I want to improve myself as a musician and as a composer. I want to find the right kinds of films and directors that will allow me to do as much creative thinking as possible. I just want to have my voice heard and hone that voice, which is a lifelong ambition. It never ends. There is no destination, just the path. You just enjoy the journey.

Marc Shaiman

Marc Shaiman's musical career began in the theater and periodically returns there, most recently with *Hairspray*—the Broadway musical for which he won a 2003 Tony Award for Best Score (the award that he confesses he is most proud of). He has a seemingly natural affinity for all things theatrical, as one readily hears in his film scores, and is equally comfortable and skilled with both comedy and drama.

Although Shaiman writes music in every imaginable style, as called for by the film projects he takes on, melody may be said to be his native language, which he speaks with great fluency. And his often-breathtaking melodies communicate directly to our hearts and create a spark for every onscreen image.

He has worked with many filmmakers, who clearly seek him out for his wide-ranging dramatic talents—from the bright orchestrations and patriotic themes of *The American President* (1995) to the sweeping melodies of *Patch Adams* (1998) and *Simon Birch* (1998) to the unabashed silliness of *South Park: Bigger Longer & Uncut* (1999). Among his collaborations with directors and producers, most notable may be his multi-film relationships with Rob Reiner, for whom he scored *When Harry Met Sally* (1989), *Misery* (1990), *A Few Good Men* (1992), *Ghosts of Mississippi* (1996), and *Alex & Emma* (2003); and Billy Crystal, for whom he scored *Billy Crystal: Don't Get Me Started* (1987), *City Slickers* (1991), *Mr. Saturday Night* (1992), *My Giant* (1998), and *61* (2001).

You have a natural theatrical sound in your writing, which leads me to believe you're among the few composers who actually sought a Broadway or film career from the beginning.

I've been a fan of all kinds of music, but I've certainly been heavily into Broadway musicals and film musicals. I wasn't a student of film music—that part of my life just sort of happened. It fell in my lap while working with Bette Midler on the songs for *Beaches*. That worked out very well for me, being the one who brought to the table "Wind Beneath My Wings," which is a song I had heard someone singing in New York. It had just been kind of languishing, and I knew it was perfect for the movie. That was a big success for her and for myself. And I got to work with Rob Reiner, whom I knew from my relationship with Billy Crystal. He asked me to do *When Harry Met Sally*, which was another great way to use other people's music as an entry into film scoring. It was my arranging skills that were called upon there.

Through those two movies, I learned how to place music into movies and a lot of the nuts and bolts. And I got to forge relationships with people at Disney and Rob Reiner. Those two movies just exploded and became a tornado of film-scoring jobs and great successes. The first few years of my career were one-hundred-million-dollar movie after another. That leveled out after a while, but for the first two or three years, every single movie I worked on was a huge success.

You are not only friends with Billy Crystal, but you have collaborated in various areas with him for a few years now. That must be a blast.

It's just great to be able to work with one of the greatest comedians. There's simply no one out there who's better. When I write material for him, like on the Oscars, it's great to know that he's going to land the punchline that's in the lyric and deliver it the best it can be delivered. That's thrilling. And we've been friends for twenty years now.

How did that start?

On *Saturday Night Live*, where I was working as a funny piano player, arranger, writer—a catchall musical kind of guy. A friend I had met on the New York cabaret circuit—playing for nightclub performers—used to do the job, and when she stopped doing it for two years, she told them to call me. That was the perfect job for me. I'm just perfectly suited to sitting at the piano, improvising with comedians and coming up with stuff. So Billy and I really hit it off. Also, Martin Short was there the same year. Those are two friendships that I've had since then.

Describe your relationship with Rob Reiner and how you started working together.

I met him when we were both working on a Billy Crystal HBO comedy special that he was appearing in and I was playing on for Billy. He also came to see Billy's act, where I used to play under Billy's monologue and kind of fool around with him on stage musically. So Billy set me up with a meeting when he heard that Rob wanted an arranger to help put together a score of American standards for *When Harry Met Sally*. Rob just gave me the job and it went really well. Then he called and said, "I'd like you to score my next movie, *Misery*." And I was like, "Terrific!" My very first compositional job was a psychological terror movie, which I didn't really have much knowledge of. That went well, and Rob just kept doing one movie after another, each in a different style. So I was really lucky to go from *Misery* to *A Few Good Men* to *The American President*. His movies have afforded me a lot of opportunities to work in different styles.

In my opinion, Rob Reiner seems to pull out the best in your work. What are your thoughts on this?

He makes me be as simple as I can be. Whereas in other movies I get more of an opportunity to be over the top, Rob prefers to be under the top or under the table. And the movies he works on are so stylistically different from one another that they give me a lot of opportunities to be that kind of musical chameleon that I happen to be. The other day, when we were talking about that, I said, "I don't mind being jack-of-all-trades, master-of-none." And he replied, "Don't sell yourself short, Mark. I think you can at least say you're jack-of-all-trades, master-of-some."

Misery was obviously not familiar territory for you, so what was your approach?

Like I mentioned, *Misery* was my first movie as a composer. I had to deal for the first time with film-scoring's mathematical side—figuring out how to write a piece of music that is going to do all the right things it needs to do at various points—which is a huge part of it. A piece of music is a minute long, and every few seconds it has to be doing something very specific. It's just an endless Rubik's Cube puzzle. So I had to learn all that. I had to learn how to work with the computer and synthesizers and deal with the director and learn how to write every day of my life—from the moment I wake up until the moment I go to sleep—which I never had to do before. And then there was the fact that it was psychological-terror kind of music.

This was a case where I was happy about a temp score, because I was able to listen to it and kind of hear how certain rhythms and textures created certain moods. I was not trying to copy it—I'm not capable of copying Jerry Goldsmith. That was a bit of schooling for me to be able to just listen to that, just how to get a vigorous sound out of violas and have a rhythm going. I just had to experiment by trying stuff. I ended up being pretty happy with the way it came out. I also had an orchestrator on that who really helped me with the timing issues, which I was just learning. It only took a few movies to master that part of it, because once you figure it out, it's no longer so daunting.

I think that horror scores would be one of the most difficult.

Yeah, it is very hard, but with *Misery*, I had no choice. Perhaps my own terror of failing helped me create the same kind of mood. But, like I said, Rob likes things simple, so he wasn't looking for the densest and most complicated music. I had that in my favor.

A Few Good Men **is another score that worked very well in the film, but it was not what I was expecting. What was the reason for creating a dark, heavily synth-based score versus using the bugles and the snare drums heard in most military movies?**

Well, that's just what he was asking for. He liked those low droning notes, so that the music doesn't telegraph too much. So that was another one where he wanted to keep it as simple as possible. Not until the last three minutes of the movie does it really fall into a traditional movie-orchestra sound. But the last few seconds were so old-fashioned and traditional that when he heard it at the recording session, he said, "I've got to have them put (The End) on the movie," which hasn't been seen in a long time. So he did that as almost a tribute to the music I had written for that final shot.

Sometimes, it's frustrating having someone who is very hands-on and controlling about the music, but in Rob's case, I've learned to accept it as something that makes the job a little easier: Someone is telling you, "I like that." "I don't like that." "This is what I want." That can be much better than someone who is going, "I don't know, I don't know what I mean," while you're just floating and floating, trying to figure out what's going to make him or her happy.

Generally, how does the director know what music he wants, and how is this communicated to the composer?

They figure out what they want the music to be: What purpose should it be serving? They can speak in thematic terms. When I say thematic, I mean moods and emotions. You know, that's any area where the temp score is useful. It can certainly be a useful tool in a musical dialogue with a director to hear what he's liking and not liking.

The bad part is where they fall in love with something in the temp score, and not only are they in love with that certain piece of music but with a certain style of music. Then it's almost impossible to even try to get them to consider another take on how to score a scene or a movie. Just getting them to not be in love with the oboe that was in the temp score or the string section coming in exactly as it was in the temp score is often impossible.

I think that *The American President* might be your greatest work. It represents the essence of excellent film music.

Thank you. That's one of my own favorites. And that was a perfect movie to be able to work on. It was humorous, romantic, serious . . . That's the kind of score I would like to be doing more of.

Your colorful orchestrations support the film beautifully. Do you ever look for inspiration outside of the film?

You know, for me it's always the movie itself. That's what always inspires it all, the images and the movie. That where the film composer's lucky. You get to sit in an empty room and just call upon the muses for inspiration. You've got the images. You've got your job to do. And it's all right there in front of you. That's doesn't mean it's easy. There are so many different choices you can make. Each choice then defines your next choice. The images of the presidential things in that opening montage was just all I needed to start writing what ended up being there. That kind of flowing of images that they created for the main title just spelled it right out. I just followed the lead.

You seem to have a natural talent or gift for writing thematic music.

I'm much more into melodies and themes than some guys who are much more into the textural or rhythmic kind of scoring, which I'm not good at. Everybody has his or her own strengths. I'm just old-fashioned in that sense, which is why I love American standards and Broadway musicals.

I finally got a chance to write an old-fashioned Broadway musical, *Hairspray*, which is what I was always longing to do. Every theme in all my film scores has lyrics to it. As I'm playing a theme, I literally have lyrics in my mind as if that character is singing a song in a musical. I don't remember any of them, so don't ask me to sing them, but I swear, on every movie, every theme has a lyric going on in my head at the same time.

You are one of the few composers today who writes mainly for orchestra. How do you feel about scores with more electronics and less orchestra?

I enjoy it. I don't ever close my ears off to any music. I've just dab-bled in it a bit. Thomas Newman is so brilliant. He can do it all. I mean, he writes beautiful orchestral stuff and yet he is so into that rhythmic textural stuff also. My hat's off to that!

So melody-driven, sweeping scores, such as *Patch Adams* and *Simon Birch*, flow most naturally from your pen?

Yeah, I forgot about *Simon Birch* until you just mentioned it. I loved working on that film. That had like eight or nine nice melodies. The director [Mark Steven Johnson] was totally into that kind of music, and I just kept writing theme after theme for him to choose from. Luckily, I've never worked with an asshole. The director of *Simon Birch* was a sweet man. He so loved what I was writing. When you know you're pleasing your boss, going to work each day is much nicer.

What about *Patch Adams*?

Patch Adams was a bit more of a committee thing. The director would come over with the editor and discuss things a whole lot more. And I actually had to kind of beg to get the job. You know, that's the kind of music that gets beat up the most in reviews. I got a review from *Patch Adams* that called the music "obnoxious." Look that one up in the dictionary. I could actually kill with it. It's poison. That was nice of *The New York Times*. Then to ironically get nominated for an Academy Award for it was balm for that wound.

How do you view people who rate CDs and rate your music? Do you ever take that stuff to heart?

It's tough to read it. Luckily, I see done it with all the other com-posers, too. So that makes it a little easier. Comedies, romances—they just beat up on those movies, and just beat up the music used in them—comedy music and romantic music, or what they call "sen-timental" music.

When they first brought me *Patch Adams* and I saw the first ten minutes of film, when I saw him smiling and dancing around in the children's cancer ward, I thought, "Oh, they're going to crucify me," because I knew what kind of music a movie like that calls for. I knew what the filmmaker wanted me to do, and I just knew that they were going to crucify me. Sure enough, they did. Meanwhile, I love writing it. It's music. Nothing deserves to be called "obnoxious." Being able to write beautiful music is a pleasurable thing to do. Luckily, real people don't feel like the critics or like the film-score aficionados, who often over-analyze. You know, it's music. It's not necessarily meant to be spoken about so much. It's meant to be heard and felt.

Orchestration is an important part of your work. What is your relationship like with Jeff Atmajian and the rest of your team?

I love them all. Jeff is especially brilliant and also a friend. We just think so much alike. Musically, we share a sensibility. I mean, Jeff is someone whom I can actually give a detailed piano sketch to and just know that the orchestration will be just what I was thinking. But it took me years and years to be able to let go to do that.

Film-composing and orchestrating is really the same thing, and the composer does well over half of the orchestration within the actual writing. The orchestrators are brought in because there's simply no time to go to a score and write it all out. Orchestrators, as they figured out a long time ago, just had to be part of the equation.

I love orchestrating and arranging. I pride myself on it, on getting into the details of it. I've learned so much about what the orchestrators do. It's not like they add notes; they just make use of all the colors of the orchestra. So, even though I may have only done something with woodwinds, Jeff will know perfectly how to have the strings mirror, or what we call "ghost," what the woodwinds are doing to make use of all the opportunities in the orchestra.

Would you talk a little bit about your work in musicals?

It's what I enjoy doing the most. *South Park*, you know, is probably my favorite movie I ever got to work on. I enjoy writing lyrics as much as I enjoy writing music and arranging music. In *South Park* I got to do it all. Trey Parker was such a great collaborator. He would write the first verse and the chorus of a song and say, "Here, you finish it." He would completely trust that I could write the second verse and chorus and make the style fit what he had already written. Once again, a shared sensibility came up. Once he trusted that we thought alike musically and lyrically, he just trusted me. Then to be able to arrange something correctly, like the brilliant song "Uncle Fucka," and be able to create that perfect *Oklahoma!*-style musical sound underneath it. It was really great for me to watch Matt [Stone] and Trey hear the orchestration for the first time. I mean, the song is funny and brilliant, but to have the traditional sound underneath it just makes it all the funnier.

Do these two careers interfere with each other?

Now that I've had the pleasure of having written a musical, I hopefully won't let movie-scoring get in the way of, or stop me from, that being my main emphasis as long as I'm allowed to do it. It's much more my heart and soul.

I understand that you have a good possum story.

One of the odder moments in my film-scoring life occurred while I was on *Hearts and Souls*. One horrible afternoon, something was sticking around middle C and then middle C was fine and D and E were sticking and then they were fine, then F and G, and . . . oh my God, is there something in there?! At first, I thought it was a mouse, a dead mouse. It must have been in there and died and it's just flopping around now from key to key. Then I could hear the sound of scratching, that unmistakable sound of a mouse in the wall. So I open the piano and, sure enough, there's a tail—the biggest tail you ever saw. So the mouse became a rat. But then it stuck its nose down and I realized that this was no rat. There's some nuclear animal in there! An exterminator came over, put on this big old glove, and stuck his hand in the piano—and out comes this possum, which he holds upside down, its arms and legs spread out in terror. It must have been living on top of the hammers in there for two or three days, the poor thing. I was holding the top of the piano and I only saw the reflection in the piano, and then I had to get right back to work. That was the most bizarre thing I've ever come across in a piano.

Ryan Shore

Ryan Shore, following in the footsteps of his uncle, Howard Shore, adds a new, talented voice to the motion-picture community. As his career began gaining momentum, Ryan wrote thought-provoking music for the Student Academy Award-winning films _Shadowplay_ (2002) and the animated short epic _Rex Steele: Nazi Smasher_ (2004). He has also done major motion pictures, including the notoriously sordid film _Vulgar_ (2000), for which he supplied a sultry jazz/avant-garde score that is truly unique, and _Prime_ (2005), a film that stars Uma Thurman and Meryl Streep.

Ryan Shore has the ability and confidence and passion to undertake any musical project, and he gives nothing short of 110 percent of himself in his work—which alone speaks volumes about who he is as an artist.

How much of a role has your uncle, Howard Shore, played in your career choice?

Howard has played a great role in my interest in film-scoring. I first became aware of film-scoring through Howard. I started getting into music around age twelve, and he gave me a keyboard for my thirteenth birthday. I began playing around on it, finding new harmonies and sounds on my own. It was the absolute beginning for me, and the discovery part of it—finding things for the first time—was fantastic. I remember thinking that I invented the major chord when I found it! Then the same for suspended chords and minor chords. It was a lot of fun.

My first instrument, which is still my primary instrument today, is the saxophone. It was Howard's primary instrument as well. I remember taking an interest in it after seeing the movie *The Blues Brothers* and watching Lou Marini playing the sax on the bar behind Aretha Franklin. I thought it was just about the coolest thing I had ever seen. I also really liked the way Zoot looked while playing the saxophone on *The Muppet Show*. It's funny how the instruments we play today we chose as kids, and then we stayed with them. It would almost be like asking a twelve-year-old what they think we should do for a living . . . and then doing it.

I grew up in Florida. Howard was in New York, so I didn't see him very often. But he did recommend the Berklee College of Music, and I went there for their summer program when I was in high school. While I was there, they offered me a scholarship to come back for college, which I did. I majored in film-music composition and saxophone and woodwind performance. After graduating from Berklee, Howard offered me one day of employment, which I accepted. It turned into four years of invaluable hands-on experiences in film-scoring. When Howard offered me that one-day opportunity, he said, "Why don't you come up to my office and see how you like it?" I knew what he really meant was, "Why don't you come up to my office and I'll see how I like you?" Since this was right after graduating, the four years I worked with Howard were almost like getting a masters degree.

One of the best parts of working with Howard was that he never asked me to get coffee or do non-musical things. He hired me on his films to do things that, if I weren't doing them, then someone else who does the job for a living would be doing them. It began with music preparation and evolved into orchestrating and some music producing. It was a great way of getting into the business because, even though I wasn't writing the music, I was processing the entire score, getting a feeling for what forty minutes or fifty minutes of music feels like in a very practical way. Especially great was going to the recording sessions and hearing the way it was translating from the page to a live orchestra or large ensembles. It was a truly invaluable experience that I'm extremely grateful for. There was a point, though, when I had gained as much knowledge as I could about working in those capacities, and it was time for me to move on and pursue my own music.

Has following in the footsteps of an established composer made it difficult for you to be your own composer without doubting your abilities?

Not at all. Creating music is a process of personal discovery and growth, and that is something that happens regardless of whether you are related to another composer. I do find it interesting, though, that there are two film composers in the same family, since it is such a unique profession, but there are other instances of that in the business.

Can you talk about how you approach scoring for film?

I usually like to watch a film a few times before writing anything, and then I walk away from the film so I can let it sink in. It's almost like when you go see a movie in the theater and then you talk about it with your friends at dinner afterwards. It's in that time that you find deeper ideas and feelings about it. I like to take time away from it and think about the overall feelings I have for the film: the characters, the performances, the storyline, the writing, the locations, the colors, the pacing, the individual scenes, and the overall impact of the filmmaking. The film needs to get inside of me and then work itself through.

Then I begin sketching ideas and improvising music for it, much like I would do when improvising on my saxophone, although I usually do it on the piano or without being in front of any instruments at all, just composing in my mind. Composing is exactly like improvising a solo, but you don't have to do it in real time. You have the luxury of being able to go back and make revisions to get your improvisations the way you want them. Once I start actually composing, I may work for twelve or fourteen hours in a day. But I find that I often come up with my best ideas at the end of the day, when I'm lying in bed and I'm about to go to sleep, because that's when I'm not thinking about any of the technical aspects of creating music for film. I'm not thinking about the physicality of the buttons and the keyboards and the machines and the computers. And I'm not tied up with having to look at the film or anything at all. I'm just thinking about human emotions, musical gestures, musical settings, sounds and colors, etcetera. It can be very abstract. There is something about that time that is so freeing. Then, of course, I have to get up and write down any ideas that I have, or I'll never remember them in the morning.

Sometime people ask how many days it takes to score a film. For me, it's almost more of a question of how many nights I have to score it. I have found that when you are truly open and honest with the film, the movie will actually tell you what to write. And when I try to force music onto a scene, it usually never works for me. I've also found that my first reactions to a film and scenes are usually my best; and, oddly enough, the less time it takes me to compose, the more cohesive and unified the music seems to be.

What do you look for in a storyline?

I generally choose films based on the collaborators rather than storylines. Given that, one of the most important things I look for in a movie is that all of its elements are working. I think for a film to be a great film, it has to be great in every aspect. I don't think that you'll ever get a great film by having any one aspect of the film pulling too much weight or making up for other aspects. Everything needs to work together in order to achieve the common goal.

You have orchestrated and conducted your own music. From the moment you sit at the piano, sketching your thoughts, to the point where you are waving your arms in front of the orchestra, what moment most excites you?

The part that excites me the most is not even the recording sessions, although those are an extremely close second. The part that excites me the most is the very moment that you hear an idea in your head during the composing process. At that very instant when you have an idea and hear it in your head, the music is in the most pure form that you'll ever hear it. The rest of the process is mostly about the work that it takes to realize that idea.

You have this idea in your mind, and then you have to go through the mechanical process of figuring out what notes need to be played to hear those ideas—how do they need to be performed to achieve this same feeling or gesture?—and then writing that down. It's all part of the mechanical process of translating music from your mind, in the abstract, to a written, concrete form. After you find those notes and performance markings, you go through many processes: You orchestrate it. You perform and record the music. You mix the music. And it's all to realize that one idea that maybe came to you in a split second. It maybe took you a hair of a second to think of it, and then took you twenty hours of work to realize it. So it is that first inspiration that is the most pure and exciting part for me.

Let's talk about *Rex Steele: Nazi Smasher*. This is an animated short. What led to your involvement on this project?

This project came through filmmakers I had worked with before. Prior to this film, I scored an animation called *A Letter from the Western Front*, which was directed and animated by Dan Kanemoto. I met Dan through a mentor of his, Cynthia Allen, whom I had met at an industry dinner many years ago, when I was just starting out. For *A Letter from the Western Front*, I put together a twenty-five-piece orchestra and recorded it live. The film went on to win a Student Academy Award and an Emmy Award, which are the two highest awards that a student film can receive. Based on my work on that film, I was asked by filmmaker Dan Blank to score his animated film *Shadowplay*, which is a very unique Claymation about the aftermath of the atomic bomb at Hiroshima. I put together a similar live orchestra and experimented by adding traditional Japanese instruments—shakuhachi, koto, and Japanese percussion. This film went on to win the same two honors. And from this film, Alex Woo asked me to score *Rex Steele: Nazi Smasher*. Dan Blank, who voiced many of the main characters in *Rex Steele*, recommended me for it.

When I met the *Rex Steele* filmmakers (Alex Woo, Bill Presing, and Matt Peters), we agreed that we really wanted to go all out for the score. So, instead of using a small orchestra, which we felt wouldn't be able to provide the sounds that we were looking for, we decided to record it with a 110-member orchestra and choir, and we found a way to do it. *Rex Steele: Nazi Smasher* went on to win the same two awards as well.

Rex Steele: Nazi Smasher is a melodic score that opens with a heavy Americana spirit and superheroish sound. What prompted the big orchestral sound for a small animated film?

We all saw the film as small only in its length. We all had large sights for what we hoped we could do within ten minutes. The animators spent about three years creating the film, which is inspired by serial comics and propaganda reels from the 1940s.

I love scoring animated films because it takes so much work to create the animation and the visuals that it is immensely inspiring for me when I score it. Scoring the film was truly a labor of love. When I first watched the movie with the director and creators, we were already thinking about a very large orchestral sound. The score I wrote for *Shadowplay* was a much more introspective score for strings and woodwinds and ethnic instruments. A small orchestra was appropriate. But *Rex Steele: Nazi Smasher* was just the opposite. With a brash, bold, exciting, action-driven, superhero film, we knew that a small orchestra would not be able to create the size of sound that we needed to match the visuals. We also wanted to explore all the sections of the orchestra in the score. So, using an orchestra was an idea we all had right from the beginning.

The Americana approach is a natural direction for the main character, Rex, because he is a confident, heroic, and strong leader who works to serve the United States.

Rex Steele is a clever piece of satire, yet your music plays a boldly serious role.

That is an approach I first became aware of through Elmer Bernstein's great score for *Airplane!*, which is a hysterical comedy, but the music plays the situations completely straight, as if it were a serious drama. By doing it that way, the film is even funnier because the music isn't trying to make it funny. It's as though the music is not in on the joke. We followed the same approach for *Rex Steele: Nazi Smasher*. With superhero animation of this kind, you just can't write large enough. Particularly with this film, in contrast to some of the other animations I've scored, the role of the music was largely to heighten the energy of the film.

I was really captivated by the choir in your score. What role did it play?

I recorded in a large concert hall, where there was a beautiful pipe organ. But, instead of utilizing the organ, we decided to use the choir, since it can, through lyrics, provide an even greater sense of impending doom with a consequence of finality. The thought is that if you were facing a torturous death, you would naturally hear the coming of the Messiah, and once you heard the choir begin, you'd know you were finished. I chose to use only the choir's females because, when the entire orchestra is playing at it's height, you really only her the women anyway. The choir is used only in the scenes with Eval Schnitzler, the evil Nazi warlord.

Tell me a little about the story of *Shadowplay*, a Claymation, and your choice for its intimate setting with the ethnic flutes and strings.

The story of *Shadowplay* is about the dropping of the atomic bomb at Hiroshima and its aftermath. It tells it through metaphor. It's a very emotional story to tell in the context of a short film. Dan Blank, the director/animator, and I knew that the film was a many-layered dramatic story that just happened to be told in animation.

The main character is a little boy, who is only a shadow, and he must discover his fate in the aftermath of the bombing. After the bomb dropped, in many instances there were shadows of people emblazoned on the walls of the buildings, because the flash of the light was so strong. It is fascinating, and horrifying. After the city was in total annihilation, you could actually see shadows permanently emblazoned on walls of the people in the same positions they were in when it happened. So Dan used that as a metaphor for the little boy who is only a shadow and doesn't know what happened to his family. Through exploration of the city and self-discovery, he eventually reunites with his family at the end.

I composed one main theme for it, and we had the idea, from the beginning, of utilizing traditional Japanese instruments. So I researched the instruments quite a bit before writing for them. I studied traditional Japanese music composition, and I learned about the shakuhachi, the koto, Japanese percussion, and how the traditional music for them is notated, since it does not employ the Western methods of notation. I also spoke beforehand with the musicians who were to perform the score and learned from them as well. For the score, I combined them with traditional Western orchestral instrumentations of strings, harp, and woodwinds to create a larger sound. It was a very rewarding film to score both from a research perspective and in the collaboration with Dan.

There's a little-known movie entitled *Vulgar*, for which the title says it all. Talk a little about this film and tell us what compelled you to get involved in this bizarre story.

Bizarre is a good way of putting it. I like to explain to people who haven't seen it that it's not a family film. The film came about because Kevin Smith's company, View Askew, has a mascot-design logo of a party clown who is dressed with high heels, a garter belt, and a clapper for making movies. Although it stemmed from a simple drawing, Kevin had the idea that maybe he would make a movie about who this character was someday. The character had no story—it was just a friend's drawing that Kevin liked and started using. But Bryan Johnson, who works for Kevin, said to him, "While you're tied up making these other movies, do you mind if I take a crack at writing a screenplay for this character?" Kevin said, "Sure, give it a shot."

So Bryan wrote a screenplay about a clown named Flappy, a kid's party clown. When things got really slow for Flappy business-wise and times were rough, he had this wonderful idea to hire himself out to bachelor parties dressed like a trashy clown stripper. Everyone would be expecting strippers to come in, but he would show up dressed like a clown and do a little strip-tease and everyone would get a laugh out of it. Then the real entertainment would show up. For these jobs he would take on the new moniker Vulgar the Clown. At the very first job that he goes to, everything goes about as horribly wrong as you can possibly imagine. Instead of it being a bachelor party, it turns out to be only a father and his two delinquent sons, who basically beat the crap out of Vulgar and rape him as well. Here's where most people probably stop watching the movie.

The movie was sent over to Howard Stern, who watched it and hated it. He watched like the first ten minutes or so and then threw it away. One of the people on his show, however, told him, "You've got to watch this movie. You've got to check it out." So, eventually, Howard did watch the whole movie, and it became a running joke-line on his show. Howard talked about it over and over again. He referenced it against other stories, like, "Well, I guess that's not as bad as getting raped while being dressed as a clown." Howard gave it great publicity. He even offered the best quote ever: "Go see the movie that grossed out even Howard Stern."

Musically, after viewing the film, I had the idea of writing a jazz score as a way of providing some levity and humor to the movie. But, because it is such a dark movie, I decided to write a very dark jazz score. I chose an instrumentation of an extended rhythm section of piano, organ, vibraphone, electric guitars, both electric and acoustic basses, and drums, coupled with a four-horn ensemble of trumpet, trombone, and tenor and baritone saxes. The score starts out optimistically—structured and light—and progresses into a very dark, free-jazz score. The idea was to have the instruments essentially take Flappy's same journey and disintegrate with him.

I had only two days to record roughly forty minutes of music, but the sessions went quite smoothly. In the rape scene—which is the scene that the film is probably most known for—I used a recording technique that I had never tried before. I didn't give any of the musicians any written sheet music at all. Instead, I recorded them individually as overdubs, and only gave them musical directions through their headphones based on pacing, volume, and intensity. We didn't use a clicktrack. I started with the drums and, while I watched the movie, I had him play completely free, giving him directions only about the emotions and the arc of the piece, but with nothing specific to play. The cue was about seven minutes long, and after those seven minutes were done, I did the same exact thing with the bass player. However, I didn't let the bass player hear what the drummer had done. The bass player heard only his own instrument and created his own little musical story based on my same directions over the seven minutes. I did the same with each of the instruments. Nobody heard each other's performances because I didn't want them to play off of each other, which is what jazz musicians are used to doing—one musician does one thing, and another responds to it. In this case, I didn't want any of that type of interplay because I wanted the sound to be as free and disoriented as possible. The only common thread among the musicians was the arc of their performance, how their intensity was shaped throughout the scene. It seemed like an appropriate way to score the raping of a clown.

By the way, at the end of the story, Flappy prevailed, although he sure didn't prevail in that scene.

Many talented young musicians want to write music for films, yet they cannot find a way to get a foot in the door. Since you traveled this road not too long ago, what bits of wisdom about it can you share?

My advice is to first make sure that film music is something that you really love to do, because it is a very long road. Learn your craft in every aspect you can, and to the fullest that you can. Meet the next generation of filmmakers and work and grow with them.

A teacher of mine at the Berklee College of Music, Michael Rendish, told me the following, which I thought was great, and it has always stuck with me. He said, "You're going to get out there and meet some young filmmakers, and you're going to say, 'I want to score your film.' And they might say, 'Well, what have you done before?' And you haven't done anything yet. So if it applies to the situation, you can say, 'Well, I haven't done anything before, but neither have you. So why don't we give this a shot together?'"

There's the saying that the journey of a thousand miles begins with one step, which definitely applies to film-scoring. Sometimes the journey can seem long, particularly when you're living it, but it is made one step at a time. My advice is to start by learning the craft as best as you can—always do your best—and begin building a reel. Through that you will gain experience and meet people and things will evolve. I think that's the best way to get started.

Alan Silvestri is perhaps best known for his bold symphonic themes to the *Back to the Future* series of films (1985-90). However, he is one of the most prolific and diverse film composers working today, and his music, as varied as the films he scores, transcends stylistic labeling. His scores range from the dark, rhythmic, heavily electronic music of *Predator 2* (1990) to the lighthearted, sweeping themes of *Forrest Gump* (1994) to the Western-flavored melodies of *The Quick and the Dead* (1995) to the wall-to-wall sonic explosion of *Van Helsing* (2004). There is no simple way to describe Silvestri's talents other than to say that he can do it all.

One of Silvestri's most fruitful professional relationships has been with director and producer Robert Zemeckis. Their collaborations have produced numerous memorable films with memorable scores, including *Romancing the Stone* (1984), the aforementioned *Back to the Future* series, *Who Framed Roger Rabbit* (1988), *Death Becomes Her* (1992), *Forrest Gump*, *Contact* (1997), *Cast Away* (2000), *What Lies Beneath* (2000), and *The Polar Express* (2004).

I find it interesting how some musicians accidentally fall into the world of film music. You have a wonderful rags-to-riches story. What were your early aspirations, and how did that change?

My earliest aspirations had to do with wanting to be a bebop guitar player. One kind of serendipitous event followed another and, to make the long story short, a call came along with an opportunity to score a film. With the tremendous assistance of Earle Hagen, who wrote the book *Scoring for Films*, which was the only such manual in existence then, I actually had a meeting with the film producer and scored a film and found myself being a film composer. Then one thing led to the next and here we are.

In your home, growing up, what kind of music was played?

There was basically no music to speak of in the house. Of course, in an Italian family, usually the oldest child bears the responsibility of being the accordion player, so that fell upon my sister. I started to play drums when I was very young, three or four years old, and did so all through my younger years. But there wasn't any real musical influence around me. My mom and dad were not musical. They didn't have record collections. So it all came from who-knows-where. There was no real musical connection that I know of, certainly not through my grandparents and not my great grandparents. So it's just one of those things.

Have there been particular musical influences in your career?

When you're called upon to do this job, the first thing you do is look around and go, "Who does this and what are they doing?" Back when I started doing this over thirty years ago, and it continues on today, you'd turn around and the first two people you saw were John Williams and Jerry Goldsmith. Unfortunately we've lost Jerry now, but that's after a lifetime of spectacular creativity. John Williams continues to do just amazing work. Those two men really raised the bar and carried the standard for film composing for all of those years. They've been a tremendous influence not to just composers, but to filmmakers and audiences for a long time.

From one film composer to the next, does there tend to be friendship or is there a competitive feeling?

I have a very dear friendship with David Newman. We've gotten to know each other very well over the years. Our wives are very dear friends. We spend a lot of social time together. I don't feel anything competitive between Dave and myself. I think the choice of a composer by a filmmaker is a very personal creative choice. I may be speaking from the point of view having enjoyed a certain amount of good fortune over the years, but I don't feel that I need to be competitive to the exclusion of a friendship with somebody really great over business. There are a lot of films being made. There are a lot of opportunities for both of us and many other composers. So I don't really look at it like that.

During your hiatus from the hit television series *CHiPs*, a phone conversation with Robert Zemeckis ultimately paved your way to success in feature films?

There was a line of demarcation between writing for television and writing for film. It was often difficult to cross. I had been involved in a very successful television series, but it ultimately didn't mean anything in terms of working on the film side.

I did that show [*CHiPs*] for four years. But there was never any long-term or short-term agreement. You went and recorded a show on Monday morning. You saw the next one Monday afternoon. It was always a weekly phone call as to whether or not you were going to do this. And after four years, there was a regime change on the show, and that phone didn't ring on Friday afternoon. So, then you go, "Wow, there must be something wrong with the phone service!" And, when the phone doesn't ring the next week, then you start to get the picture: There's nothing wrong with your phone.

After having this twenty-eight-week season of a hit television show for four years, you potentially can get lulled into thinking that this is how life is going to be now. So you really enjoy your time off and then that phone rings after ten weeks or whatever it is and there you go again. When that stops, it can stop cold, which it did in my case.

When Bob Zemeckis called, I don't think I had worked for a year in television, and it was very difficult to get anything going. It wasn't like I was working on this successful television show and then the phone rang and it was Bob Zemeckis and I went and did *Romancing the Stone* and that was the start of the film side of my career. It wasn't like that at all. I had been out of work for a good while.

Right at that time came the real emergence of electronic instruments. The first really good electronic drum machine had just come out. There had been a few electronic keyboards that had been out for a period of time, but great strides and great revolutions were occurring in that world, and the Yamaha DX-7 [synthesizer] had just appeared.

What I came to early on in that gap was, if you're going to be in this business, somehow you need to find a way to get your work out before the people who need your work, i.e., producers and directors. Before this electronic renaissance, if you wanted to get music to play for a director or producer, you had to have recorded it with an orchestra, which was, of course, very costly. There was now this possibility for someone with very limited means to at least find a way to put their ideas together and have something to play in order to try to get work as a film composer. So that's what I chose to do.

So I went out and bought a LinnDrum [drum machine]. We really didn't have the money to do this, but we seemed to have no choice. My wife was behind the business plan a thousand percent. I then went and bought a Yamaha DX-7 and there was a Japanese manual and a power converter. I bought a small board and I started to put this little group of components together and, literally, at the very beginning of that process, that phone call came in for *Romancing the Stone*. In that phone conversation, Bob introduced himself and explained a scene in the movie, which was the gorge scene, where they're running away. He said, "Al, here's the deal, this guy and this girl, they're running through this jungle. It's raining. They have machetes. They're being chased by the Federales. It's a nightmare. It's this big chase in the jungle. Can you do about three minutes of something like that and come see me tomorrow morning?" I was actually able to say yes.

So I wound up going in with these boxes of things that I newly purchased and stuck them all together and stayed up all night and I put together this little three-minute demo based on what Bob Zemeckis had just described to me. I got in my car at eight-thirty in the morning and drove to Warner Hollywood and played it for him.

The following night, the phone rang, and it was Michael Douglas, who was the producer of the movie, talking to me about hiring me to score *Romancing the Stone*. So it was kind of a miracle story.

Romancing the Stone was a unique set of circumstances and an amazing opportunity. I think it's now eleven films and twenty years later with Bob, who has become a very dear friend and the most amazing creative collaboration for me.

When we think of Alan Silvestri and Robert Zemeckis together, it becomes more than a collaboration, but a friendship that has sustained for almost thirty years. Talk about how this developed and what has kept this bond inseparable.

When a film director develops a project, shoots it, endures all of the obstacles that a filmmaker has to endure in order to bring a piece of film to the screen, he or she is carrying a tremendous amount. Like anyone who bears the full responsibility on that level, in the end, directors look for help, and they look for people who can be part of the solution, as opposed to part of the problem.

I think Bob was bearing this tremendous responsibility for this film. It was a very important film for him. It was very important for Michael Douglas as a producer. It was very important for both Kathleen Turner and Danny DeVito as artists. A lot of folks had a lot at stake in this film.

I entered late in the game, and Bob was just an amazing person to work with. I worked very hard on that film, and what I brought to the film seemed to really work for him—it seemed to feed back to him his vision and his direction for the music of the film. I think our personal relationship was born at that point through our professional creative relationship, because one of the things I think that underlies any kind of strong ongoing personal relationship is a feeling that you're really communicating. The person that you have that relationship with sees a lot of the world the way you do and expresses what they see the way you do.

We both have grown over the years. Bob has always been a very challenging filmmaker for music. It really just comes from the fact that he is always challenging himself first. So you're happy to get in his wake and try to do your best.

When one talks about memorable themes in film music, the first two names that come to mind are John Williams and Alan Silvestri. From *Back to the Future* to *Forrest Gump*, your themes come to mind at the mere mention of the titles. Would you talk about your process for developing main melodies? And are they where you begin on your canvas, before adding color and other details?

First of all, it's a supreme compliment that you even mentioned my name with that other name. His name comes to my mind first with regard to what you speak of. I have always felt the amazing power that a theme, a clearly definable theme, can bring to a film. I have been greatly influenced by John Williams and have aspired to learn from that and try to, when it's appropriate, find a very clearly definable theme that captures either the essence of an entire film or an aspect of it. It is absolutely, when that is the mission, where I start.

Both films that you mention, *Back to the Future* and *Forrest Gump*, had themes that were the first things created in all of the music for those films. They both served something for me creatively—they musically kind of "essentialized" the feelings of the entire films. But they each had very different lives in the films that they were a part of.

The theme for *Back to the Future* is used in all kinds of forms and aspects everywhere, front to back, in the movie. I wrote the feather theme for *Forrest Gump* after a meeting with Bob. There was no feather to be seen yet. It was very early on in the film's life. There was only a camera-move in that town square, no feather. Bob described the feather to me in terms of what it would ultimately be, and I went back and I wrote that theme for that movie. Bob seemed to take to it immediately, so I knew I was on the right track. I said to myself, "Wow, I've just found a key to this film! It will guide me as I go ahead and score the film."

I scored *Forrest Gump* front to back in sequence. I got to the first piece of music that we had to have for the film, and I thought, "Here we go, now I'll use the theme." But it didn't work. So I had to write a new theme. Then I got to the next place for music in the film, and it didn't work. I went through the whole movie looking for a way to use that theme, and I didn't even use three notes of it until the very end of the film, when this feather appears again. It seemed to be the most appropriate bookending for the film.

With both the *Forrest Gump* and the *Back to the Future* themes, the attempt was to really "essentialize" in music the feeling of the films. One had a very limited use in the film and one had a very wide and expansive use. You just never know until you try and bring these things together.

How do you know when it's appropriate to start thematically?

Very often, I'll go to a very key dramatic moment in the film. For instance, my entry into the ultimate score to *Polar Express* came through the scene in the last third of the film where the kids are all in the town square and the bell breaks loose from the sleigh and winds up at the feet of our hero, who says, "I do believe. I do believe." And all of a sudden he can hear the bell for the first time. I just knew that whatever I would write for this film had to really work and capture this whole event we're about to see—Santa talking to the boy—and it had to be somehow connected to this bell. So that was the place that the score really started.

To answer your question, this now becomes a resource for you as the composer of the score. As you move through the film, you make the determination whether it is appropriate at a given instance or not. And if it isn't, you need another resource. For instance, there may have been four or five independent themes in *Forrest Gump*. Some of them recur periodically through the film. Some of them don't. In each instance, I faced that piece of music that needed to be written from the point of view of: This is thematic material that we've already heard. Is any of this appropriate to use here, in terms of how it resonates with the film? If not, I need to go back to the drawing board, begin again, and find out what is appropriate for this film.

Writing great themes—is this something that can be taught, or is this a strength that's developed from within?

I don't know if it can be pigeonholed one way or the other, and I don't mean to be evasive about it. It's always a very difficult question. Obviously, many things can be learned in music and in many other disciplines, and need to be learned. There is the craft of putting notes together. That is undeniable. However, on the other side of the coin, there is one's sense of taste, which comes from one's experience with music, one's experience with living, one's likes and dislikes. And there may be this inherited genetic propensity to prefer this note following that note as opposed to another. I don't think anyone would say that *anybody* writes a memorable theme for a movie if they just work hard enough. I wouldn't say that,and I don't think anyone else would. I also don't think you can say that, anyone, if they work hard enough, can go out and pitch a no-hitter in major-league baseball. At some point, there are other attributes and factors beyond one's hard work that enter into the mix.

Although I think of the main body of your work as melodic and orchestral, you use synth rhythms and sounds in *Predator 2* or, more recently, *Lara Croft Tomb Raider: The Cradle of Life*, for example.

Let's use painting as the analogy. If you're painting in color, why not have this vast array of color? So you have this amazingly powerful orchestra, but you also have this very amazing palette of new sounds, new colors, new ways to combine things. I love all of it—it's all part of the creative process to use the tools at hand, whatever tools they may be. I love the technology. I love how it has progressed. I've always been involved with it in some way, shape, or form. I love the orchestra, also, and what it can accomplish. As you know from my list of films, I traditionally use very large, powerful orchestras. But, that doesn't exclude the fact that there are amazing colors available through the electronic side of life.

Blown Away **opens with a solo soprano voice and choir. Why did you use voices instead of a full orchestra or perhaps bagpipes and a fiddle, for example? How do you pick a sound palette?**

That film had a very dramatic opening. It was this long tracking shot. It was a very rugged coastline, but it was beautiful at the same time. The arrival of all of this beauty was basically hell. It was this terrible prison. So it seemed like there was the possibility to do something very beautiful, and its contrast with where we wound up would ultimately be as powerful as what the filmmaker was doing in his shot.

That was one aspect. The other thing was that this was a story about a man who had, in the name of doing something right, lost touch with his innocence and something childlike in himself and had become basically a monster. There was something very pure about the idea of this solo voice that I thought could be a very interesting tone and layer to what would ultimately unfold in the film. So that's kind of where I went.

What is being sung? Does it impact the story?

It comes from an old song called "The Prince's Day." I don't have the lyrics here in front of me, but they had a tremendous kind of relevance for the subject content of the film. So, all in all, it just seemed to be a really wonderful choice to begin the film.

Cast Away **is a captivating, profoundly emotional score, yet it was used so sparsely in the film.**

Once again, Bob went to a very unique place in his creation of that film. When you sit, as a film composer, and confront a film like that, a lot of things go through your mind. You know you're working on a movie, but there's the sense that anything cliché would just be devastating to everything that both Bob and Tom Hanks were trying to create.

As I saw the film, I was just salivating, waiting to jump in there and make my contribution, but I keep watching and watching and I just keep saying, "There's nothing I could do that would be right, that would add anything to what I'm seeing." It was a very strange experience, actually, to keep watching and watching and watching and have Bob looking at me, saying, "Nothing yet, Alan?" I answer, "I don't think so, Bob." "Nothing yet?" "I don't think so." Now we're over halfway through this movie and his composer hasn't heard any music yet. Bob's like, "Okay, Al, nothing yet?"

The first time that I felt that there might be a place for something was when Tom left the island. What ultimately came to me was that, as terrible as that island was, it was known to him. He was very proactive or could potentially be proactive. And basically that's what we saw through that whole time on the island. But, when he broke over that wave, all of a sudden it was a new game. He had made a choice, and now he had to count on forces beyond himself for the outcome. That was, to me, what that whole movie was really about. That was the point where I felt that that character had really transformed, had really come to this focal point of his arc—and that was the first time I heard music, that I felt music might have a place there.

It was a very simple musical statement. From there on out, we hear the same simple theme played in a number of settings. It was always exactly the same, and I used very simple, very pure orchestration. The oboe is notoriously one of the purest sounds in the orchestra. It's the instrument used to tune the orchestra. The stings also have a very simple, organic feeling and sense. So those are the only two timbres that we hear. I didn't want to complicate even the timbre palette because I felt that, if we start feeling like the music is doing something here, we will just destroy everything that everybody worked so hard to create. It was a very interesting process for me to restrain myself. If you hear other things that I've done, you know that I'm not shy about going out there and making a ruckus.

Cast Away, to me, is a masterpiece.

That's fantastic. I will pass that on to Bob. He would love to hear that. He cares very deeply about what he does, and no comment like that is wasted on someone who works that hard.

Outside of writing music, what are your passions in life?

I have a number of different things that I love to do. I love to fly airplanes. I've been doing that for a good while. I'm jet-type rated and have flown alone in a jet at 41,000 feet. That's a great passion. I continue to fly.

About eight years ago, we started a vineyard here [in Carmel, California] from absolutely nothing. That's been an amazing experience for me and for the whole family. We're drinking our wine, which comes from our land, which we all have been a part of. We are just about to release our first wines. The chardonnay and the pinot noir are bottled and labeled. The syrah is being bottled in about a week. The website, sylvestrivineyards.com, is up and running.

As a film composer, you marry sound and picture. Do you ever just want to write music to life or freely express from within without film images in front of you?

So far, and that doesn't mean that it couldn't be different once I hang this phone up, I have really enjoyed and been inspired by watching film. That's been the motivating factor in my sitting down and putting notes together. But, like I said, that could change at any time.

As composer Brian Tyler and I sat in his Los Angeles studio, discussing his experiences as a relatively new addition to the film-music industry, I found fascinating his intoxicating excitement for what he does. Film-scoring seems amazingly natural for him, as if he were meant to walk down that artistic road from day one.

Tyler's scoring opportunities have been spread across an array of genres, from the introspective *Panic* (2000) to the sci-fi epic *Children of Dune* (2002) to the dark, haunting thriller *Darkness Falls* (2003). His score for the epic *Timeline* (2003) is overwhelmingly powerful. His chameleon-like ability to tell a film's inner story without imposing his musical personality on the picture is evident in each score he writes.

Let's first talk about your musical upbringing and how it led to film music.

I suppose it all started with my grandparents. My grandfather was an art director for films and my grandmother was a pianist. That's where the actual collision of film and music first happened. My grandfather [Walter Tyler] was a really wonderful, Academy Award-winning, art director who did films for Cecil B. DeMille, like *The Ten Commandments* and those types of epic features. He'd tell me about his experiences. Then I would hear my grandmother playing Chopin.

I took to music, playing piano and drums, very young. After a few years, I would play music that I composed more often than not. That led to an early mini-career as a composer. I composed concertos and things and ended up touring Europe and all around by my teens, playing the piano. I think my last gig was when I performed at the Moscow Radio Hall for [Mikhail] Gorbachev when I was probably sixteen or seventeen.

Meanwhile, my parents were influencing me with rock and jazz from Led Zeppelin to Cole Porter. So the music industry came to me early. It was my life. Film music always interested me. I think the first record that I bought was either *Midway* or *Star Wars* by John Williams. I would actually watch videos with the volume off and re-score the movies for fun. I never formally studied film-scoring in school, however. My trial by fire was my first movie. I dove into the deep end. I didn't know what timecode or spotting was. That came much later. When I had started my film-music career, I was still in a band. I crossed over to scoring because a song that I had written was going to be used for an end title to a movie called *Bartender*.

I told the movie's director, Gabe Torres, that I wanted to score it, but he wanted to use someone more established. So I convinced the producer to give me the director's address, and I went over to his house with a DAT player with some of my music on it. We sat down and watched the movie as I plopped in this music that somehow fit the scene that we happened to be watching. I got the gig. It was one of those flukes.

That was pretty gutsy.

It was one of those calculated risks. I guess I had nothing to lose. I thought that the worst he could do was throw me out of his house, crushing my ego. Other than that, I had nothing to lose.

What is your approach to a score?

There's a process that I go through every time: I'll watch the movie for the first time either with the temp music or without. Then I'll watch it silent or just with dialogue. During this second viewing, the first thing I think of is the thematic material. During this early stage, themes somehow emerge, and they are almost always melodic. I'll be driving in the car or I'll be in the shower when a theme occurs. Then I'll have to find a piece of paper and write it down. If I don't write it down, it might be gone. Then I go through the project and get more specific: I watch the film again and begin jotting down where the different motifs and themes go and the style that I want for each cue. From that point on, I can launch into writing specifically. In today's film industry, as you know, the post-production process has become shorter and shorter. One of the main components in film-scoring is, of course, speed. Writing comes fairly quickly to me.

Does a temp track become a hindrance?

It can. The number-one thing that the temp track does is act as a placeholder for me. It shows me where a director wants music.

I've done movies where there was no temp track. At first it was a bit scary, but now that I have scored a few films like that, I actually prefer it, because it's just wide-open—you can do what your natural instincts tell you to do, which is, I think, why they hire you.

The first twenty movies I did were temped with all sorts of famous scores. But in the last year or so, I think every film I've done has been temped exclusively with my music, with the exception of maybe three or four cues. That's even weirder, because I know exactly what I did. I almost know it too well. There's no mystery. It's potentially more dangerous.

The danger is in repeating your own music?

Yeah, because you know it so well. I try to flee the temp track so I don't become unduly influenced by it. I'm still perplexed why the filmmakers don't bring the composers in on the early stages of production. With *Children of Dune*, for instance, I got the script and I started composing. Then the director, Greg Yaitanes, would send me dailies of the film. This is really great because you can just sit with the themes and let them percolate over time, even if you're doing other films at the same time.

I've been anxious to hear about your brilliant epic score to *Children of Dune*, which displays all your strengths as a composer.

It was a challenge. My first reaction was that I couldn't believe I was going to write a *Dune* score, because when I saw the original *Dune* in 1984, I just loved it. I watched it many times. I have the score for the original one. I got really sucked into the *Dune* universe. I read all the books and I became this kind of *Dune* nerd. Early on, I re-scored *Dune* for myself. No one ever heard it. Coincidentally enough, the very first thematic motif on the soundtrack was something that I wrote for *Dune* all those years ago and has stuck with me ever since. It was like one of those great serendipitous things. It was a dream that I was able to score something that I had read beforehand. That was the first time that ever happened.

I knew that the score would primarily be orchestra, but there would be voices and all sorts of percussion in it as well. It needed something that isn't typically associated with something shot for television, so I took my budget and put it directly into recording the orchestra. I needed massive percussion and string ensembles aside from the orchestra to achieve what I was writing down on paper. I wasn't going to use samples. I wouldn't abide by that in terms of this earthy percussion and Eastern-stringed-instrument vibe, so I was lucky that I played most of those instruments. I ended up tracking about eighty-three different Brian Tylers playing all sorts of weird instruments. It was probably the most complex thing that I had to do in terms of instrumentation and orchestration. Luckily, the process started very early and I was able to write all the way through the filming of the movie.

***Four Dogs Playing Poker* has a diverse sound.**

Yeah, it was a really interesting project because the storyline starts in Argentina, then it goes to Los Angeles and then New York. Right when you think everything is going smoothly, the plan goes horribly wrong and the film progresses from a lighthearted heist movie to this really dark, intense nightmare. You can see why the music took a complete turn. It starts off with an Argentine guitar over the orchestrated motifs. Then it goes into that cold, industrial, rhythmic electronic score. The only thing remaining from the heist part of the movie is that there's an Argentine guitar over it. Then the score just completely loses all of the orchestra. There's none of it left except for the very last piece, "Insomnia", which is orchestra combined with beats.

That might be my most eclectic score, and it's exactly reflective of this intentionally disorienting movie's changing scenery. There is a little bit of a red herring at the beginning, where you feel that you are in more of a *Catch Me if You Can* vibe, and then it just throttles you.

Panic is probably your coldest-feeling score, but in the same breath, it's melodic and passionate. Talk about your approach to this film.

Panic was a huge revelation for me. I actually saw the film before I scored it. I had another movie, *Shadow Hours*, that was in dramatic competition against *Panic* at Sundance. I went to see *Panic* because I wanted to see the competition, and I loved it. It was one of my favorite movies immediately when I saw it. I just had to do this movie, so I immediately went out into the parking lot and called my agent and called around: "Who's directing this?" "Is the director here?" "I've got to find this guy. I must score this movie."

Talking to the filmmakers, I expressed that it should be really wide and sparse and kind of minimalist, but I also wanted it to have emotion. It could be cold in the way the orchestra played, but in the way the music was written it could be really emotional, because this main character in this movie, played by Bill Macy, was this guy who completely suppresses everything. He really *feels* it under the surface, but you don't see anything on his face that would be a sign that there's actually emotion underneath that skin. But you know it's there.

I wrote a very emotional score, but I had the orchestra play with no vibrato and completely cold and stark. I had never really done this combination on another movie. It's kind of unique unto itself and somehow it's heartbreaking in a way.

You perform, including vocals, on most of your scores.

Yes. I'm on almost all of my scores. If you go through *Children of Dune*, my voice is all over that. It's a go-to thing for me. Some composers have a synth patch that they always like to go to or something like that. For me, it's about three or four layers of my voice. And I'll bring in a female vocalist for a different part. So it's a combination of things. I also love using large choirs when a film calls for it.

I've been a singer most of my life. But I'm not in there belting out a tune or something in the score. I don't want to do that.

Tell me about *Timeline.*

Boy, it's a massive tapestry! That's for sure. The idea behind it is to create a really intense score that has a lot of scope—a very wide, kind of epic quality to it. Although the film partly takes place in the present, it is really about futuristic technology. We're dealing with contained wormholes and the ability to travel back and forth between the fourteenth century and the present. The music does something similar in that it constantly weaves from a more ancient sound to a more modern musical sound. In the present, there is always orchestra, but it's complemented by other things, such as electronics. But when the story travels back to the fourteenth century, the music has a purely orchestral sound with medieval percussion. During this time, the score has a really rough, warlike feel and is contrasted with a new love theme. It's very melancholy. So there are three elements to this score that are in sharp contrast with each other.

I would say that ninety percent of the movie is in the fourteenth century. So the majority of the score was played by a ninety-one-piece orchestra with a fourteen-piece medieval percussion ensemble and a choir. It is relentless. In fact, one cue in the movie is probably the most relentless thing I have ever had to write because there are these giant, epic battles between the French and the English armies that are just unbelievable. The French developed this weapon called the trebuchet, which has this amazing ability to launch objects through the air. I was told that it could launch a piano four football fields. When the people from the present went back in time, they brought knowledge of modern technology. They aided the English with things like "Greek fire." So there's this battle in medieval times, but it's got explosions that you wouldn't see in *Braveheart*. The music has to create this hyper sense of reality and war. But these scenes are very long. I think the longest stretch of music that I had toward the end of the movie is fifteen and a half minutes. To keep up a solid piece of action music for fifteen minutes, keeping the energy building up and getting bigger and faster, is practically impossible. When I just watched the scene last night at the scoring stage it occurred to me how long it was. I don't know if I could do it again. But it was really a lot of fun.

Academy Award-winning British composer Stephen Warbeck, who has an extensive background in theater music, is greatly skilled at creating film music that is naturally dramatic, poetic, and serene. With his scores for such highly respected and popular films as *Shakespeare in Love* (1998) and *Billy Elliot* (2000), he has earned an admired place in today's movie industry.

With his eccentric score for Philip Kaufman's film *Quills* (2000), he wove a wide spectrum of abstract textures into a period piece that told a dark, erotic tale of lust and insanity. This score differs greatly from his epic and emotional music for *Captain Corelli's Mandolin* (2001) and *Charlotte Gray* (2001), displaying well Warbeck's ability to adapt his musical personality to fit any cinematic environment.

You won an Oscar for your *Shakespeare in Love* score. What did this work mean for your career?

Having an Academy Award does make a difference in terms of the fact that people who wouldn't necessarily have thought of approaching you do now. I think that effect is a kind of wave that happens just afterwards and then it all dies down again. Immediately after *Shakespeare in Love*, people would phone me up or phone my agent without actually considering who I am or in what regard if I might be the right composer for this job. Certainly it puts you slightly more in focus in terms of reputation.

Quills stands out to me as your most creative work. Talk about your choice of colors in this score.

One of the exciting things about _Quills_ was that Philip Kaufman, the director, continually encouraged me to be more daring and experimental. Philip would tell me to be as eccentric and individual as I wanted to be. So, I agree with you: I think that it resulted in some of the most interesting textures I've come up with for a film.

What influenced your choir music in _Quills_? Was that original music?

That's original. I think it came from the fact that I wanted to counterpoint the rather extreme apparent innocence of those young girls who were taken, and then they've no idea what's in store for them.

What do the water sounds and the ethnic percussion symbolize in _Quills_?

We were trying to create a landscape of sound that would be indistinguishable from the effects. By using the groans and creeks of the building itself, I wanted to find an abstract palette that wouldn't be defined by European art music or anything. We made quite a few instruments especially for that film as well. We came up with a variety of strange inventions, like bits of tubing and buckets of water.

Dreamkeeper is another colorful, diverse work. How challenging was this film for you?

That was very challenging. I haven't seen it yet, so I can't quite imagine what the whole effect is of the thing in sequence. I saw it in sections when we were working on it, but because it hasn't been broadcast over here in England yet, I haven't seen it as a whole.

I certainly loved the visual material. I thought it was very bold, and the way it was shot and cut was magnificent. Recording some

Native American musicians in the States was also great, because that was literally fed back into the score.

The Native American voices sound like they are far away.

When we recorded them in the States, they were recorded quite dry, and then, once we mixed them into the score, effects were added so that the music and the voices all became part of the same world.

You were originally chosen to score *The Hours*, but two composers later, Philip Glass ends up scoring it. We often hear of the rejected score, but a series of composers seems a bit unusual. Can you tell me how this all took place?

I was the first composer, Michael Nyman became the second, and finally, Philip Glass was hired, as you mentioned. Basically, it was one of those things where the director wants one thing and the producer wants another. The problem is that you end up not being able to please either of them because you're trying to please both. I spent a few months attempting to find a path between them. Then Michael Nyman had a couple of months of the same sort of thing. Then Philip Glass finished it all off.

Can you give me a take on your interpretation?

I loved the script, and I thought it was very nicely shot. I spoke to Scott Rudin, the producer, and expressed to him my thoughts of a minimalist score. He loved the idea. About two or three months later, I started to think that maybe it didn't need a minimalist score and, at that stage, the director agreed. But, by then, Scott Rudin had got very set on how that's how it should be approached. So our ways started to diverge.

How do you feel that Philip Glass's score relates to your first impression of the film, and do you feel it worked well?

It's not that dissimilar, in fact. Although it's a minimalist score, it has a considerable emotional charge to it. So I'd say it's a lot less minimal than some of his work and, therefore, probably functions quite well.

I have seen mention of a group that you are involved with called The Clippers. What sort of group is this?

The Clippers is my band, which I have had for about fifteen years. We play at little jazz clubs in London. We only play about five times a year because it's quite difficult to get everybody available at the same time.

You're also involved with theater at the Royal Shakespeare Company?

I stopped being head of music at the RSC. Because of family commitments and film-work and so on, I didn't have enough time to do it. But I'm writing a musical, a theater version of *Matilda*, by Roald Dahl, which was made into a film by Danny DeVito. But this is a theater version.

Gabriel Yared

"Spiritually inspiring" might be a good way to describe Lebanese-born composer Gabriel Yared's film music, which can quite ably express a character's soul and a story's essence.

Yared, who lived in France for many years, has worked with an enviable list of filmmakers that includes Jean-Luc Godard and Robert Altman, and formed enduring relationships with Jean-Jacques Annaud, for whom he scored *The Lover* (1991) and *Wings of Courage* (1994), and Anthony Minghella, for whom he scored *The English Patient* (1996), *The Talented Mr. Ripley* (1999), and *Cold Mountain* (2003). Yared's music for Minghella's films have enjoyed both popular and critical success: His *The English Patient* score won an Academy Award for Best Score, and his *The Talented Mr. Ripley* and *Cold Mountain* scores received Oscar nominations.

His scores for the tragic love stories of *City of Angels* (1998) and *Message in a Bottle* (1999) and the cold journey of *Map of the Human Heart* (1992) are further testament to his wide-reaching abilities and musical passion.

Would you talk about your discovery of music while growing up in Lebanon, and how it eventually brought you to write music for films?

I was born into a family with no musical or artistic traditions and a very strict attitude toward education. I was sent at the tender age of four to a Jesuit boarding school. My family felt it was an important place to get a respectable education. So I was thrown very early into great solitude. I did not have a musical role model, so I don't know where it comes from actually.

I believe that I have an angel watching over me all the time. I think I was born with music; I didn't discover it. In my non-musical family, I was considered a black sheep. Nobody understood my interests.

My first approach to music was with a teacher at the Jesuit school who used to play the organ in the church. He would give me a half-hour a week. The first thing I realized was that I most enjoyed reading it. I was not interested in being a virtuoso of Chopin or whomever. I just wanted to learn how to read it. I continued to do this until the age of fourteen, when my teacher died. It is sad, because he used to feel that I would never be a musician or do anything in my life in music. I felt surrounded by enemies.

When my teacher died, I still had the key to the organ. So I used to go there to read and play all the works I could of Bach and Handel or any music I could find. At the time, I was not influenced by Arabic music, which I did not like, although I used to hear it coming from a radio outside the walls of the boarding school.

After boarding school, I discovered that I was attracted to some pop music, like Stevie Wonder, Marvin Gaye, and The Beatles. At the same time I was discovering Schumann, Beethoven, and Mozart. This all went together for me. I have never made any difference between pop and the classics and world music. For me, any music is interesting as long as it brings you into consciousness, into discovering that you are a holder of a diamond and you have something beautiful to deliver.

My influences have been very diverse. Very early, like at the age of seventeen, I was interested in what people today call "world music," because I thought of myself as a son of the world. I'm not really born Lebanese or born whatever. I'm just born a composer and musician. I was attracted to almost all music. Bulgarian singing, pygmies, Bali's music—all of those things were influences when I was young.

How did this lead to film music?

I went to France, where I ended up staying until two years ago. I became an orchestrator for French pop singers. Among them was Françoise Hardy, an icon in France from the sixties until now. She was married to Jacques Dutronc, a very famous French actor who worked with Jean-Luc Godard. As I was producing his wife's work, he was very interested in my music composition and orchestration, and when Jean-Luc asked him if he knew somebody who could adapt some work from Ponchielli, a nineteenth-century Italian composer, he said, "Yes, Gabriel Yared." This is how I stepped into film music.

Before stepping into Jean-Luc's project, I had no interest in going to the theater or going to see a movie. When I was very young, I would see *Spartacus* and *Ben-Hur* and the other big films then. And I saw the Hitchcock and Bergman films, but I didn't have any culture in films because I was much more interested in internal images versus external images. This is because all of my inspiration comes from being silent and completely focused inside. I always felt that the images outside were less interesting. They don't appeal to my imagination. And this specific lack of interest in external images kept me from imagining that I might become a film composer one day.

It's not that I don't have an interest in films, because I think there are great artists who have directed great films. It was that all of my money went to buy records and music scores by Bach, Schumann, Stravinsky, Bartók, etcetera. It's not because I dislike images, but I have devoted much more of myself to music and only music. I don't see myself looking at a moving picture and being inspired to compose music. I am inspired by looking into a painting or a sculpture or at Mother Nature. A fictional picture doesn't speak to me in a direct enough way to be inspiring.

Jean-Luc came to me and, by a great coincidence, he said, "I don't want to show you any picture. I just want to tell you the story for which I want themes. Just read the script and, then, let's talk." So my first approach to film music was through a man who didn't even want or didn't care to show me the picture. He just told me the story. We talked about music. We talked about the main characters. Then I dived into my work—my first film music.

I have a very special approach to film-composing, and I don't specifically see myself as a film composer. I'm just a composer, and I approach all my work—whether a film or a ballet score or even a ten-second jingle—with an equal sense of conscience. I feel that the cinema audiences are as worthy of hearing high-quality music as the concert-hall audiences. Music should not be written for less-sophisticated audiences. Music for different media or different functions should be quite simply music—different music, maybe, but still music.

I don't see myself as a good film composer because I don't have all these methods for scoring a battle or a fight ... I don't know how to do that. I know there are methods to that, but I don't want those methods. I don't want to go through the Hollywood vocabulary of film music as it has been established through the past sixty years. I would like to escape from that vocabulary.

You say that images aren't all that important to you, but I find that your work produces so much imagery in the way that, for example, Jean Sibelius's *Finlandia* captures an image of the land.

It does, because the internal images that are within you are expressed as external images. So the idea is to close your eyes and listen to your heart, not to look at the picture and say, "I will do this music from here to there." Listen to all the things in your memory— the script, your conversations, going to the shooting stage, your meeting with the actors—and try to express the main feeling that you get from that and not look to a specific scene. It has to do with grasping the emotional things inside the film. We should seek to capture the very sense of the narrative within the music.

As a film composer, how have you changed through the years?

I have a very special technique. For me, the music fits the spirit of the film first and the details are second. I think composers should be involved from the very beginning of the project. There is no way you can help a film if you just devote three months to it. We should be involved in the preparation of the film and propose some themes, for example, during the shooting process. I think this is the only way to produce good music and a beautiful osmosis between the picture and the music, which is there to serve the picture.

I can tell you how this worked with one of my most well-known works in France, *Betty Blue*, a 1985 film by Jean-Jacques Beineix. This music was written eight months before the shooting. I talked with the director and we read the script together, exchanging ideas. I had also met the two actors. I wanted to know what their skills were in playing the piano, because they had to play a piano piece in this film. All this work that was done before the shooting made me discover the music, which helped the film as it was shot. The cinematographer would act like a choreographer—listening to the music and shooting at the same time. Being on the picture very early in the process brings to the film and the director many ideas of how to shoot and direct and just many things. So, for many of the films that I did in France, I wrote the music before the shooting. Then I adapted the themes to fit the picture before delivering the actual score.

What I find most beautiful in your composition is the flow throughout the album, telling its own story, which allows the listener to experience your creativity on its own, while having the marriage to the picture at the same time.

Yeah, but at the same time, I'm helping the picture. I'm really serving the picture. I want to say, "Yes, you can produce real music built with a beautiful sense of respect for music and also help the picture." That's all. I would like people to listen to my music and say, "This is music! Also, this music was for a film, and has really matched the film." If I achieve only one thing, it is that I may be able to elevate an audience and say to them, "You are watching something beautiful, but you are also listening to something beautiful, and you can also take this opportunity to elevate your souls."

The more time I can spend on a film, the happier I am, because I can search. This is difficult in this industry. I spent eight months on *The English Patient*. On *The Talented Mr. Ripley*, I spent almost a year. This is what you need, really. I mean, I don't think that any composer, unless he's a genius like Mozart, could write an opera in fifteen days. We need to spend a little more time. We need to forget about our habits. We need to unite in a collaborative effort.

Unfortunately, a lot of directors have no background in music. The film schools and universities teach a lot about the focus, how to direct an actor, how to direct a set, and all those things, but there is no education in music. If there is, it is education in film music, which is just a small part of music. There is a proverb: "One hand alone cannot applaud; you need two hands." I wish directors would become more educated in music in order to be more demanding of composers. Not to direct them, telling them to do this and that, but to have the ability to go further, to go beyond your habits, to try several different musical approaches on each scene, experiment, etcetera . . . "What could we do to go beyond that?"

I respect my colleagues and I love their work, but I don't think that film music is really experiencing a harmony between director and composer. I would like to do my best to create great music that serves a picture, but composers cannot really do the job by themselves. We need directors around us who know about music and who could be involved in the music process and not just ask us to cover the film safely.

I hope that directors will read this. I hope this makes a difference for them.

Christian, I hope that the universities will make a move in this direction. Where film is taught, there are teachers who should give strong music courses—not just film-music courses, but also the history of music. The director should know the difference between Bach's and Mozart's work and what an oboe and a French horn are. So, when he comes to the studio, he is not naïve. Instead, he has the ability to establish a relationship with a composer and to discuss music. He can talk to a cinematographer, to an actor, to a director of special effects. He should be able to talk to a composer.

Certain directors and producers seem to desire the same sound of music, again and again. So, I often sense that a score written to serve a certain picture could be used for numerous films.

It means that the directors are not awake inside to analyze the music and to say, "I've heard it before. Please serve me something else." It's like a dog biting his tail. Music is repeating.

An example of the perfect collaboration with a director is my work with [author and director] Anthony Minghella. He is, in addition to being my soul mate, an educated, refined person. He's a musician. He plays piano. He reads and loves music, and he pushes me beyond the ordinary. He asks me to renew myself each time. We talk about his film as soon as he has finished writing his script. I am among the first people to read the script. All his scripts have literal comments about music here and there. We meet and discuss the music.

Then I start composing, even though he has not started shooting. And now we are in the process of starting the score, with my themes set to the picture and very efficiently commented on and experimented with by [editor/sound designer] Walter Murch. We know where we're going at this point. We can only improve. I don't even have to think about the themes. I like all the colors that I've established, and now I just have to paint.

Is this what has kept you more in the European productions versus getting involved with Hollywood, so to speak?

I have said this to the Hollywood filmmakers many times: "Hire me for one year and pay me for only three months. Don't change your contract." They're not opposed to that, but they've never heard of it.

I know that now my colleagues are starting to consider my point of view, and many of them are saying that they would like to work before the shooting or before the end of the editing process.

When you get married, you just don't decide to get married in two weeks. You need to be engaged. My point is that you need to be engaged with the director, and then you get married during the scoring.

This is a real relationship. And sometimes this kind of relationship will last beyond films. Then, you can slowly open the ears of your director to new music. Listen to music other than film music. Go to concerts. Start a relationship that is based on art because it's an artistic relationship that becomes a human relationship.

You've done a wide range of films but might be pigeonholed for a master of heavily emotional romantic dramas.

I know. It's very ironic. *The English Patient* is a drama where the characters die in the end. Immediately after that, I composed *City of Angels*, *Message in a Bottle*, and then *Autumn in New York*. The characters die at the end of all these movies. I told my agent, "Stop it! It's becoming ridiculous." I'm not specialized in this kind of music. I don't want to be pigeonholed. I've done some comedies in France. I've done many different things. I'm now doing *Troy*, which is a period epic film. I'm very open to different projects. The only films I'm not interested in are violent films. I hate violence. One of the reasons I don't go to the cinema is because you don't know when violence will hit you. I'm very sensitive to that.

Your music is heartfelt, and it is obvious why you were chosen for these pictures.

Yeah, but at the same time if you listen to my score for *The Talented Mr. Ripley*, I could go in very different places. I don't want to be stuck to romantic, dramatic, lyrical films. I'd like to do something else and people should listen to what I've done in the ballet field, which reflects much more of the things that inhabit me. It doesn't mean that I am excellent at everything. I like to laugh, I like to eat, I like to drink, I like to smoke, whatever. I'm not stuck to only one style because the more you ask me to do this, the more I become reluctant and disgusted by myself.

Autumn in New York really touched me. It is a unique score with romantic themes, but it also has ethnic sounds and beautiful vocals. This is a work that I feel is richly authentic to your technique.

I love to bring into the music something that is ethnic and that is so beautiful or ancient that it really shines. But I'm interested in that only if there is a purpose for it, not just to make a hit or to be looked at as a new sound.

I thought that *Autumn in New York*, since it was in New York City, should have something like a little color of ethnicity. Before that I've used the ethnic sound in *A Map of the Human Heart*, which is a score that I like very much because it's very simple—it's only synths and samples. I was able to study Eskimo music, which makes the score to *Map of the Human Heart* more interesting. It's so real. In *The*

English Patient, we used this Bulgarian-Turkish-Hungarian song in the beginning of the film, which was a real traditional folk song.

Let's talk about *The English Patient* a little bit more. Your score won an Oscar. How did that affect your career?

When I got the Oscar, I was very happy. The Oscar has been very good to me. Of course I enjoyed it. But it also brought about a misunderstanding, because people thought that if I did *The English Patient*, I'm only capable of doing *The English Patient* and nothing else. I was hired on so many similar films, as I mentioned before, because of *The English Patient*. All the things I did for three years were kind of similar: *City of Angels*, *Message in a Bottle*, *Autumn in New York*, *Possession*, and *The Next Best Thing*. But if you'll listen to each score, they are very different from one to the other. I don't think I have really repeated myself, although they do have the same lyrical feeling.

After that, I was very lucky because I was nominated for an Oscar for *The Talented Mr. Ripley*. I thought that maybe people would understand me differently after listening to *The Talented Mr. Ripley*, which is very different from *The English Patient*. If *Cold Mountain* is a huge success, maybe people will listen to me as an Americana composer, because *Cold Mountain* takes place during the American Civil War. I must say that my music is very far from *The English Patient* on this one. So I look forward to not being pigeonholed again.

The thing is, Christian, if you really live with music every second of your life, you don't mind any opportunity people give you to write music. It's fantastic for your soul and for your skills and for everything. So I shouldn't even be complaining that I have been pigeonholed because I produce music and I have no regrets and no resentment about all that as long as I write.

You score movies that need to be absorbed and thought about if one is to understand their stories. Do you consciously choose such projects?

I am very sensitive, as you may notice when you listen to my music. I don't socialize a lot. I never go out. I live almost like a monk. But

I'm very attached to people. If I meet someone, I really want to know him or her. And it takes me time to know somebody. It takes me time to deliver myself, to become really who I am.

I am not interested in simple relationships or stories or people. I find it really interesting when you have to go deeper and deeper to understand something. I like situations, people, music, a work of art in which you can endlessly discover new things.

Which of your scores is most dear to you?

Actually, I never listen back to my scores. I look sometimes at the scores themselves, at the sheet music.

You always love the one that has been the most painful, that made you really suffer. I don't know why that is. The one that really made me work a lot, and search a lot and be perfect is *Camille Claudel*. This is, for me, the one that seems like me. It represents me the most.

You also write for ballet.

I write for ballet because I like choreography. One of the most beautiful and the most modern is *The Rite of Spring* by Igor Stravinsky.

You can be completely bold when writing for a ballet. You can take all the risks you want, and it's all so rhythmical. What all the people who have pigeonholed me don't understand is that I'm a very rhythmical person. I don't only like beautiful strings with melodies and beautiful, lyrical, and romantic things, I also like rhythm. I am very happy to use my rhythmic skills in ballet. I make people dance to my music in ballet. My music is really a dance.

So how does writing a film score differ from writing a ballet?

There is not a difference to me. It's just the crafting that changes a little. We know how to craft a stone into a beautiful diamond. You just cut it, and then you put around it the things that you want. This is crafting. But finding the stone, this is more important. And whether we have found the stone for ballet or film music, it's just some elements that change.

Your music has affected my life profoundly. How does it feel to know that your music touches people or reaches their souls on many different levels?

Wow. That's very tough. Listen, I'm just a man of great passion who sees music as a gift he has received and that he must not betray or destroy. My musical ideas come to me as if they're given to me from somewhere outside of myself. As a result of that, I feel myself to be less the author of my own work than a channel for it. I see everything that I do as an opportunity to deliver my inspiration received from above and to elevate an audience to the highest understanding of our world in this universe and, also, to make the picture and the music shine.

I'm not responsible for the things I'm doing; I'm just a good translator. And to be the best translator, you must never stop digging and searching. So, at the end of the day, if my music hits you, I'm very happy for this angel who inspires all my music. So thank you to my angel. The music will always come to me as long as I respect her and as long as I worship her.

Christopher Young

I feel compelled to share a short story about my initial experience with Christopher Young, who was my first interview for this book. Chris and I sat in his Culver City studio and talked for nearly two hours. I was so engrossed in what he was saying that I forgot to pay attention to my tape recorder, which had shut off a half-hour into our conversation. Needless to say, once I noticed this problem, I started to sweat bullets, not even sure if I should mention my error to Chris. The only thing I thought of was jumping out his second-story studio window and, if still alive, running for my life. Finally, I built up enough courage to tell him about the recorder. Being as kindhearted as he is talented, he chose for my "punishment" an evening of dinner, drinks, and conversation. The next day, we finished the interview, talking as if we were friends. And today, I would call him a friend.

Young writes very, very well for every imaginable genre, but for a good portion of his early Hollywood career (mid-1980s through the early-1990s) he was not given opportunities to show off the diversity of his talent. He was a prisoner of his own success, pigeonholed as a horror-movie composer because of the wild, pioneering music he wrote for a string of highly successful horror films, which included *Hellraiser* (1987) and *The Vagrant* (1992). Once his career was given a chance to blossom, free of the horror-movie label, he immediately began turning out wonderful scores in all genres. While maintaining his unique musical voice, Chris writes in diverse styles, from his melodramatic, emotional score for *Murder in the First* (1995) to his jazzy, comedic score for *The Man Who Knew Too Little* (1997), and including *Runaway Jury* (2003), *The Shipping News* (2001), *The Gift* (2000), *The Hurricane* (1999), *Rounders* (1998), *Hard Rain* (1998), *Copycat* (1995), *Tales from the Hood* (1995), *Dream Lover* (1994), and *Jennifer Eight* (1992).

Were you aware of film music while you were growing up?

I am embarrassed to say this, but outside of my James Bond matinees, I don't have memories of being affected by the music in films. Certainly, in the James Bond movies, I did. Like most everyone else, I did not experience the film music but the songs. As a child I was raised on songs. It is like now. You can't walk out of your house without being bombarded with a string of pop songs or whatever is current. So, growing up, my musical diet was whatever was on the radio. I didn't even know anything else existed.

How did you get involved in film music?

In my teens, I started out as a drummer, planning to do the rock thing. At that time, I was so in love with The Beatles, and still am for that matter. I cursed the stars for not making me Ringo Starr. Then I got into jazz and cursed the stars for not making me Buddy Rich or . . .

There was a time, however, when I stopped thinking entirely rhythmically. I wish I knew when it was. It was a time when my mind opened up to being able to invent pitched material. I had an encyclopedia of music in my head that I had heard throughout the years, but I was never able to invent stuff until the time I started hearing melody and tried this out by bringing my charts into a jazz band that I was involved with.

One day, I walked into a record store in my hometown of Red Bank, New Jersey, and I discovered a soundtrack section—three rows, three-feet deep, of film-music records. While I was browsing in there, I found a record with the coolest-looking cover. It was called

The Fantasy Film World of Bernard Herrmann. I remember turning over the cover and reading, in Herrmann's own words, a description of what these science-fiction and fantasy films were about and what he chose to do with the music. I found this interesting, as I was going through a heavy science-fiction craze at the time. So I swiped this record up.

I thank God they had that record in the store that day. When I first put that record on and played the opening bars to *Journey to the Centre of the Earth*, I realized that I had found the missing link to what I had been hoping to find in music. The chords, the melodies . . . this was it! So I became obsessed with Bernard Herrmann's music and bought every record I could find, which wasn't that many at the time. Then I started watching the late-night movies on television, where they would sometimes play a movie with Herrmann's name on it. I used to put up my reel-to-reel tape machine and record the audio track off the television. Then I could listen to it on my headphones. I could listen to the music under the dialogue. I tried to remember what it looked like, what the visuals were. So, my interest with film music started with my obsession for Bernard Herrmann's music.

What is the film music composer's goal?

I have an analogy for you: Have you ever played Pin the Tail on the Donkey? It's a game where you are blindfolded and spun around and then a person gently guides you toward where you have to blindly pin the tail on the donkey on your own. The job of a film composer is to gently push the audience toward the emotional meaning of a scene. It reconfirms what they often already expect. A composer simply guides them on the path.

The horror genre seemed to attach itself to you immediately. How did this happen? What was your main goal as a young film composer?

It wasn't necessarily to work in horror films. That's for sure. It just happened when I moved out here and started going to school at UCLA, studying with David Raksin, who had a tremendously positive effect on my life. He was my Rock of Gibraltar. He was the guy who kept me from packing up. He was the one who encouraged me to continue to pursue this nonsense of a dream when I moved out here. He was the only person I took a film-music class with.

It just so happened that there was this group of students who put together enough money to make a feature [*The Dorm that Dripped Blood*] for their senior thesis. I was desperate to get it. It just happened to be a horror film.

Back when I moved out here in the eighties, because of the success of the *Nightmare on Elm Street*, *Halloween*, and *Friday the 13th* films, everyone felt like they could make a quick in into the industry by putting out low-budget horror films. So these guys made a low-budget horror film and they hired me. You know how it goes—your first picture sort of defines who you are. And my next film was their second film. They would call it a supernatural horror film, but it was basically another horror film. It was called *The Power*, a low-budget, supernatural thriller. That sort of defined what I did. I was the horror guy. The whole slew of jobs I got at the outset was about horror. Do I regret it? Absolutely not. Fortunately, over the years, I have been able to slowly move away entirely from thrillers or horror films.

As you know, horror films can offer a composer, number one, the opportunity to experiment. Number two, they allow you to be excessively dramatic in your music. As a matter of fact, you are encouraged to be excessively dramatic. With a lot of the dramatic movies, your job is to keep yourself in reserve. But, in horror movies, I'm always vomiting up as much sound as I can.

Like in your experimental score for *The Vagrant*?

Yeah, that was very experimental. There were other things before that, too, like the thrown-out score for *Invaders from Mars*. I have a love-hate relationship with horror, as I think most people who work in the genre do. There are not many people I've met who work in horror films and say to me that they want to do nothing more than that in their entire creative careers. Everybody who gets typecast wants to be doing something else. Marc Shaiman will tell you that he's sick of doing comedies. I was the horror guy who got sick of doing horror films, and all I could dream of doing were dramas like *The Hurricane* or *The Shipping News* or *Bandits*. I've done other dramas all along, but if you look at my credits, you'll see *Bright Angel* and *Getting*

Even, a cop-action-urban thing and a drug/action film, wedged in between *Hellraiser* and A *Nightmare on Elm Street Part 2*.

Now you're getting a lot of dramas and comedies, with maybe one horror thrown in the middle.

I like going back to horror every once in a while. I would never ever want to flush that out of my system. I'm just waiting for a really great horror film to come my way. I'm not a slasher guy. To me, my favorite moments in horror are those that play on your mind. They put you in a state of cerebral fear that is entirely induced by things unseen. It's implied, not stated.

In the beginning you did all your own orchestrations. How big of a role does Pete Anthony play in your orchestrations now, and how do you keep your present sound consistent with your original sound?

You'll hear me say this often: I thank my lucky stars. I'm very fortunate that, at the beginning of my career, I went into this Herrmann phobia—Herrmann refused to let anyone orchestrate his music, and I thought that I would sort of fly on that same plane for a while and try to orchestrate everything myself. By doing that, I learned that a composer who doesn't have that experience of orchestrating his own stuff would never have it. So, by the time it got to the point where I had to move away from that, I had it. Why did I have to move away from it? First, it was so time-consuming. I was getting more jobs that they wanted produced in shorter periods of time. Also, after I had been married for a couple years, my wife said, "I can't go on like this with you never being around. Why don't you do what other composers do and bring in an orchestrator? It will free up some time so we can have a life together." Well, I slowly but surely worked in some people. Jeff Atmajian was the first orchestrator I allowed into the circle. Jeff did an excellent job.

What project was that?

He orchestrated a couple of cues from *Hellbound* [*Hellraiser II*]. I orchestrated the majority on that one. I think it was on *The Fly II* that he took over the entire show.

It took me a long time to adjust to writing sketches, going from doing the full-blown score in which you are responsible for laying out every note for every instrument to a reduced sketch in which you're telling them what you want everyone to do. With the sketch, you're still doing it, but in a reduced form. It took me a long time to adjust to that. I went into it fighting. "Oh, it's not going to work. I can't stand this concept." But, over the years, I learned how to get everything on the page—the sketch—that I needed to get there.

Why weren't your scores for *Sweet November*, *Wonder Boys*, and *Bandits* publicly released?

Wonder Boys and *Bandits* both had song releases. In my case of the scores, I guess they felt that they weren't worth it because the pop CDs were what they were promoting. My suspicion is that the record companies with whom the film studios made the deals stated in their contracts that under no circumstances would another competing CD be released at the same time. In situations like that, no film company will want to touch a score with a ten-foot pole if they have to put out the money to pay for the re-use fees but can't have the CD in the stores at the time the film is released.

What about Danny Elfman? *Spider-Man* and *Batman*, for example, have compiled soundtracks as well as score releases.

Danny Elfman is a superstar. He's got an arrangement with MCA. If you hire Danny Elfman, he's guaranteed a score release.

Swordfish is completely different from what you normally work on in that it' s abstract, metallic, and energetic. What went on with this project and the use of Paul Oakenfold's music?

That score, for me, was rushed, but it was exciting to work with Paul Oakenfold. I had never done anything quite like it before. I embraced it with open arms. When I was hired, it was my choice to have Paul. The idea of fusing his world and my world seemed pretty good on paper. Unfortunately, when it came time to score the film, he was off touring, so I used some of his loops, his drum loops, his sequences, and his sounds. Above and beyond that, when it came time to score that movie, I was on my own. But at least I had his language in my head, so when I was doing the synth stuff I was coming from that point of view.

So you actually wrote most of the score?

I wrote all the score.

Why is he credited as a composer?

It's funny that you should mention that. I remember the director and the editor saying to me, "You should make a stink about this, get his name off the credits. What's the matter with you?" My feeling was, "Are you kidding me? Paul Oakenfold is a star. To have my name on the same bill with Paul Oakenfold is a good thing."

Your score for *Swordfish* didn't get a release.

Right, the score will never get released. But it was just about having the credit with him. I've been told that the future of film music may be in guys like myself, trained composers, working with people who come in from the pop world. I don't know if that's going to come to fruition, but I'm hearing that you have to be willing to do this. I want to do it. If Shania Twain wants to do a film score, but she doesn't know how to make her stuff work, you better believe I'm interested.

I'm fascinated with all kinds of music. You're going to learn something from anyone who's sincere in what they do. I learned something from Paul.

As a footnote, at the end of the day, orchestral film scores are always going to be around, no matter how great the effort is to get rid of them, because they are the main hits. If one thing has been proven during the approximately hundred years that film music has been around, it is that orchestral music works. It is the language that seems to win audiences, even though it's not hip. It is very much responsible for making classic films classics, and it definitely extends a film's shelf life. A score that hangs on an idea that's popular at the moment it's conceived will do extremely well upon its initial release, but it will date the picture very quickly. All those disco scores and all those light-jazz comedy scores from the sixties and psychedelic rock scores from the sixties date movies in more obvious ways than orchestral scores.

Composers often develop a special rapport with certain directors. You seem to have done so with Jon Amiel. How does this affect your work?

Before I worked with Jon, I had already worked with a variety of directors, whereas a lot of close relationships start at the beginning of a composer's career. In Jon, what I got was my first long-lasting relationship with someone who was actively making movies. I had done three of Dwight Little's movies, but he's not making movies anymore. I think he's working in television. The last movie of his that I worked on was *Murder at 1600*. Before that I did *Rapid Fire*, and before that something called *Getting Even*.

I'm fortunate in that Jon's movies are successful and he's usually making a movie every two or three years. The movie we met on was *Copycat*. After completing that, I was thrilled to hear him turn to me while we were mixing the music and say, "Chris, by the way, my next film is going to be a comedy and I'd like you to score it."

Was that *The Man Who Knew Too Little*?

Yeah. I was stunned. I was touched that he would give me the opportunity to do something I've never done before, just on blind faith. I had never done a comedy at that point. I had done some comedic moments in action or dramatic films, but I had not done a straight-ahead comedy. I still had that reputation of doing doom-and-gloom movies. But he knew, after working with me on *Copycat*, that I'd bust my tail, and I'm sure he just saw in me the same thing he saw in himself—a guy who is capable of doing a variety of different things and who wants to get the opportunity to so. What's so special with Jon is that I get diversity and a belief in my ability to conquer all odds.

Jon likes the idea of having one composer he can work with on a regular basis. Some directors, as you know, don't really like that. From movie to movie, they want a new composer to come in so that they can redefine the sound of the movie. They don't like the consistency. Norman Jewison, whom I worked with on *The Hurricane*, never goes back to the same composer. Well, that's not true. If he does, it's usually after a period of time in which he's gone out and worked with others. He casts each picture based on what he thinks is right for it.

Does this have any effect on you, especially given the opportunity and prevailing with Norman Jewison's *The Hurricane*, for example?

Well, it hurts. Even though you've done your homework, you realize that in all probability he's not going to use you again. No matter what kind of score you deliver, no matter how great it is, no matter how happy he is, he's probably not going to change his pattern. So I go into these experiences knowing that there is a high probability that I'm not going to get asked back. But, inevitably, after you have delivered the score, you're always hoping that you're going to be the one to change the pattern, and it hurts when you're not the one.

I know Norman was thrilled with what I did for *The Hurricane*, and he has helped me get other jobs. He has put in good words for me, which is a wonderful thing to do. When I was up for *Bandits*, Norman called Barry Levinson and recommended me.

I hear something different in your work on Amiel's films. From *Copycat* to *The Man Who Knew Too Little* to *Entrapment*, they have a flow that seems particularly effortless and confident. I think that one can hear that they're scores written from the perspective of a consistent relationship where you are believed in wholeheartedly.

Oh, it's great to hear that. We do love each other, and he does trust me, which touches me deeply. And what is terrific, also, is that he's a musician himself. He studied sitar for a while. He gave that up, but he knows music. He can look at scores when we're in the booth recording a cue and go, "Chris, can you change the cello to a D-flat for me?" So we have a shorthand. I don't have to mock the cues up for him.

He can already hear what the orchestral sound is going to be in a sense?

Yeah, it's amazing. Sometimes, when I play the piano, trying to create a full orchestral sound on the keyboard, I think that it doesn't sound good and wonder, "How is he going to understand what is going on?" But he does.

I had to watch *Virtuosity* over to make sure that it was really you. It is hip, rhythmic, synthetic, and " kick-ass," for lack of a better description. What happened here that made you change directions in your style?

That is very true. I was thrilled that Brett Leonard, the director, hired me on that. But there was very little time. This film was rushed like you wouldn't believe. I've heard that its post-production schedule was one of the shortest in recent history. What I remember most about that was having to knock that music out at the speed of light.

When I spotted the film, I knew there was going to be a lot of electronic, techno, heavy-metal songs laced throughout the picture. Every time we spotted it, we would go through one of the songs or the beat things that Brett had in there. I got the feeling that, even though Brett couldn't articulate what it was what he was looking for, he's a beat guy who loves it loud, just blasting. He also is a friend of Peter Gabriel's, and Peter Gabriel contributed a very nice song for the end credits. Brett wanted me to interpolate Peter Gabriel's theme for those sentimental moments in the movie and at the end of the movie. Also, I wanted to utilize some of Peter Gabriel's percussion loops, so some of those were sent over.

I decided it would be a mistake to jump back and forth between orchestra and songs. We see this in action films a lot, where they have a song and then immediately go into orchestra. Then we jump back into a song. Then we're back into orchestra. Those are two different worlds that collide. I don't care how well-crafted the orchestral stuff is—as a unit it's distracting because it's from such a different sonic world. So this became the first score that I had done in quite some time that was ninety-percent electronic. The orchestra doesn't make its appearance until the very end of the movie. I was very particular about the moment when the orchestra could make its first big appearance. At that moment, I said, "The synths are not going to be enough. We have to throw in some orchestra."

In terms of electronic stuff, what did I use as my guideline? I just listened to what Brett had in the temp or at least the songs he had in the temp. I think most of them were used in the movie. On a very short order, I created this palette of sounds, and a lot of that electronic stuff was written on the fly, which means that I came in with very loose sketches and made it work on the spot. We blocked out a studio for all-night-long sessions, and I would have to run back here to write the orchestral stuff, and then work on the electronic stuff until like four or five in the morning, and then come back and do some more. It was really crazy. There was a lot of music in that movie, as I remember.

I guess the spontaneity of that score is what made it great.

Did you like the electronic stuff?

I absolutely loved it. You have a strong feel for every medium that you work with, and using the rhythmic pulsing and the metallic sounds, you really shined!

I'm thrilled that you liked it. It's amazing what one can manufacture when you're under that much pressure.

Your *Tales From The Hood* score has it all, from the thematic side to the ethereal sounds. You take so many directions—from its opening organ that seems to be inspired by Bach to some of violin motifs that hint at Rimsky-Korsakov's *Scheherazade*. What is taking place with this mixture of styles?

I can't remember what that second track is and so fourth, but the first was an organ piece. The inspiration for that was [Charles-Marie] Widor's organ symphonies. I borrowed that rhythmic pattern from him. How did I know of his work and how to use it for this film? I sang in a boys' choir when I was a kid. It was one of my favorite preludes or postludes.

What I remember most about that score was that the director originally wanted a different a composer to do each of the different segments because he was afraid there would be too much similarity from one to the other. I understood his concerns. I think he was afraid that I was going to slap one kind of sound on top of all of them. Now, there is definitely similarity. I hope you can sense that it's from the same pen when you hear these different sounds. But, at the same time, I hope there is enough diversity among them so they sound like self-contained units specifically written for each episode.

Absolutely. I am glad you mentioned the Widor, because I think a strong point about you is that you don't conceal what is inevitable with every composer—influences—yet you put your own unmistakable signature to every score you write.

This is incredibly kind of you to say. I am touched.

I can remember one other situation that was a concern to me, and it still is to this date, actually: the *Tales From The Hood* episode about the voodoo doll. Corbin Bernsen plays a redneck Southern politician who's chased down by this voodoo doll that's trying to kill him. I remember thinking that this would be perfect for a fiddle solo but, shit, if I used the fiddle as the principle instrument, it would be like one of those *Twilight Zone* episodes that [Jerry] Goldsmith scored. I know he used a lot of tri-tones. There are a lot of things I do that are different, but you can tell the source of the seed.

You have one of the most individual sounds in Hollywood. You are one of only a handful of composers whose scores I can almost always recognize.

[Laughing] That's funny and great to hear, because the thing that always haunts me is diversity. I don't constantly write in one style. I think it's good to have that diversity, but I have always been concerned that I am a jack-of-all trades and master-of-none. The more you spread your wings and try to diversify your music, the more diffused your sound is going to be. I always wondered, when someone like you heard my diverse scores—from comedies, dramas, action films, horror films—if you thought they sounded like the same guy.

PART II

Orchestrators and other members
of the film-music team

Conversations with Orchestrators

Film scoring is an industry of many hands, as it has been since the days when the major studios reigned in Hollywood. Orchestrators play a vital part in the production of large- and mid-scale film scores. In the following interviews, the work of the orchestrator will be discussed by some of the best in the business.

Pete Anthony

What does an orchestrator do?

Technically speaking, I create the orchestral score, which is the master plan of the music that is to be performed by an orchestra. The way I describe it in non-musical terms is that a composer is the master architect and the orchestrator is the associate architect. What this means is that it is up to the orchestrator to carry out the composer's wishes based on the composer's shorthand representation of the score.

How did you become an orchestrator?

I started as a composer. I went to Williams College, and then I came out here to the film-scoring program at USC. I studied music composition and orchestration privately with a number of different people. In my college years, I was primarily into jazz and avant-garde music. When I got out here, I started falling behind in my classical studies, so I became more well-versed in standard repertoire. Then I taught school and did gigs at jazz clubs and stuff like that, and I met a guy by the name of Pat Russ, who was working with Elmer Bernstein and Maurice Jarre at the time.

He became my mentor and teacher. I proofread and started learning things as we went along. Pat would give me a sketch that he had already orchestrated and say, "Here, go orchestrate this." So I would take the sketch, orchestrate it, and then I compare what he did to what I did. I would listen to the recording of what Pat had done and I would make notes about my own work. Pat was an important influence. I sort of modeled my career on what he was doing. So I started doing it, and now, I can't afford not to do it.

What was your first introduction to film music?

Star Wars. But to go a step back, I used to ask my mom for the soundtrack albums to all these Disney movies, and I listened to them from the time I was two years old. So I guess I was listening to film music earlier than *Star Wars* but didn't realize it. I was really interested in the instrumental music. It didn't need words for me to take interest.

How do several orchestrators on one project blend the styles in the score?

You do hear differences in style, but teams of people who work together usually work out the details so that you don't hear large contrasts when going from one orchestrator to the next.

The orchestrator is responsible for being well-rounded. We are all trained similarly. Some of us have gone through traditional classical training, and some of us have worked with jazz ensembles and then gone back to study the classical literature and sort of bring a different set of skills to the table. Some orchestrators are known for their styles in jazz or classical, but we all have overlapping skills. We all speak the same language.

You developed a good relationship with composer Christopher Young early in your career. How did this begin?

I met Chris through a mutual friend, composer Dan Licht. I had just done a couple of films with Dan, who recommended me to Chris. I met Chris at the studio when he was recording the score for *Rapid Fire*. He asked me to consult with him for an arrangement that he was doing for a band. It was source music that was supposed to sound like Chicago blues. He asked me to look at it and offer my thoughts. I didn't know anything about what authentic Chicago blues was. So I went to the library and listened to whatever music I could and decided that what he had done was pretty good. He called me up on his next film, *Jennifer 8,* because the orchestrator he was working with was tied up on another project and Chris needed somebody. Based on our brief experience with *Rapid Fire* and the referral from Dan Licht, he used me for the project, and I have been with him ever since.

How difficult is it to change gears between genres or composers and find that right voice?

When I have to change gears and go into different musical worlds, it is a slow start for me. Chris is one of those guys who listens to records all the time. He has this voracious appetite for different types of music. He listens to music and absorbs it, and it starts coming out in his scores. So how do I adapt to it? I have to listen to some of the music he listens to. If I get something that I am completely unfamiliar with, I'll ask him about it, and he will refer me to his source.

A lot of times you are just expected to know. For example, I worked with James Newton Howard on *Signs,* and the very first time I heard the main title, I pulled out all my Stravinsky recordings and started listening to them just to get that stuff back in my head. The whole job is about styles. So, I listen to the music and I refresh my memory, filling my head with that kind of sound. Then I start working on the project.

I need to determine what are the critical elements and what are the instruments and so on. I need to make sure I have all that covered before I start a project. In the case of *Rounders,* Chris basically dictated to me what all the orchestrations will be, so there's not a whole lot for me to do. What I have to do is make sure that I have taken his shorthand sketch, which is on only six or eight lines, and made it work as a thirty-two-line score, with everything voiced properly. As for decisions about whether it's strings or woodwinds, he has pretty much made most of those. Some composers may leave more to me.

What is tough is when you are working on two different projects from two different composers. A cue from one project may be an about-face—a totally different musical world—from a cue from another project. I work with people who have different tastes or concepts about the way it should be done. Some want the whole orchestra busy. Some like it to be very still, their concept being that it should be about subtle color differences. So that part can be jarring. It can be almost schizophrenic.

Do you take on multiple projects simultaneously?

Well, I try not to, but the way our business works now is that projects come up so fast that rarely is there time for an orchestrator to do a whole film. Years ago, when I first started out, the composer would work four to six weeks, and I would get a steady stream of sketches that I would orchestrate. So, at the end of the project, I would've worked on the whole thing myself. But now, films require that scores get orchestrated in a shorter period of time and, thus, I have to work on more films just to keep the business going. So, yes, I work on more than one film at a time because I work on a small part of one film at a time.

You are also one of the most sought-after conductors in the industry. How do you balance your orchestrating and conducting projects?

Obviously, I can't be at more than one recording studio at a time. Fortunately, a lot of the people I work with have the same contractor, Sandy DeCresent, who sets up great scheduling. Usually, I can go from one place to the next without missing out on projects because I am scheduled somewhere else.

James Newton Howard's *Dinosaur*, *Atlantis*, and *Treasure Planet* were big Disney animation projects. How challenging were these scores for you in comparison to other scores that you have worked on?

I think they were challenging for everybody. They were one-hundred-plus-piece orchestras, and they were big, thematic-based scores that were old-fashioned in the sense that they were so dramatic and carried the films. A lot of films aren't like that these days. They were great and rousing and from one of the best young composers, and we had the best players and orchestrators, which was just glorious. It sounded wonderful.

When you're orchestrating these scores, it's slow-going because there's so much music that you have to get on the page. Big music is a lot of work, and it takes a lot of hours to orchestrate it. It is difficult, but the payoff is that you have all this fun music for the orchestra to play and you get this huge sound. I'm a lucky guy to be able to stand in front of an orchestra and hear that.

What are your favorite projects that you have worked on?

I had a great time working on *Signs* by James Newton Howard. I had a great time working with John Debney on *The Scorpion King*, which had the old-fashioned approach where the music is so heavily involved in the movie. That was just a great time and a wonderful score. The three James Newton Howard Disney scores were absolutely fabulous. I had a wonderful time conducting for Danny Elfman on *Spider-Man*. With Chris Young, I had a terrific time working on *The Core*, which was a big production. Another thing that was fun about this film is that Jon Amiel and Chris have such a great collaboration. Jon communicates what he wants very well to Chris, and Chris is very responsive to Jon. It is gratifying and fun to watch what they do. Chris writes the score but he gets a lot of input from Jon, and I think that what they come up with is better than what either of them would do on their own.

My favorite scores are often the result of a long-going composer-director relationship. Christopher Young's music is tremendous anyway, but his work on Jon Amiel's scores has some little extra touch that I love. It's the same thing with James Newton Howard when he works with Lawrence Kasdan or Michael Hoffman.

I don't know what it is, whether there is a personal connection or if it is a creative energy that is so positive, but these guys always do their best work with these certain directors. I think with Jon and Chris, Jon pushes Chris to another level. Chris probably works harder than anyone I have known, but Jon is able to focus Chris's energy in a way so that he gets more.

How did you get started in orchestration?

After years of piano lessons and studying scores and writing for different groups, I knew I wanted to work in music. So, after graduating from the university in my hometown of Fresno, I moved to Los Angeles. I then graduated from the film-scoring program at USC. At that point I didn't know if I would be composing for films or writing songs. To "pay the bills," I played piano and did a lot of copying and arranging.

I met Christopher Palmer while working as a copyist/librarian on the film *Three Amigos*. [Christopher Palmer was an orchestrator/film-score expert who worked with many leading composers in the seventies, eighties, and early nineties.] I really learned so much from him and enjoyed many rare and wonderful musical opportunities through working for him. This was how my living and working in England came about. The work was available and I really took to the culture, so I began to spend much more time there. Then, a short while later, Bruce Broughton introduced me to Chris Young. I believe I was Chris's first orchestrator. Then, through Christopher Palmer, I also began to work as George Fenton's orchestrator. What finally brought me back into the L.A. scene was meeting Marc Shaiman in early 1993.

Why didn't you pursue a career as a composer?

Probably because of a lack of certainty that I had what it took. But mostly because I got caught up in a whirlwind of orchestrating and arranging. Though I have always taken time to write, I never found the ability to pursue it because my career in orchestration started so rapidly. I am happy to say that I am now in pursuit of more composing projects.

What was it like working with James Newton Howard at the height of his career?

I may have come to James with a strong orchestral background, but working for him really gave me the chance to learn about the ways orchestra and synths can work together. James always seems to surpass himself. Every time he does a film, I think, "Wow!"—and then he does the next one even better or differently. I feel that I am always driven to expand myself and push that much harder because of his material. May I also add that he is a truly gifted and kind person, and that also inspires me?

In general, how complete of a sketch do you get from the composer?

Each composer is different. I have always been given clear intention if not clear direction. With schedules so tight these days, most composers give out synth demos and transcriptions. My greatest goal is to represent in the orchestra what they are hearing and portraying in their demos and transcriptions. Sometimes it is a matter of doing a bit of final crafting; other times it is making sure what comes through on synths also comes through clearly in the orchestra. Sometimes I am trusted to really flesh out a sketch from a piano part. Always, I am there to make sure that the score is clear and offers options of weight and color through the use of cued parts.

Do you ever get handwritten sketches anymore?

Only from Rachel Portman. Most composers write into sequencers. They have to because they often must give demos that sound complete. This has created a bit of a minefield for orchestrators because, to make a demo sound complete, you often make orchestration and color choices based on the synth samples and the way they come across sounding in the synth world. Sometimes that is the opposite of how you would do it with the actual orchestra. It may also be the case that, in addition to what's been written for the orchestra, there are big hits or dissonant clusters that are represented by a little dot or a triangle on the sketch. For those, we need to recreate the sound that the composer gets with a single sample. Another difference is that we don't get dynamics and phrasings. They come via demos so, ironically, with all of this technology, we still have to spend time doing aural takedowns!

The Rachel Portman projects that you have worked on—*Cider House Rules*, *The Legend of Bagger Vance*, and *Chocolat*—seem to have a lot more color in their orchestrations. Is this a change in her style, or does she rely on your talents to fill in the color?

I can claim very little credit for Rachel's scores. I think I'm the one who has learned new colors from her!

Do you find it difficult to blend styles with other orchestrators who work on the same score?

It has never really been an issue, because we are all working for the same composer with the same intention. The thing that is amazing is seeing how often we each do similar things, even though we work separately. It is also a great chance to learn new things from the other guys. We all seem to have our unique ways of getting certain sounds from the orchestra, but things always coalesce.

How does a composer choose an orchestrator?

I would look for a sympathy of purpose. If I were a composer, my first requirement for an orchestrator would be that he or she understands my music and, thus, would be able to follow my musical lead. And the willingness to put in extra effort also makes someone more desirable. It is a given that they must have a great knowledge of the orchestra. Knowledge of synths and the composer's mental process is also important for understanding what the composer may imply, even if it is not spelled out.

What is the average timeframe to complete an orchestration for a score?

These days it is one to three weeks. When I started out, it was nearer to six weeks. This partly explains the greater number of orchestrators on a film. When you see six names, it often means that two or three orchestrators did the majority of the work and the rest picked up the slack. Truthfully, I would say that there is never enough time!

Since you work almost exclusively with a handful of composers, how do you choose your projects when more than one score is due at the same time?

So far, I haven't been confronted with this situation. Quite often, when I am really busy, I will be finishing one score and then starting on another, but I never actually work on two scores at the same time. If the situation you mention ever did arise, I suppose I would choose to work for whomever asked me first and/or whomever I had the longest association with.

Brad Dechter

Let's start with your upbringing in music and how your music career developed.

I came from a musical family to start with. My father, a musician and music teacher, was my first inspiration and teacher. I started taking piano lessons when I was about six. I hated it. Well, I hated the practicing part. One day my father brought home a clarinet and said, "Here, try this." So I started playing clarinet. As junior high school came around, I really became interested in jazz and saxophone. So I added saxophone to my repertoire.

Fast-forward to high school: A counselor at school, who used to write for name big bands, taught a jazz arranging class. I took his class and fell in love with writing music for jazz bands. Basically, I wanted to be a bebop saxophone player and write for jazz bands. I soon learned that was a fairly unrealistic thing. But that never stopped me, so that's what I did.

I grew up in the Los Angeles area, but went back east for college. After college, I spent a year teaching at Western Michigan University. Along the way, I learned how to copy music—making the parts for the individual player—and found out that I could make some money doing that. I was lucky in that some of my father's friends shepherded me and mentored me into that. So I came back to Los Angeles, where I played jazz and did whatever sort of jobs I could do, and copying music became my main source of income.

Stan Sheldon, a great teacher mentor friend, was the source of most of my music-copying gigs. Some composers for whom he worked occasionally needed a big band arrangement or a redo of a chart for a new instrumentation or a sound-alike [a re-creation of some piece of recorded music]. At one point, Stan asked if I could and would like to do some of that. And I said, "Sure, of course!" It all blossomed from there. It was serendipitous.

I had taken orchestration classes in college and played clarinet in classical orchestras as well as doing the jazz thing, so I had a lot of broad knowledge, thanks to my father, mainly. When the opportunities came along to do some of these simpler types of writing and orchestrating jobs, I grabbed them and, frankly, I learned on the job. I had good ears and I knew what was needed and I knew how to get it done. I learned a lot in those beginning years. Then recommendations came and it sort of blossomed. I would say that my real entrée into my major career as an orchestrator started with a couple people: number one, Lee Holdridge, who was one of the fellows I did some of this preliminary work with. Then, he recommended me to a then-new composer, James Newton Howard, who was looking for somebody to redo some arrangements for Elton John, of all things, for a concert tour in Australia. That's when I hooked up with James and I guess you could say that the rest is history.

Where did you go to school back east?

I went to Yale as an undergraduate, and I also did my master's degree work there. I got a degree in saxophone, but I was very active in the composition department there and the new music that was going on.

How did your James Newton Howard/Elton John work eventually change into the film-music work?

James and I got along famously at the beginning with the Elton John things, and then James starting coming into his own as a film composer. Up to the time when I met him, he had done one or two, primarily synthesizer, scores. Then he got the opportunity to use a live orchestra. And I became his orchestrator. That's how I developed my reputation as a film-music orchestrator. Then, from there, people heard of me. John Debney, who has also been one of my major colleagues for over a dozen years now, called me up one day because he had heard of me. He similarly wanted me to just do an arrangement for some Disneyland project. And when he started doing films, I became his orchestrator. So that's what happened. All of the other things that I've done were just through word-of-mouth—people heard of me and called me up.

You were the only orchestrator for James Newton Howard's early scores, such as *The Man in the Moon* and *Dying Young*. When and why did he start adding other orchestrators?

I was his only orchestrator to begin with. Adding orchestrators really had to do with the time and ability to get the job done. A short schedule would dictate that I couldn't do it all. There were also times when he wanted to have another point of view from the orchestrating end. So, due to a combination of time and styles, it has evolved into me and Jeff Atmajian now. Jeff came on a few years ago. Once again, for the most part, there isn't time anymore for any one person to do a whole score in the time given. Occasionally, yes, but most of the time, no. So that is a huge consideration. But the other consideration is that James really appreciated the different creative input.

James Newton Howard's scores have grown from intimate scores such as Dying Young or *The Man in the Moon* to scores such as *Dinosaur* or *Treasure Planet*. Does this have any sort of impact on your side of the production?

James is such a complete musician, and he has the ability to orchestrate if he wants to—and he has. He just doesn't have the time to do that. But he creates everything in his own studio, especially with the synths. Then he'll add the orchestral element when that happens. So, whenever there is a project like that, he simply gives me or any of the other orchestrators a demonstration CD or MP3s on the Internet. That gives us his rendition of the score, which he obviously has been playing for the director and getting approvals for. Then we just orchestrate accordingly.

I did most of *The Prince of Tides*, a pure orchestral score, myself. Right around the same time, we did the movie *Grand Canyon*, which was one of his brilliant scores that had a fabulous mixture of synthesizers. I took what he intended for the live orchestra and just orchestrated accordingly. To me, the synthesizers are just another element that I hear on the demo. It suggests drama and style, but it doesn't really change how I do things. If anything, James will say, "That sound is covered by the synthesizer. You don't have to orchestrate it. That's a very particular synthesizer sound." He will be very specific that way, sometimes, in that he has some exotic ethnic flute, for instance, which is really a synthesizer sound. So I won't deal with that.

Every project is unique—and that's probably more telling than the use of synthesizers. I really have to look at each project as its own entity. It's not like the last one. It's not like the next one. It's not like anything else I've ever done. I just come in with fresh ears. What is this about? What is it I need to do? Then, looking at the clock, I realize that I'd better get going because there's usually only that much time to think about it.

His sound, though uniquely his own, is always evolving. Like you said, *Grand Canyon* is very different from *The Prince of Tides*, so this doesn't allow you to fall into any sort of patterns, I presume.

James is, to me, as good of a film composer as there has ever been. Based upon his obvious absolute mastery of music in many idioms, he has the great ability to create music for a movie, not impose music on a movie. In other words, James really creates something unique for a film; it's not just James Howard doing a film score.

He has a style. He has, in fact, many styles, in a way. I can recognize many aspects of his work throughout very disparate types of scores, because they all still have a thread of James that goes through them. But he adapts himself to the movie, and he realizes that he is serving the drama of the film. That's his job. That's how I would categorize his chameleon-like abilities. He never fails to amaze me.

In every single picture I've worked on with him, he has come up with something new and interesting that is not only wonderful musically but perfect for the film from my points of view and, apparently, the point of view of many directors and producers, because he certainly has been successful. I think that's probably a great part of his success, not to mention that he's a very charming and affable person who is not only nice to be around but also makes everyone feel that he's very with them in spirit and heart on a project, because he is.

All of that being said, he also has that great ability to write music that stands alone without the film. That is a great composer.

The Prince of Tides, to me, is a prime example of a perfect film score, if there is such a thing.

That's probably my favorite that I've worked on. I think that was a turning point for both of us—for him as a composer and for me as an orchestrator. I learned so much because of the scope of the film and working with Barbra Streisand, which was a remarkable experience.

Because of the way that particular process worked, I developed a great affinity for the musicians in the room. There was a lot of alteration and reworking of the original parts because of Barbra's needs and requirements, which were absolutely "right on." It took a lot of hard work, but it was a whole step up in another world for me, and for James, too, I think.

You worked with Trevor Jones on Cliffhanger and The Last of the Mohicans. Jones most often uses orchestrators Geoff Alexander and Julian Kershaw. Why did Trevor bring you onto these projects?

I'm not really sure how that all worked, to be honest with you. I know that, though he lives in England, he was spending a lot of time out here, and I believe I was recommended for these films, which were done in the States. What was interesting with Last of the Mohicans was that Trevor ended up doing only half of the score, and Randy Edelman did the other half of the score, which was a mixture of many different musical ideas. Then Trevor started staying in England and, for obvious reasons, he used guys over there who were recommended to him, including Geoff, whom I've met and talked to. He's a very nice guy and a wonderful orchestrator. Coincidentally though, Trevor is actually over here doing a film now. He just called me up, and I will likely work on his next film, so I think that I tend to work with him on his "in the States" projects.

I have to tell you a funny, human-interest story that happened during *Last of the Mohicans*. If you recall, it was in the early nineties when we in Los Angeles had the so-called "Rodney King rioting"—a horrible few days of rioting and curfew and all that. We were in the middle of recording one of the sessions for *Last of the Mohicans* at Fox Studios' scoring stage. I recall that it had just gotten halfway through the afternoon session when some people of authority came in and said, "We have to close this session down now because the National Guard is using Fox Studios as a home base for this situation. So you all have to leave." What an amazing experience—that certainly colored my whole feeling about the film. That was quite a tumultuous film in many ways, including this odd situation. You know, we all relate experiences we have with current experiences, positively and negatively. If a horrible thing happens on a birthday or a holiday, people will often recall that holiday or anniversary with the same feelings of the negative thing that happens.

That's sort of an interesting memory I have. Nevertheless, I was just so fortunate to be a part of that score because I think it was a monumental work, and that theme especially was one of those moments of music that not many people ever get to. That's such a memorable theme, and it just was remarkable.

Do you have other favorite scores and/or memorable work experiences that stand out?

Absolutely. *The Prince of Tides*, as I mentioned before, was definitely one of my favorites, and so was *The Man in the Moon*. I happened to have watched this movie a couple of times in the last couple of months when it was on some cable channel. I absolutely love that film. There's a movie called *Some Girls*, which also has an alternate title, *Sisters*. It was one of the very first films James and I did together. I just love that score. I don't know why except that it just makes me feel good.

There've been some great ones with John Debney. I have to say John Debney, though he is starting to gain recognition, is almost a secret in movies. I know that a lot of movie-music buffs are certainly aware of him. But I think that John is probably as fine a composer as there is in the style of John Williams, in that he just has a command of the orchestra and the depth of music. Almost every project I've worked on with John has been an absolute joy because he makes it so easy for us to do our work, number one, but the outcome of the music is just always so wonderful and just feels so good. There was one movie in particular—one of the very first ones we did—*Hocus Pocus*, which was a Disney kid-oriented film with Bette Midler and Sarah Jessica Parker. I tell you, the score John did on that was just priceless, and I absolutely adored working on that one.

So what becomes challenging for you?

The worst challenges I've had in any score have had to do with the clock, not the music. As I said, I tend to view each project as almost starting over in music. I don't just rely upon, "Okay, I've done this before," and scribble it out. I really think about what I'm doing. The hardest part is when there is not enough time to do it all. And, subsequently, as we spoke about before, we often have to engage other orchestrators to assist. That has been the case on virtually every picture in the last six or seven years at least. With John, it's a little bit of a different relationship than with James, in that James has a particular way of working and he hands out the cues to each orchestrator, whom he handpicks. John leaves a lot of that up to me. So I become the principle orchestrator, and it has fallen upon me to distribute the cues to other orchestrators whom we may need for any given project. So I spend a good deal of my time with John listening and going through all of the music, deciding who should get what. When the clock bears down upon me, trying to do my own work and to supervise other people becomes an interesting challenge.

But, once again, musically, I never really find anything that is particularly more challenging than any other. It's all just something fun to work on, and I think how lucky I am to be making music for a living. I am not being patronizing here, but I sincerely feel the absolute genius and creativity and completeness of the two main guys I work with, James and John. Their music is very clear and very defined by the time I or my colleagues get it. So the creative input we have is often minimal to the point where the real challenge becomes knowing when to be creative, when to add something or when not to. The music is all there. I would say that only five percent of the time do I really need to do something. I think that my particular talent is knowing when to do it. I know when to leave the rest alone. I mean, we have to still configure ranges of instruments and coloring and know that the trumpet players have to take a breath once in a while—otherwise their lips will fall off—and all of these aspects of orchestration that are important and that go beyond just knowing about chords and how to write out rhythms. But beyond that, it's just knowing when to do something and when not to. I'd say, once again, that we all have to have a very good knowledge of music—harmony, orchestration, etcetera. But that being a given, the real key to being a successful orchestrator in the film business, working with a composer, is to know when to do and when not to do. That's the real ticket.

Although I am not stating that film composers can't or don't usually do their own work with their own creativity, there must be times when orchestrators lend their own brush strokes. Can you shed some light on this?

I think that really varies by picture. It depends on what the style of music is. You mentioned about James and synthesizers. When he has a synthesizer-heavy score, I think that the orchestral colors would tend to be less noticeable. Of course, you know, orchestration really consists of many elements. And, of course, James and John contribute most of the orchestration ideas. I am taking what they are doing and, number one, cleaning it up, and, as I said before, adding my five percent.

Now that's not to say that I don't have creative input at times. Sometimes I figure it out myself, or occasionally John or James will say, "Fill this section out for me." Those are rare moments, I have to say. I'll get an emotional direction on occasion. They'll say, "Here's the drama, here's what's going on in the film, make it bigger or smaller or more poignant or sadder or whatever." I will certainly add my own voicing or counterpoint if it's appropriate. But, in terms of me having a style, I've heard people say that they recognize my style, but I wouldn't be surprised if my style is really more defined by James Newton Howard's writing.

I guess all of this is really a collaborative effort, and it's really hard to pick out a very specific thing that's an orchestrator's input. It does happen, but I'm working to try and make the composer's music on which he's worked so hard to be dramatically correct. I'm trying to make it even better than his demo is. That's really what it comes down to. I think it's my job to work in the whole style and approach that the composer is using in a film. I really feel like I'm more of a chameleon than a creative voice when I'm doing film orchestration.

Have you ever considered composing yourself?

Oh, of course I have. I've shot it down immediately because I don't feel I have the personality or strength of character to be able to deal with the extra pressures—dealing with directors, producers, and studios, and agents, and a lot of issues like that—that come with being a composer. Those are very real issues, and not everybody is suited to that.

I know that there are some great composers in the world and there are some great orchestrators who are also great composers, and not everybody is suited to the business of being a film composer. I think that is a real key, and I think that's why James and John are equally successful at that aspect of it as they are as musicians. That's why they are so good and at the top of their game. For me, I don't really feel like that's something I have the time or stomach for, to be quite honest.

If there were a small film that was maybe a jazz-idiomatic thing, because that's really what I love the most, and if I didn't have to do it in one week, I think I would enjoy doing that at some point. But as a career goal, no, it's not something I'd like to do. I'm much happier being creative doing arrangements for either instrumental groups or for a vocalist or things like that. I've done quite a bit of recording-type arrangements, and I like doing that a lot. My wife's a great singer and I do a lot with her. I have a jazz octet that I work with occasionally and write for and lead in the Los Angeles area. That's where I find my creative output.

I think that it's important to understand what orchestration really is. This is a little history lesson, I suppose. Composition and

orchestration really go hand in hand and, initially, the art of orchestration, especially in the nineteenth century, was part of the composer's venue. However each composer would construct a big
orchestral piece of music, the orchestration was a natural outgrowth
of that. In other words, composition and orchestration were inextri-
cably linked and, for the most part, orchestration was not a separate
entity for a composer. As time has gone on, the art of orchestration
has evolved, just as music has evolved and gotten more complex,
with the different instruments, the different capabilities. And, as film
music has evolved, the big issue that I mentioned before—time—has
a lot to do with the reason why I have a job as an orchestrator. The
composer, especially today, generally doesn't have the time, even if
he could or wanted to orchestrate.

Another reason that my profession as film orchestrator has come
into being is that some people just don't have the ability to do all that
may be required on any particular project. There are people who are
wonderful composers with a wonderful sense of drama and music and
that ability to work with the director and the producers and all of
those people, but may not have complete knowledge of the orchestra
and the ability to do a full orchestration. And I say that with no dis-
respect; it's just the way it is.

In the early days of film, most of the composers could do all of
it, but they would run out of time and hire people to help them do
some of the work—and that was called "ghostwriting." So somebody
may have done some of the work for the composer and not really
gotten credit for it. That happened, and probably still does to a certain extent. Once again, I say this without any animosity or judg-
ment. It's just the nature of the beast. So the good composers were
smart and hired good orchestrators, some of whom were fabulous
composers in their own rights; and that's how it has evolved.

I just think it's important to understand that composition and
orchestration are really one, but, by the nature of the business, have
evolved into two distinct professions that are totally linked together.
You can't have one without the other.

**In terms of approach, what is your point of attack, and does this
vary from a team of orchestrators on a project?**

I try to always make each part make sense in that the notes are not just thrown in—this note's a part of this chord, and this note's a part of that. I try to make everybody's part flow; make musical sense. As a general way of approach, that's what I do.

But I really have to come back to the composer. He's the one who sets the tone for the people whom I work with. I really just go with that, and I think that's why we gel so much. Yes, I guess we all have a style. If you sat me in a room and Jeff [Atmajian] in a room and said, "Do an arrangement of this," I'm sure we'd come up with something different. But I still think we all have in mind the goal that the composer dictates. It's hard for me to go beyond that.

I don't really believe that my style as an orchestrator is as important as the job I do as an orchestrator to support the composer. That's what I want to be clear on. I don't sit down and say, "I'm Brad Dechter trying to figure out how to make a Brad Dechter sound in this film score." I would only do that if I were the composer.

What have you gained most from your career?

The knowledge that there's a big difference between music and the music business. In other words, I grew up loving music. I wanted to be a part of music. I have learned that the making of music does not require making money at music and, conversely, making money at music doesn't mean you're making the music you want to make.

Now, it doesn't mean that it doesn't happen the other way. I've plenty of times made money at music I loved to do or been given assignments that I like to do. The music business has taken me places I never would have dreamed of or never would have thought of or never would've had the opportunity to go on my own. I've been to Australia with Elton John. I've been to London with Elton John. I've been in movie-score recording situations, sat next to Barbra Streisand, and met people like Jerry Goldsmith; I once worked with John Williams on the Olympics music. I've done arrangements for Johnny Mathis and Jack Jones and Bette Midler. I've just had a wonderful blend of musical experiences that I never would have gotten had I not become a professional musician.

On the other hand, I have to say that some of the most satisfying music I have ever done is the music I have created on my own for me, my family, and my friends. I've recently taken the time to try to take control of my own musical destiny. It's not always easy! I don't want to just be somebody who works for somebody else. As much as I love that, I think it's important for our souls to create something that comes from within us.

I've done this for over twenty years. I've worked really hard and had a lot of time taken up from my family and my friends and from my life in general because of these crazy deadlines, and they will still continue to happen. But I realized there was a point when I needed to take control and either say no to or limit my involvement in a project so that I can do things that I want to do, whether they be with my family, or my own music, or with friends, or whatever it is. That's what my career has done for me. It's taught me a lot about priorities.

Robert Elhai

What, in general, is expected of an orchestrator?

An orchestrator is basically responsible for creating a detailed orchestral score that specifies exactly which instrument is supposed to do what in order to be able to perform the composer's music. This involves many aspects: copying detailed written sketches into a score, transcribing detailed orchestral sketches done with MIDI, transcribing/arranging an orchestral "mockup" in order to realize the composer's specific orchestral intentions, filling out a composer's sketch that doesn't necessarily specify orchestration but nevertheless makes it clear exactly what the music is supposed to sound like, creating an arrangement/orchestration based on what the composer hums into a tape recorder. Obviously the amount of skill and creativity that is required of the orchestrator ranges hugely, depending on the requirements of the particular project.

How does one develop a relationship with a composer or a project? What is it that a composer will look for in terms of qualities or strengths?

My experience is that the most important aspect of a successful collaboration between a composer and an orchestrator is a basic compatibility that is both musical and personal. Orchestrating is a super-elite field that is narrowed to a handful of professionals in the business.

How did you become an orchestrator? What inspired you to walk down this road to begin with?

Well, throughout my training as a classical composer, I was always drawn to the art of orchestration, but never thought of doing it at the film-scoring level until my collaboration with Elliot Goldenthal. I began assisting him on theater and concert projects, and this extended into film-scoring.

Why not be a composer yourself?

I am a composer. My interest as a composer is in the world of theater and concert music.

You have worked on many large projects and developed relationships with, most notably, Elliot Goldenthal and Brian Tyler. You began with Goldenthal. When did Tyler enter the picture?

I was introduced to Brian by Sam Schwartz, the famous super-agent, who represents both Elliot and Brian as well as the late, great Michael Kamen, with whom I also had a lengthy, enjoyable, energizing, and much-missed collaboration. When Brian was hired to score *The Hunted*, his first major orchestral score to be recorded in Los Angeles, Sam thought that I could be a great help to Brian during the process of producing this score.

Does your involvement with these two composers differ from one to the other?

My collaboration proceeds along pretty much the same lines with both composers. Both are classically trained, have very clear ideas of what they want orchestrally, and create sketches that are quite detailed— not just orchestrally, but also dramatically and compositionally—by which I mean that there is an abundance of textural, dynamic, contrapuntal, etcetera. detail as well. From the detail in their sketches and the close collaboration that I enjoy with them, what I need to do in order to accurately realize their intentions is pretty clear.

As I listen to Goldenthal's *Final Fantasy* and Tyler's *Timeline* I am overwhelmed with the intensity and grandeur of the orchestra. On projects such as these, versus projects of smaller scope, what sort of special challenges present themselves to you?

The challenge that you speak of has to do mostly with the disconnect between what the score needs to be and how much money there is. It constantly amazes me how often supposedly experienced producers insist on a big orchestral score without actually providing any money to pay for it.

Do you often discuss different approaches with a composer, or are most things simply black and white?

Nothing is black and white except a piano keyboard. My work with composers is a collaboration with a constant back-and-forth.

Although James Newton Howard is known for his collaboration with Brad Dechter and Jeff Atmajian, you've worked on occasional projects of his, including *Waterworld* and *The Sixth Sense*. Why were you brought in on certain James Newton Howard scores?

I originally was brought in by James to work on *Outbreak*. He had heard my work for Elliot on *Alien 3* and thought that some of the orchestration for that score would be great for *Outbreak*. This was before he started working with Jeff on a regular basis. Brad was his main guy, and I was brought in for the "weird stuff." James and I hit it off, and I worked on his next few projects. But when I got very busy with *The Lion King* musical, Jeff was brought in on a more permanent basis. I've always felt like I'd like to work with James again. I really enjoyed the projects I did with him!

Time constraints on the scoring process seem to get tighter by the decade. Why is music so often kept on the sideline until the very last moment?

The main thing here is the advent of digital editing. It has become way too easy to keep on messing with the picture edit, and the music isn't really supposed to be recorded until there is a locked picture. Of course, even when the music is done, they keep messing with the picture edits, and then the music editor has to keep cutting the music, sometimes to shreds, in order to keep up with the edits, or else they have to schedule more recording sessions, which is really expensive!

Another thing is that so much of the picture these days is created during post-production, which pushes back even further the time that the film is finished enough to score it.

What is the most exciting thing about your work?

I think that the most exciting thing is staying up all night orchestrating a big orchestra cue, and then getting to hear it played the next morning by some of the best musicians in the world. Talk about instant gratification!

If one orchestrates well, will one excel as a composer?

First of all, composing, especially for media such as films, and orchestrating are two different things. They certainly draw upon similar knowledge and techniques, but composing is primarily conception, the one-percent inspiration, while orchestration is realization, the ninety-nine percent perspiration. It is something like the difference between creating a building as an architect and drawing up the plans as a draftsman. It is certainly not true that excelling at one means that you can—or should—excel at the other.

Secondly, I enjoy orchestrating. As a film composer, one rarely gets to orchestrate anything, by which I mean get really into the details of writing out the score and figuring out exactly how the sound of the orchestra is to be created.

Any final comments?

I just want to emphasize that the real work of composing is conceptualizing and creating, not so much realizing. Much is said about how much Composer X relies on Orchestrator Y to write out his scores, but the composers who have help with the realization of their concepts can spend more of their time thinking about the big picture, so to speak. I love the collaborative relationships I have with the composers I work with, and have never felt like I was "doing their composing work for them."

Sandy De Crescent discusses her role as a music contractor

What does a music contractor do?

My clients are the composers. I have about fifty clients, and when they get a movie, I schedule, budget, and put everything together—hire musicians, get the place to record . . . I just sort of coordinate everything to do with the scoring of the movie.

How do you balance multiple projects that happen simultaneously?

Sometimes I'm working on ten or twelve movies in a six-week period. I have a great staff. I have two wonderful guys who work with me. It's a lot of teamwork and I've been doing it for a very long time. I'm not saying it's easy, because it isn't. Sometimes it's mind-boggling: I mean, we've had three movies going in the same week. That's awful. Two are manageable. We very often have two going, and the ideal situation is to have one go at a time, but I don't have much to say about that.

How did you get into the business?

I went to work for the old agency MCA when they were in Beverly Hills, and the man I worked for there was one of the top agents for composers. When they dissolved the agency to buy Universal and start producing television, he took me with him to Universal, where he became the head of music. I worked for him for a number of years. Eventually, he did just the contracting there. And, when he died, I took over.

What is it like being a woman in your position, or does gender even play a factor in your work?

Oh, my God! It's a lot better now! It's been thirty-three years. But at the time . . . I have a daughter who is thirty-five years old. She's a labor lawyer, and she thinks it's really hard for women today. Boy, she hasn't got a clue about how much better it is. It was horrible. I had death threats. My car was vandalized time after time after time. I got terrible hate mail that was so disturbing that it doesn't really bear repeating. And, at that time, people thought there was only one way that a woman would get that position. It's just the way it was. It was basically a boys' club. There were very few women in the orchestras. It was awful. It was tough. Fortunately, I have a very loving, supportive family. My husband was just fantastic. He helped me get through it, and I'm a very strong person.

So what made you want to stick with it?

I loved music. I kind of grew up with it. When I was not quite twenty and in the music business, it was a huge opportunity for me—just huge—to become the contractor of what was then the top television-producing studio. We had eighteen one-hour shows at that point. It was so different from now, where everything is a half-hour sitcom with two minutes of music. And, in fact, of the eighteen shows, two were ninety-minute anthologies. So when I say it was a lot of work, I mean it. And I did it by myself. But it was very organized and unlike movies. Television has air-dates, so you don't have dates that cancel all the time. You would almost never cancel a TV date. In many ways, and as horrendous as the volume was, it was a lot easier than what I do now.

What are some of your challenges that you face on a daily basis?

Work going out of town. There's so much runaway production. A good deal of work, more than I probably would want to know, is going to London. A large amount is going to places like Salt Lake City, Seattle . . . It's very disturbing, so I have been dedicating a good chunk of my time at this stage of my career to trying to keep work in L.A. It's not like the old studio system, where everything was done here. Once in a while something went to London or New York, but not very often, and that's all changed.

I think I've had a few goals. One of them was that the women in the orchestra would have dignity and be treated equally, and that there be many more of them. I would say that my orchestras are anywhere from thirty to forty percent women now. I'm very pleased with that. And the women are treated with the utmost respect and dignity. In fact, all the musicians are.

I've also tried to make sure that the musicians are protected and treated as artists, which they are. You listen to John Williams' orchestra or James Newton Howard's or James Horner's—any of the marvelous orchestras—and you hear that these people are sensational. There are no greater musicians anywhere in the world—and no musicians anywhere in the world with their versatility. I mean, I just finished a movie with Marc Shaiman where we had a classical orchestra and within it, a big band. We've done that so many times. It's just incredible. One minute they're playing like the L.A. Philharmonic and the next minute they're playing like they're in a Broadway show pit. You know, they're just unbelievable!

How closely do you work with the composers?

Pretty closely. Some of them have been my clients for a good many years. I also have many new, younger clients. I feel very nurturing toward them. I try to show them the ropes and be protective of them and make sure they're getting the best orchestras. Then, I'm on the stage with them while they're recording. So we see each other quite a bit and talk a lot.

You touched on this a little bit earlier, but how has the industry changed since you started?

There is very little leadership today. I think it's a lot of inexperience. I think a lot of it is that there isn't the leadership at the studios. Directors are given free reign.

We used to have leadership. You had producers who knew what they were doing and things went smoothly. You didn't have the constant previewing. I mean, every movie that I work on is previewed, almost without an exception, besides Spielberg, who is among the very few who do not preview. He makes the movie that's his vision and, hopefully, everyone will see it as he does.

With previews, somebody in the back row of a preview says, "Gosh, I didn't like that ending," and they'll re-shoot the ending or they'll re-shoot this or that. So there's never a schedule you can keep to. Sometimes I hire orchestras out and cancel them two, three, sometimes four times, because they're constantly previewing and if they don't get good numbers, that's it, they pull it back and they start with the editing again.

With digital editing, it's very simple or fast to go in and do it, but what this means is that the picture is always changing. We sometimes record without a locked picture. It's just very difficult for the composer. I've been on some films where it's been brutal, where changes were made and the composer doesn't even know it. We're on the recording stage and up comes the picture, and it's not what they've got.

So yeah, it's changed. And all those things certainly have made the cost of making movies just tremendous.

Where do you see the changes going in the future?

I would like to be very optimistic, but at the moment I don't have a reason to be. I know that the constant re-shoots and all of that are very bad because, when they get down to music, they have no money left. Obviously that doesn't bode well for us.

Is that why there is a battle about recording in L.A. versus London or elsewhere?

Believe me when I tell you, a lot of the recording in London is a free trip and a great vacation because, by the time you pay first-class air-fare, they're not beating us at all. Airfare is tremendous for first-class, or even business-class, and most of them fly first-class. Then they stay at the best hotels, and there's the per diem, etcetera, so recording in London costs a huge amount of money.

With Seattle, it's awful! They work for cash, no benefits, no pay-roll taxes. Even with our low-budget agreement—which we have for films twenty-nine-million and under—it's hard to match Seattle. And, needless to say, I've heard some of the scores done in Seattle, and I feel terrible for the composers, because they come back and they're miserable. They've written a good score, but it has been played so poorly.

PART III

Directors and Producers
on Film Music

Jon Amiel

Where did your interest in films begin?

Probably at an extraordinary local movie theater called the Everyman Theater, which played classics and world cinema. I think that's where I first got to sort of love movies. Loving directing movies is a whole different thing. I didn't decide I wanted to be a film director until I was about thirty-eight.

You also have a musical background. Tell me about that.

There were three specific times when I almost did music for a living, and I'm deeply glad I didn't because, quite frankly, I just didn't have the talent. First, when I was about seventeen, I was offered a scholarship to do classical guitar at the London College of Music. I ended up declining that in order to go to Cambridge, where I wrote a lot of music for theater—which is the main reason I got into theater and then into television and finally into film. When I was twenty-one, I went to India for six months to study Indian classical music and was told that with another two years of work I could become the foremost Western exponent of the sitar. For reasons that must be fairly obvious, I decided that that probably wasn't the direction my life lay in. When I was twenty-eight, I went through a particularly painful

period of divorce and ended up writing a whole swathe of pained personal songs and got off a publishing deal, which I finally declined in
order to go on with a career in theater at that time.

**How much of a role does music play in your films, especially given
the fact that you have developed such a strong relationship with
Christopher Young in your latest works?**

I think it's fairly obvious that it's enormous. I mean, it's automatic
that film music changes the way we perceive an image. You can take
an image, for example, of a man walking, smiling, toward a child
who's in the foreground. If you put cheerful music to it, you know
that that man is the child's father. If you put melancholy music to it,
you start to see that the smile on the man's face is, in fact, deeply
sad and he knows he's dying of cancer. If you put sinister and men-
acing music to it, the smile on the man's face will suddenly have a
curiously twisted and sinister look, and you'll immediately start to
believe that the man is a child-abductor. That's a simplistic example
I can give you of the way in which music changes the significance of
the image you have seen. I love an abundant use of music in all my
movies. I think *The Core* is a total of 125 minutes, of which at least
105 minutes are music. That's a very high percentage for the average movie.

Sommersby **is a remarkable film. How did you come to choose
Danny Elfman for that project?**

I like to cast creative people to do something they have never done
before, because I always think that the results are a lot fresher. It was
obvious that he was a brilliant, charismatic, and inventive composer,
but he'd never done anything that was romantic. I really enjoyed the
idea of working with somebody brilliant on something they've never
done before.

And why did he not carry on to your next projects?

It was one very simple reason, actually: The company that I was
working with on my next project, *Copycat*, felt that Danny was too
expensive for a low-budget film.

Out of all the film composers, how did Christopher Young come into the picture, and what is it that you took to versus other composers?

The story goes as follows: James Newton Howard was slated to write the score for *Copycat*. Several weeks into the process, he unceremoniously dumped our movie because he had been offered a large sum of money to do the score for *Waterworld*. I was suddenly put in a very difficult position. I had to find a composer very quickly.

As you know, in every movie, when you're editing it and indeed sometimes when you're previewing it, you put a temp score on it. A temp score is a thing of shreds and patches. It's music snatched from other movies from all over the place very often. I had temped *Sommersby* with a score from a movie called *Bat 21*, which, to this day, I've still not seen. During the editing of *Copycat*, I absolutely smothered it with a temp score from a film called *Jennifer 8*. These are two very different scores from two very different films. But I suddenly realized that they had one thing in common—they were both composed by a guy named Christopher Young. It was very obvious to me that I loved this guy's work and that he had immensely diverse talent. That was the point at which I contacted Chris. From that point on, the primary question was, "Were we going to be compatible personally?" And that very quickly became obvious that we were. Chris has incredible energy and, I believe, the most prodigious talent of any composer working in Hollywood today. And he has a complete lack of what I call an "intervening ego," the kind of ego that's more about his ego than about the work itself. Chris is one of the most humble and amenable composers whom I have ever worked with.

With *Copycat*, you have this temp score, but, what sort of direction did you give him to support the music used.

I said that I want to make things very scary, very creepy. I want to use natural sound—the drip of a tap, the tick of a clock, the creek of a floorboard—to really heighten the tension. I'd like to create a score that's got great transparency and will allow those sounds to come through. So let's use high-frequency strings and sustained strings

and low-frequency pads and pulses, but leave enormous transparency in the middle-frequency range to let all of those other small
sounds come through. This has really a lot to do with areas where we
particularly tried to create tension. There are also passages of enormous lyricism in *Copycat*. Chris ended up using piano with a small
string section to create very simple, very lyrical counterpoint to the
electronics—the more psychotic sounds of the serial killer's mind.

I need a director's point of view on the temp track.

I think that the temp track is an absolutely essential tool. Firstly, a
director can't judge the effectiveness of a sequence without music on
it if he or she believes that they are going to have music on it.
Sometimes you absolutely have to put music onto your image in
order to know whether it's working or not. Again, a very simple
example: If you take *Copycat*, there are a series of very long tracking shots, as, for example, Holly Hunter moves through the apartment. Until you put the right music on those shots, they are empty,
devoid of tension and unquestionably overlong. The moment you
put the right music onto them, they become almost unbearable as
each corner she turns becomes a sort of hiding place for the killer.

Equally, a romantic scene very often has a turning point. There
is a moment when suddenly, after they put the teacups down, his
eyes catch hers and suddenly in comes the music and we know that
something intensely emotional has begun. Without the music, the
moment is dead. With it, it's suddenly full of significance. So you
have to have music in order to gauge the effectiveness of your
moment.

When you come to the composer with a film that has a temp
track on it, that track serves several functions. Firstly, it tells you
where essentially you want to spot the music, where you want it to
start, and where you want it to finish. The music then serves as a
point of reference. You can say, "I think this music is shit. I don't
want the final music to be anything like it." You can say, "I like the
way the strings come in at this particular moment." So, in other
words, you can use the music as various reference points for the
writer. If it's somebody else's music or if it's his or her own music,
immediately there is a certain invitation to the dull-minded to pla-
giarize or to self-plagiarize. I think for a really creative composer,

who can simply take the temp as a reference point and as a discussion point and go on and build from there, it works.

In my conversations with composers, the temp track comes up a lot as a hindrance to their work, mainly because the filmmakers become so tied to the temp.

I think very often that the problem is that the director or the studio gets very used to hearing a certain score against a certain scene, and they get very locked into it. But I think, provided that the director enfranchises the composer to take the intention of the music rather than the notes of the music, all is well.

What do you look for in film music, and how do you know what sound you want by viewing a scene?

Music is entirely emotion. Essentially, I look for the music to enhance and reinforce the emotion of any given scene at any given moment. That's a very simple answer to a very complex issue. There are various ways different pieces of music can invoke similar emotions. So, obviously, there is a question of style and scale. If the movie is a gritty, spare, melancholy piece of work you're not going to want Mahler, even though Mahler is deeply melancholy. You're not going to want 120 swooping strings, even though the emotionality may be appropriate. It's a combination of emotionality and stylistic confluence that I look for in music, to put it very simply.

***Copycat* and *Entrapment* were amazing scores that fit those movies like gloves. I find it wonderful that you have so much faith in Chris Young's music.**

You missed out on *The Man Who Knew Too Little*, which is one of the most delightful, syncopated and jazzy, swinging scores you're ever likely to hear. That's a score that I'm incredibly proud of, and so is Chris. So basically look at the quadrangle that's formed by those four movies—*Copycat*, a psycho thriller; *The Man Who Knew Too Little*, a kind of Mancini swing score; *Entrapment*, a technoheist thriller; and *The Core*, an epic end-of-the-world movie—and tell me that Chris Young cannot write any damn movie he chooses.

Quite simply put, there isn't a movie that I wouldn't make without Chris Young. As far as I'm concerned, he can do anything he chooses in any genre.

So many reviewers seem to think that they have this answer, but in your opinion, what makes the extraordinary score versus one that is simply in the film?

That's as an elusive and impossible question as, "What makes a great novel?" It's a synthesis of many things. The first is that it has to fit the movie like a glove. A film score, however extraordinary, that doesn't work with the image will not work. The first time I ever understood what a great film score was was actually long before I ever thought I might end up directing movies. I saw *Chinatown*. I loved the film. Was that a great score? I have no idea. I can simply tell you that it was a great movie. I'm not even sure, although I'm a musical kind of a fellow, but I think the music was great. It must have been great because the movie was great and the music never intruded. But I could not have told you specifically much about the music.

Ten years later I went and saw the movie again. I sat in the movie theater. The opening credits started. The opening theme music started, and I started to cry because the music instantly, across a span of ten years, brought everything—every mood, every feeling that the movie had evoked in me—back in an instant. That was the moment in which I finally understood the power of great film music. It's sometimes almost invisible. Sometimes when it's not invisible it's not right. That's one of the paradoxes of great music. And yet it is like the wind that fills the sails of the ship at sea. Can you see it? No. Is it moving the ship? Absolutely.

There's no simple definition of great music. Is a great score one that you come out of the movie theater humming? Actually not. There's a fashion in movies currently. I'll take *The Last of the Mohicans* as an example. I personally do not think this was great movie music. It was one theme repeated over and over and over and over again. Did it become a hit? Absolutely. Did people come out of the movie thinking they heard great theme music? Yes, probably because they could come out of the movie theater humming the tune. Do I think it was great movie music? No, not at all. Do you come out of *Psycho* humming Herrmann's score? No.

But you remember it.

You'll never forget the movie. Listening to the music, you'll understand how it worked on you. But when you see the shower scene for the first time, do you remember what the music was? No. You only remember what the overwhelming emotional effect was of those screeching, syncopated high strings. Great movie music should be expertly camouflaged within the texture of the image. At the same time, in my opinion, it is at least fifty percent of the image that you see. The only way you'll ever know that is to see the image without the music. You'll suddenly feel it's half empty.

Do you listen to film music outside of films or do you feel that this is a craft that should be strictly meant for the film?

I don't tend to listen to music outside of films, no. Funny enough, I don't tend to listen to opera outside of an opera.

I have incredibly wide range and taste in music. I listen to everything from acid house to techno and hip-hop through to medieval choral music with pretty much everything in between. But I don't instinctively put on a movie-music album. Movie music is an applied art. It's like looking though the clothes without looking at the person who's wearing the suit of clothes. At it's crudest, put a Versace outfit on a supermodel and it's a luscious thing to behold. Hang it on a hanger and who cares? The person wearing the outfit gives it meaning, context, personality, and image. Without the person, it's clothes.

So what are your views on someone like me, who does enjoy film music outside of a film?

I think it's great. Maybe it's because I work in film that I just don't listen to film music as my entertainment. I don't watch a huge number of films either. One of the great problems with filmmakers today is that the only experiences they've ever really had in life are inside movie theaters. So they end of up making movies that are actually not about their own lives or their own experiences. They end up making movies about other movies. I love movies that bring a sense of a life lived—that bring a sense of a kind of world that the film-maker has experienced.

I love film music that brings with it a sense of other worlds and other lives too, outside of the movie theaters. Which isn't to say that I have anything against anybody who clings to film music. In fact, I wish more people listened to film music and bought more film-score records. I think it would make film composers' lives a lot more comfortable. I'm really glad that people are buying all of those Varèse Sarabande issues and so on because it's an enormous help to film composers. It helps to keep them away from taking jobs they don't want.

Atom Egoyan

What led you to film?

It was theater. From a very young age, I was fascinated by theater. I used to put on plays at school that I would write and direct. When I went to the University of Toronto, there was a film club and I started playing with the camera. I realized as soon as I started taking images that it was really exciting to me, that the camera was a very powerful instrument that could transmit the notion of a personality outside of the physical or literal characters that were in front of the lens, that there was a spirit that the camera itself possessed. That, to me, was a powerful concept. It enabled me to find my voice much more than theater did.

Your voice in films is very deep and true-to-life in both Armenian and Canadian cultures. What do you look for in a story?

I look for a story that hasn't been told. I look for something that is not immediately apparent, but which haunts the lives of the characters and the environments that I'm portraying. That there's a story other than the one that is immediately apparent is an essential element for me.

I like the notion of denial. It's a very powerful concept for me because it not only reflects on the idea of self-delusion, which is interesting, but also the mechanics in which characters can delude themselves into believing something other than what is there. It's also a way of exploring notions of how we construct realities in a more political context. This is where my relationship with Mychael [Danna] has been fundamental because, very often in my films, the emotional life is somehow withheld. You're not quite sure what it is that roots the characters. The music often connects us to something in the subconscious before we understand the literal level of what's going on. It's a very careful balance that Mychael and I try to orchestrate.

What filmmakers or films themselves have influenced you?

I would say that I was very influenced by Ingmar Bergman and Robert Bresson. I was also very influenced by many American films of the seventies—films like Francis Ford Coppola's *The Conversation* and Martin Scorsese's *Taxi Driver*—but more by European tradition. There are a number of individual features, films like [Pier Paolo] Pasolini's, *Teorema* and Bergman's *Persona*. Above all, perhaps, is a film like Alfred Hitchcock's *Vertigo*, which I consider to be one of the best films ever made. *Vertigo* is just so stunning, and it's an exciting film for me to watch and revisit. The more I work in opera, the more I think of the synthesis of image and music in that production.

In your youth, were you aware of music in films?

In my early teens, the one film that left a very strong impression on me was *Jesus Christ Superstar*. The musical changed my life when I heard it at the age of ten. I'd been raised with bible stories, but they didn't really resonate. Suddenly, this rock opera came along that I thought made a lot of sense. I became so excited that I listened to it endlessly. It was a defining moment for me because, through this film, I realized how cinema, and camera movement especially, could really accentuate and give definition to certain musical concepts. It stays with me as a great example of music and film married together, though obviously in a pop way. I loved the music of the Bergman films, the really atonal scores that were used to convey notions of alienation and unease in films like *Persona*.

So how did your relationship with Mychael Danna evolve?

I was aware of his work because Mychael has had a curious trajectory. He started as a composer of New Music and then, in the mideighties, composed more—environmental, ambient scores with his brother. I was also very influenced by Brian Eno's music, such as *Music for Airports* and these ambient scores that he released for film collaborations, as he did with Harold Budd, for example. When I heard Mychael's music, it struck a chord. There was an affinity in some of the tonalities and ideas he was expressing emotionally. We met and collaborated for *Family Viewing*, which is still one of my favorite films. The music is able to show the emotional interior long before the film gives it away. I realized that the film was not working until I actually put the music on it. It was really a revelation. And working with Mychael has been an incredible journey.

Looking at a project, do you often have a view of how you want the music, or do you leave this to Mychael's creativity?

Going back to *Family Viewing*, I remember the very early session during which we played each other some of our favorite music. I have always been interested in music that skirts on the edges of tonality, and so I think a lot of the early music sort of does that. It was just really great to use that type of instrumentation on a film like *The Sweet Hereafter*. *Exotica* is one of the few films where we actually developed the theme before we shot, because it is played out in the scenes. For instance, when Sarah Polley's character is getting ready to babysit, she plays it on the flute and then plays it on the piano. It was very important that we establish those things beforehand and, of course, that's a very rare situation. But it's also great to be able to have a theme in mind as you're shooting. It's a close relationship. It's unusual perhaps. It's not one of those situations where I wait: Music is something that I am thinking of all the time as I'm putting the piece together.

Have you used other composers?

No. I certainly work with other composers in opera. I've worked with Gavin Bryars. I did a collaboration with Philip Glass on a film. It was

a ten-minute film for his series *Philip on Film*. I've worked with
Steve Reich's music as well. But these are all sort of more experimental projects or opera projects. In terms of my narrative work or
my feature work, I've always worked with Mychael's music or source
music.

What has sustained your relationship with Mychael?

Our relationship sustains itself on a mutual sense of intimacy that
we feel toward each other's artistic process and sensibility. We also
are very honest with each other and very demanding with each other
as well. The thing Mychael hates most is when I use his scores as
temp music for my films. He wants to reinvent himself, and that's
great. We challenge each other, and we are very close to each other
emotionally as well.

**The music for *Ararat* is just beautifully written. Talk about this
movie and what it means to you and how much of a role this music
plays in this film.**

The music here is so emotionally invested because some of the
themes are like themes that my grandmother, a survivor of the
Armenian genocide, would sing to my father. There were themes
that I needed to have in that film. The opening theme of the film is
a very important piece in terms of the Armenian national identity,
and I wanted it to be the theme throughout. Mychael resisted this
because there are easier themes to work with in terms of his development, but he finally got used to it and created something quite
magnificent from what is not an easy theme for variations. There are
four main themes running through this film. It was the first time that
Mychael and I were able to work with a huge orchestra. That was a
very fun part of the film to score.

**What I find most fascinating is that *Ararat* was largely recorded in
Armenia.**

Mychael has an incredible desire for authenticity, which is sometimes supremely impractical, yet which he'll fight for and defend it.

In the case of *Exotica*, there was a shanai sound, and he wanted the real thing. He had to get on a plane, go to India, go to the village, and then record it weeks before the final mix.

In the case of *Ararat*, there were musicians whom we could have used in Los Angeles, but it was very important to Mychael that he go to Armenia and find musicians there and record it there, and especially record the choirs in a church. He felt that all of those elements would find their way into the score on a subconscious level. I feel that with the camera lens as well. There's an ability to capture energy that is not literally dependent on what the person who's photographing that image may feel. I think that Mychael feels that way about where and how instruments are recorded. It's not enough to just use the sound, but you have to invest yourself physically within the production of that sound.

You actually recorded with him?

Yes, I wouldn't have missed the experience for the world, but I was also there to help with the translation.

This goes back to your roots, making this an extra-special event?

Absolutely. That's about as close as you can get.

What was this experience like?

It was overwhelming. It was great to share it with Mychael, because we're also friends. It was just great to take him on that journey and for him to see that country, which is so meaningful to me. While there, we both knew that it was what we had been working toward for almost twenty years.

Norman Jewison

When you first started out, how aware were you of film music, and what scores have stuck in your mind?

I was very much involved with music all the way through my career. I realized that the marriage between music and the motion picture is the most powerful visual communication we have. When I was working in television, I found that you could take almost any edited sequence and change its emotion with the use of music. Many of the composers in my films have been nominated for Academy Awards, which shows that the scores played an important part in the films, whether it's Georges Delerue in *Agnes of God*, or whether it's John Williams, who won the Academy Award for *Fiddler on the Roof*. Look at Bernard Herrmann. *Psycho* without the music would be nothing. Everybody talks about the suspense and Hitchcock's brilliant designed editing, but what they don't talk enough about is the tremendous power of the musical scores in Hitchcock's films—and a lot of them were Bernie Herrmann's scores.

Music in your films has a wide range of flavors. You seem to seek different talents for each picture. How does this approach work for you?

Most artists think that they can do everything, and a lot of them can—just like I make musicals, comedies, and strong dramas, so I, too, like to think that whatever the story is, I can tell it well. But all of us, every single artist, has a strength in a certain area. Every artist has his or her own milieu. Every composer has an identifiable original sound. There are some composers who, in my opinion, have a great sense of a lyrical line. They are total romantics, and most of their strongest scores are ones that have soft, romantic feelings. So this is what I think about when I cast a composer for a film.

What inspired the jazzy tempo with a dramatic undertone for *The Hurricane*?

It was a matter of finding the right sounds and the right tempos. I think it was a matter of experimentation.

What was your input on that score, for instance?

Chris Young did a lot of temp cues that we would sort through. Then we would discuss which ones were working.

I think that there is a very close collaboration between directors and composers, especially in the early stages, but once the theme is kind of established, then it becomes less of a collaboration.

What is your process for discovering the right music for your vision?

I work with a lot of temp music. Out of that, I usually find certain things that work and certain thing that don't work.

Some composers consider temp music a hindrance.

A lot of composers hate it. There are certain composers I've worked with who won't listen to the film with the temp score. There are other composers who like it because they can see what works and what doesn't work.

I actually get a little embarrassed when I show a composer someone else's music behind the film. I explain to the composer why it
works—because of the orchestration or instrumentation or because
of the lyrical quality and so on. That's what you have to do.

Index